Wittgenstein in Swansea

Wittgenstein in Swansea

Philosophy and Legacy

Edited by Alan Sandry

UNIVERSITY OF WALES PRESS

2025

© The Contributors, 2025

All rights reserved. No part of this book may be reproduced in any material form (including photocopying or storing it in any medium by electronic means and whether or not transiently or incidentally to some other use of this publication) without the written permission of the copyright owner. Applications for the copyright owner's written permission to reproduce any part of this publication should be addressed to the University of Wales Press, University Registry, King Edward VII Avenue, Cardiff CF10 3NS.

www.uwp.co.uk

British Library CIP Data
A catalogue record for this book is available from the British Library

ISBN: 978-1-83772-225-9
eISBN: 978-1-83772-226-6

The rights the Contributors to be identified as authors of this work have been asserted in accordance with sections 77 and 79 of the Copyright, Designs and Patents Act 1988.

For GPSR enquiries please contact:
Easy Access System Europe Oü, 16879218
Mustamäe tee 50, 10621, Tallinn, Estonia
gpsr.requests@easproject.com

Printed and bound by
CPI Group (UK) Ltd, Croydon, CR0 4YY
Typeset by Marie Doherty

Contents

Acknowledgements		vii
Preface		ix
Contributors		xi
1	Wittgenstein: The Swansea Years, 1942–1947 *Ray Monk*	1
2	The Cultural Milieu of Swansea in the 1930s and 1940s *Jeff Towns*	13
3	The Place of Swansea on the Road to *Philosophical Investigations* *Jonathan Smith*	37
4	'It's good to be away from Cambridge & to be here, & among friendly people' – Wittgenstein's letters to Ben Richards and his philosophical work in Swansea *Alfred Schmidt*	51
5	The 'Swansea School' *Mario von der Ruhr*	67
6	J. R. Jones and Wittgenstein: Resisting the Demise of the Welsh-language 'Neighbourhood' *Huw Williams*	85
7	Wittgenstein, Communitarianism, and Welsh Cultural-Linguistic Identity *Rhianwen Daniel*	111
8	'Change and decay in all around I see': The Wittgenstein School of English at Swansea *M. Wynn Thomas*	133

9	Strange Country: The Cosmopolitan Particularism of Ludwig Wittgenstein and Ralph Ellison *Daniel G. Williams*	151
10	The Psychogeography of Swansea as a Stimulus for Wittgenstein's Cerebration *Alan Sandry*	187
11	Wittgenstein, Rhees and Philosophy: James Kelman in conversation	201
12	Family Recollections of Wittgenstein in Swansea *Jamie Bill*	215

Afterword: Wittgenstein's Swansea Legacy and Contemporary Relevance 217
Alan Sandry

Select Bibliography 227
Index 231

Acknowledgements

This volume emanates from a series of events over several years. I am extremely indebted to so many people for their advice, interest, and curiosity about all things Wittgenstein and Swansea. Special mentions and praise, however, must go out to:

Professor Terry Stevens for facilitating my lecture 'Wittgenstein in Swansea: Language and Langland' at the Kepler Salon, Linz, Austria, July 2017; The late Professor Hywel Francis for inviting me to write 'Am I Glad to Be Here!: Ludwig Wittgenstein and Philosophy at Swansea' for the Swansea University Centenary Essays 2020; Radmila Schweitzer (Wittgenstein Initiative, Vienna) and Dr Waltraud Dennhardt-Herzog (Austrian Cultural Forum London) for kindly agreeing to allow the exhibition *The Tractatus Odyssey* to visit Swansea in June 2022; Sian Williams (South Wales Miners Library, Swansea University) for her ongoing support and expertise across the board; Dr Simon Mackley (Richard Burton Archives, Swansea University) for his archival and curating skills for the exhibition *The Tractatus Odyssey and Wittgenstein's Swansea Years*, displayed at Swansea University's Singleton Library, June 2022; Alan Figg for his wonderful original print of Ludwig Wittgenstein, which was unveiled at the exhibition; All the team at the Richard Burton Archives for their guidance and depth of knowledge; Dr Elaine Canning for her kind assistance with the Wittgenstein events in Swansea in June 2022; Jeff Towns for being an Ambassador Extraordinaire for Swansea's literary history, and for his conversion to all things Wittgensteinian; Geoff Haden and Alun Gibbard ('the Cwmdonkin Pirates') for allowing Wittgenstein a place at Dylan's table; Professor John Tucker for interweaving Wittgenstein with Richard Price, and his remarkable History of Computing Collection at Swansea University; Professor Alan Dix for breakfast debates on Wittgenstein, Artificial Intelligence and Pedagogy; Nigel

Acknowledgements

Crowle for masterminding *Wittgenstein: From Austria to Abertawe*, our 2022 documentary for BBC Radio Wales; Professor Mererid Hopwood for explaining the wider role that Wittgenstein played in the development of Welsh literature and society; Jonathan Smith for his detailed tour of Wittgenstein's Cambridge on the hottest day of the Century; James Kelman, for his inspirational conversations regarding Celtic literature, Chomsky, and radical philosophy; Dr Christopher Stray for coffee, Classicism, and intellectual stimulation; the late Professor Marjorie Perloff for a fascinating dialogue on Wittgenstein's Private Notebooks, and the wider literary field. Thanks also for her encouragement to publish on Wittgenstein in Swansea; David 'Dai' Hughes for his germane, incisive poetry, and for his seminal work on the history of the Uplands, Swansea, and Wittgenstein's important place within that story; Ian 'Zag' Seaton for numerous conversations about Wittgenstein, Swansea, politics, and games; Helen Nicholas for her boundless enthusiasm for Wittgenstein, and her exhaustive knowledge of Gower's history and archaeology; Hannah and Dan Hanratty for being perfect hosts and for sharing their home with Wittgenstein; Robin Campbell for Architectural insight, and Sally and Roger Moss for conversations about Ian Hamilton Finlay's interest in Wittgenstein; Llion Wigley for his pointers and professionalism. Last, but certainly not least, a profound *diolch yn fawr* to all the contributors to this volume for their time, efforts, and insights. I wish, particularly, to thank Professor Ray Monk for floating the idea that a volume of this kind was 'much needed'. Finally, quite naturally, my foremost thanks must be extended to Rush Rhees, for his metamorphic decision to apply for a position at Swansea University, and to Ludwig Wittgenstein for simply being Ludwig Wittgenstein.

Preface

This volume covers aspects of Ludwig Wittgenstein's time in Swansea from 1942–7 and looks at his philosophy and legacy through various eyes, and from different perspectives. These include explanations and assessments of Wittgenstein's time and work at Swansea from Ray Monk, Jonathan Smith, and Alfred Schmidt; historical and cultural scene setting from Jeff Towns; analyses of the Swansea School from Mario von der Ruhr, and Huw Williams; literary comparisons from Daniel Williams; ideological evaluations from Rhianwen Daniel; and a range of intimate reflections and commentaries from James Kelman, Jamie Bill, and M Wynn Thomas. The editor, meanwhile, offers some psychogeographical observations, and considers Wittgenstein's present-day significance within Swansea.

The genesis of this volume was a mid-Covid conversation with Radmila Schweitzer (Secretary-General, Wittgenstein Institute, Vienna) and Dr Waltraud Dennhardt-Herzog (Austrian Cultural Forum London). This led to the staging at Swansea University, in June 2022, of the *Ludwig Wittgenstein: An Austrian in Swansea* conference, which ran alongside the touring exhibition *Ludwig Wittgenstein's Tractatus Odyssey: The Great War and the Writing of the Tractatus Logico-Philosophicus*. This exhibition was supplemented by material on Wittgenstein, Rush Rhees, and the Swansea School, which was curated by Dr Simon Mackley, Sian Williams and the team at Swansea University's Richard Burton Archives. Around this time, Professor Ray Monk, whose chapter commences this collection, kindly suggested that I compiled a Wittgenstein in Swansea publication. This is it!

Whilst the Wittgenstein in Swansea years of 1942–7 naturally occupy the minds of our contributors, it is his legacy, be it in his interaction with Rush Rhees, his stimulus for the Swansea School, or his broader influence on students, academics, and writers from a plethora of disciplines and interests, which act as a leitmotif. The chapters are designed for an audience of Wittgensteinians and non-Wittgensteinians alike. The overall message is to celebrate, and mildly interrogate, Wittgenstein's association with Swansea, and I hope this volume encourages further discussions, research, and publications.

Contributors

Jamie Bill is the son of Barbara Clement, and grandson of Albert and Mary Clement of Cwmdonkin Terrace, Uplands, Swansea, with whom Wittgenstein lodged. Jamie has detailed family reminiscences of Wittgenstein, many of which have never been previously published.

Rhianwen Daniel is Lecturer in Philosophy at the School of English, Communication and Philosophy, Cardiff University. Her PhD thesis 'The Impact of Language on Cultural Identity: Implications for Linguistic Justice and Liberal Nationalism' explored Wittgenstein and the Welsh language. She is the author of 'Standardization and vitality: The role of linguistic purism in preventing extinction' (*Language Problems and Language Planning*, 47/2, 2023).

James Kelman is a novelist and short story writer. He won the Booker Prize for *How Late It Was, How Late* (Secker and Warburg, 1994), and is co-author with Noam Chomsky of *Between Thought and Expression Lies a Lifetime: Why Ideas Matter* (PM Press, 2021).

Ray Monk is Emeritus Professor at Southampton University. He won the John Llewellyn Rhys Prize and the Duff Cooper Prize for *Ludwig Wittgenstein: The Duty of Genius* (Vintage, 1991). He is also the author of *Bertrand Russell: The Spirit of Solitude* (The Free Press, 1996), and *The Ghost of Madness* (Jonathan Cape, 2000).

Alan Sandry is Senior Lecturer in Philosophy and Strategy, Swansea University. He is the author of *Plaid Cymru: An Ideological Analysis* (Welsh Academic Press, 2011), *Am I Glad to Be Here: Ludwig Wittgenstein and Philosophy at Swansea* (Swansea University Centenary Essays, 2020), and *From Linz to Langland: A Journey with Ludwig Wittgenstein* (Cambria Books, 2024).

Contributors

Alfred Schmidt is a historian and Archivist at the Austrian National Library, Vienna, Austria. He is the author of *"I think of you constantly with love …" Ludwig Wittgenstein's Correspondence with Ben Richards 1946–1951* (Haymon Books, 2022).

Jonathan Smith is Curator of the Economists' Papers Archive, David M. Rubenstein Rare Books and Manuscript Library, Duke University, Durham, USA. He is the former Archivist of The Papers of Ludwig Wittgenstein, Wren Library, Trinity College, Cambridge, and co-author with Nuno Venturinha of 'Wittgenstein on British Anti-Nazi Propaganda' (*Nordic Wittgenstein Review*, 2018).

M. Wynn Thomas is the Emyr Humphreys Chair of Welsh Writing in English, Swansea University. He read Philosophy (Year 1) at Swansea University under Rush Rhees, Peter Winch and J. R. Jones. He is the author of *R. S. Thomas: Serial Obsessive* (University of Wales Press, 2013), and *All That is Wales* (University of Wales Press, 2017).

Jeff Towns is an antiquarian bookseller and expert on Dylan Thomas. He is an Honorary Fellow at the Cultural Institute, Swansea University, editor of *Edward Thomas and Wales* (Parthian Books, 2018), and co-author with K. G. Miles of *Bob Dylan and Dylan Thomas: The Two Dylans* (McNidder & Grace, 2022).

Mario von der Ruhr is Honorary Senior Lecturer in the Faculty of Humanities and Social Sciences, Swansea University. He is the author of 'Rhees, Wittgenstein and the Swansea School' (*Sense and Reality: Essays out of Swansea*, ed. John Edelman, De Gruyter, 2009).

Daniel G. Williams is Professor in English Literature, Swansea University, and Director of the Richard Burton Centre for the Study of Wales. He is the author of *Wales Unchained: Literature, Politics and Identity in the American Century* (University of Wales Press, 2015), and editor of *The Werner Sollors Reader: Ethnicity, Cosmopolitanism and Particularism* (Edinburgh University Press, 2025).

Contributors

Huw Williams is Reader in Philosophy at the School of English, Communication and Philosophy, Cardiff University. He is the author of *Credoau'r Cymry* (University of Wales Press, 2016), *Ysbryd Morgan* (University of Wales Press, 2020), and co-editor of *The Welsh Way: essays on neoliberalism and Welsh devolution* (Parthian Books, 2021).

*Gyda chariad a diolch i Jill,
Tom a fy mwnci bach*

1
Wittgenstein:
The Swansea Years, 1942–1947

Ray Monk

Wittgenstein liked Swansea – its people, its surrounding countryside, and the wonderful coastline of the Gower Peninsula – but what first drew him there was the opportunity it provided for discussions with his friend and student Rush Rhees. Rhees was an American whose family contained many distinguished academics and clergymen. His father Benjamin Rush Rhees was a Baptist minister and the president of the University of Rochester, while one of his more distant ancestors was the Welsh radical evangelical preacher Morgan John Rhys, who left Wales in 1794 and emigrated to America where he changed his name to Rhees.

In 1922, at the age of sixteen, Rush Rhees enrolled at his father's university to study philosophy. In his second year he was expelled from his ethics class because his questioning of the professor who gave it was considered rude and insolent. As a result, Rhees left both Rochester University and America and went to Scotland to study philosophy at Edinburgh where he flourished, graduating with a first-class degree in 1928. He then taught at Manchester for four years before going to Innsbruck to study with the Brentano scholar Alfred Kastil. In 1933, he enrolled as a PhD student at the University of Cambridge with G. E. Moore as his supervisor.

At Cambridge, Rhees later told me,[1] he had been put off attending Wittgenstein's lectures by the mannerisms of his students; but, in February 1936, he overcame those misgivings and attended all the remaining lectures of that year. Wittgenstein evidently took to him very quickly and within a few months was inviting him to tea and taking him into his confidence. In June 1936, for example, Wittgenstein discussed with Rhees his future plans. Should he get a job of some sort, or should he concentrate on finishing his book? 'I still have a little money,' he told Rhees, 'and I could live and work by myself as long as that lasts.'[2] In the end, that is what he did, spending most of the next eighteen months alone in Norway working on *Philosophical Investigations*.

In December 1937, Wittgenstein left Norway and moved into his family's opulent mansion in the Alleegasse, Vienna, where he stayed for a month or so before heading for Dublin in February 1938, to be with his friend Maurice Drury. He was still in Dublin at the time of the *Anschluss* on 12 March 1938, when Austria became part of the Third Reich. Wittgenstein responded to this development by returning to Cambridge, where he resumed lecturing, with the long-term aim of becoming a British citizen.

For Wittgenstein it was essential that his lectures were also discussions and so he insisted on keeping his classes small. His lectures were therefore not announced in the usual way in the *Cambridge University Recorder*; rather attendees were individually selected from the students of John Wisdom, Richard Braithwaite, and G. E. Moore. One of the students chosen by Moore was Rush Rhees, who during this period became one of Wittgenstein's closest friends. Unusually, the subject of these lectures was aesthetics, though it is impossible to place them in the standard literature devoted to this topic. What Wittgenstein was doing, he told his audience, was 'making propaganda'[3] for a style of thinking that was at odds with the worship of science, which Wittgenstein considered to be characteristic of the modern era. The idea that aesthetics was, or should be, a kind of science itself was, he said, 'almost too ridiculous for words'.[4] After Wittgenstein had talked about the deterioration of the German music tradition, Rhees asked him about his theory of deterioration. Wittgenstein reacted strongly against the idea that he had one. 'Do you think I have a theory?' he asked rhetorically. 'What I do is describe different things called deterioration.'[5] Theories belong in science.

At this time Wittgenstein had prepared for publication a typescript that is now regarded as the earliest version of *Philosophical Investigations*, which, on Moore's recommendation, he asked Rhees to translate from German to English. In working on this translation Rhees met regularly with Wittgenstein, but when, in the New Year of 1939, he showed it to him, Wittgenstein was horrified at what he saw. He nevertheless submitted a revised version of it as part of his application for the Chair of Philosophy at Cambridge University, which had fallen vacant after Moore retired. On 11 February, he was elected professor. This helped enormously with his application for British citizenship, which was duly granted in June.

In 1939, Wittgenstein gave what has become a celebrated series of lectures on the philosophy of mathematics, which was attended by none other than Alan Turing, the great logician, computer scientist and codebreaker. Rush Rhees does not seem to have attended these lectures. He had by then taken a factory job as a welder. Wittgenstein repeatedly encouraged his students to seek work outside of academia. His lover Francis Skinner, though an extremely able mathematician, became, at Wittgenstein's urging, a factory mechanic at the Cambridge Instrument Company. Another of Wittgenstein's students, who might otherwise have been destined for an academic career, Yorick Smythies, became a librarian; and yet another, Rowland Hutt, went to work in a branch of Woolworths. Wittgenstein tried to persuade his American student Norman Malcolm to become a cowboy, but Malcolm was having none of it and became a professor of philosophy instead. In 1941, Rhees took a similar path and abandoned his work as a welder for an academic position at Swansea University.

In the same year, so determined was Wittgenstein to contribute to the war effort that went in the opposite direction, leaving Cambridge to become a dispensary porter at Guy's Hospital. His job there was to deliver medicines from the dispensary to the wards, where, apparently, he advised the patients not to take them. It was while he was thus employed that he first visited Rhees in Swansea in the summer of 1942. Together, the two would take walks along the Gower Peninsula, talking philosophy as they walked. When they returned to Rhees's house, Rhees would write up these conversations; a practice he would maintain for the rest of his acquaintanceship with Wittgenstein.

Though Wittgenstein's writing at that time centred on the philosophy of mathematics, what he and Rhees discussed that summer was Freudian psychoanalysis. Wittgenstein told Rhees he considered himself in some sense to be a 'disciple of Freud'.[6] He was, however, an especially critical disciple. In particular, he rejected Freud's claim to have established a new science, one that discovered new *laws*, whereas, Wittgenstein told Rhees, 'the fact that there *aren't* actually any such laws seems important.'[7] For example, Freud's idea that anxiety is always a repetition in some way of the anxiety we felt at birth has not been established scientifically, using evidence, hypotheses and laws. Rather, '[i]t has the attraction which mythological explanations have'.[8]

Wittgenstein remained at Guy's until the spring of 1943, when he moved to Newcastle to join a team working for the Medical Research Council on an investigation of the condition known as wound shock. The team had, until the end of 1942, been based at Guy's and Wittgenstein had impressed two of its members, Drs Reeve and Grant, with the intelligence and relevance of his questions and suggestions concerning their work. When the group moved to Newcastle, therefore, Grant requested that Wittgenstein should join them, nominally as a laboratory assistant. Before he left for Newcastle, Wittgenstein returned to Swansea to spend more time with Rhees, resuming their discussions about Freud.

Again, these discussions centred on the contrast between Freud's work and science. The interpretation of dreams, for example, Wittgenstein insisted, is not the application of a theory. Theories typically take a multiplicity of phenomena and try to pick out something common to them all, they generalise. The interpretation of a dream, however, is more like the understanding of a poem or a novel or even a person. As Wittgenstein puts it in *Philosophical Investigations*, what we are after here is 'the understanding that consists in "seeing connections"'.[9] He told Rhees, 'When a dream is interpreted, we might say that it is fitted into a context in which it ceases to be puzzling. In a sense the dreamer re-dreams his dream in a surrounding such that its aspect changes.'[10]

A similar issue arose in a different context when Wittgenstein accompanied Rhees to a meeting of the College Philosophical Society in Swansea to hear the classicist Benjamin Farrington give a paper on 'Causal Laws and History'. Farrington was a Marxist and a Communist Party member, and his talk endorsed a version of historical materialism according to which societal progress is made in accordance with a general law of historical development. In the discussion Wittgenstein said that something that looked like progress might, when seen from a different point of view, appear as decline. For example, the mining of iron and coal in the area around Swansea made it possible for industry to develop, but at the same time it scarred the valley with slag heaps and old machinery. Farrington responded: 'With all the ugly sides of our civilization, I am sure I would rather live as we do now than have to live as the cavemen did.' 'Yes, of course you would,' Wittgenstein replied, 'but would the caveman?'[11]

After his return to Newcastle, Wittgenstein, though remaining a valued member of the research team, began to long more and more for philosophical discussion and time to finish his book. 'I am feeling rather lonely here,' he wrote to Norman Malcolm, 'and may try to get to some place where I have someone to talk to. E.g., to Swansea where Rhees is a lecturer in philosophy.'[12] When Grant and Reeve left Newcastle for Italy in the New Year of 1944, therefore, Wittgenstein left too and, after a few weeks in Cambridge, returned to Swansea with the intention of staying there until the autumn.

Rhees had found him some lodgings in the home of a Mrs Mann, who lived by the coast at Langland Bay in the Swansea headland known as the Mumbles. It is a delightful, scenic spot. Wittgenstein found it so ideal that when Mrs Mann wrote to him to tell him that she had changed her mind about having him as a guest he refused to accept it and insisted on moving in regardless. He stayed with her throughout the spring of 1944, and she proved to be a good landlady, taking care of him when he was ill.

Presumably at Mrs Mann's request, Wittgenstein moved out of her house by the summer. He then moved into the home of a Methodist minister, the Revd Wynford Morgan, who lived in Cwmdonkin Terrace, situated in the Uplands with views over Swansea Bay. Around the corner is 5 Cwmdonkin Drive, famous as the birthplace of the poet Dylan Thomas. At that time, Thomas was no longer living in the area, but he was extremely well known to everyone in that part of Swansea and a great talking point, so it is perhaps surprising that there is no record of Wittgenstein ever mentioning him.

Wittgenstein liked the Morgans. On his first visit to their house, Mrs Morgan kept asking him whether he would like first some tea, and then this or that other thing. 'Do not ask, *give*,'[13] her husband shouted from another room. It was a remark that Wittgenstein repeated several times to his friends. On religious matters, Wittgenstein was less impressed. When Revd Morgan asked him if he believed in God, he replied: 'Yes, I do, but the difference between what you believe and what I believe may be infinite.'[14]

Next door to the Morgans lived the Clement family, with whom Wittgenstein became good friends. He particularly liked Mrs Clement, who invited him to have Sunday lunch with her and her family every week. 'Isn't she an angel?' he said once to Mr Clement. 'Is she?' came the reply. 'Damn it all man, of course she is!'[15] Wittgenstein roared back. Indeed, he was so impressed that, as he had done with Mrs Mann, he insisted on moving in and would not take no for an answer.

The Clements had two daughters, Joan aged eleven, and Barbara aged nine. They had trouble pronouncing his name ('There weren't many Wittgensteins in the Swansea area,' Barbara's grandson explained many years later, 'Joneses, Thomases, yes, but not many Wittgensteins'),[16] so they called him 'Vicky'. It was, however, made clear that they were the only people allowed to do so. Wittgenstein took an enthusiastic part in Clement family life and particularly enjoyed playing Ludo, and Snakes and Ladders, with the girls. Once, when a game of Snakes and Ladders had gone on for over two hours, the girls had to plead with Wittgenstein to leave the game unresolved.[17]

Wittgenstein's most consequential intervention in the family life of the Clements took place when he came home to find Joan in tears. She had been told that she had failed her examination for entry into the local grammar school. 'We'll see about that!' said Wittgenstein, who, with Joan and her mother following behind, marched down to Joan's school, Terrace Road in Mount Pleasant. 'I can tell you,' he stated to Joan's teacher, 'that she *must* have passed.' When the teacher checked the records, they revealed that there had indeed been a mistake and that Joan had passed after all. This was a relief to everyone concerned, but Mrs Clement never showed her face in that school again.[18]

Wittgenstein took to Swansea the 1938 typescript of *Philosophical Investigations* and the notebooks he had written in the intervening years, and he set to work on a revision that he hoped to deliver to the university press when he returned to Cambridge in the autumn. At that time, Wittgenstein intended the discussion of language that opens *Investigations* to lead into an analysis of mathematics, and for the first half of his stay in Swansea in 1944 the philosophy of mathematics provided the focus of his work. Rhees told me that during this time Wittgenstein received for his consideration a short paragraph about him written by the Cambridge philosopher John Wisdom for inclusion in a biographical dictionary. Wittgenstein made just one change, a final sentence that read: 'Wittgenstein's chief contribution has been in the philosophy of mathematics.' Nevertheless, after the summer of 1944, he ceased writing about the philosophy of mathematics, concentrating instead on the philosophy of psychology. The last line of *Philosophical Investigations*, however, reads: 'An investigation entirely analogous to our investigation of psychology is possible also for mathematics.'[19]

Wittgenstein's investigations into mathematics and psychology are entirely analogous in a very special sense that strikes at the heart of his later philosophy of language. *Philosophical Investigations* opens with a discussion of a picture of language that Wittgenstein illustrates with a passage from St Augustine's *Confessions*, but which, he insists, is one of the main causes of confusion in all of philosophy. The picture in question sees words as getting their meanings from the objects to which they refer: tables, chairs, etc. When we apply this picture to mathematics and psychology, we become confused. To what does the word 'six' refer? Or the word 'anger'? Numbers and mental states do not seem to be objects and yet the sentences containing the words for them do not seem to be meaningless either.

Wittgenstein's proposed solution to this problem is to emphasise the *variety* of language. Not all words are names for objects and not all sentences are descriptions of states of affairs in the world. '2 + 2 = 4', for example, is not a truth-claim about a special kind of object (numbers); it is a *rule* telling us that whenever we see '2 + 2' we can replace it with '4'. Analogously, 'I am angry with you' is not a description of my mental state; it is an *expression* of a mental state. It has more in common with a scowl than with a statement about tables and chairs.

Connected with this, and another thing that connects his thoughts on mathematics and psychology (and also with his thoughts on aesthetics and history) is Wittgenstein's insistence that mathematics is not itself a science. As he had put it in a typescript that he wrote in the 1930s, and which was posthumously published as *Philosophical Grammar*:

> Confusions in these matters are entirely the result of treating mathematics as a kind of natural science. And this is connected with the fact that mathematics has detached itself from natural science; for as long as it is done in immediate connection with

physics, it is clear that it isn't a natural science. Similarly, you can't mistake a broom for part of the furnishing of a room as long as you use it to clean the furniture.[20]

It is difficult to know why Wittgenstein abandoned his work on the philosophy of mathematics in the summer of 1944, but, with the autumn looming and with it the necessity of returning to Cambridge, he spent the last few months of this stay in Swansea concentrating on incorporating his thoughts on psychology into the 1938 version of *Philosophical Investigations*. He had some success with this, enough to have a typescript prepared of the new, extended version of the *Investigations*, but he had no intention of delivering this to the press. As far as he was concerned, the book remained unfinished.

Wittgenstein was to spend just three more years teaching at Cambridge, and during that time Swansea was the place to which he retreated in the vacations. He was more than usually unhappy at Cambridge during this time. 'I have no hope whatever to finish my book in the near future,' he wrote to Rhees. He was also unhappy with his students: 'My class is exceedingly poor. I have so far 6 people, none of whom is really good.'[21]

Things looked a bit brighter after his Christmas vacation in Swansea and he returned to Cambridge optimistic that the time for publication was near. The final version of the book's preface is dated: 'Cambridge, January 1945'. In it, he describes the book as 'the precipitate of philosophical investigations which have occupied me for the last sixteen years',[22] and says about his remarks:

> I make them public with doubtful misgivings. It is not impossible that it should fall to the lot of this work, in its poverty and in the darkness of this time, to bring light into one brain or another – but, of course, it is not likely.[23]

He still did not deliver his typescript to the publisher, however, but kept working on it throughout the two remaining terms of that academic year. In June 1945 he wrote to Rhees:

> The Term's over & my thoughts travel in the direction of Swansea. I've been working fairly well since Easter. I am now

dictating some stuff, remarks, some of which I want to embody in my first volume (if there'll be one). This business of dictating will take roughly another month or 6 weeks. After that I could leave Cambridge.[24]

In August, when he finally made it to Swansea, he wrote to Malcolm: 'I might publish by Christmas.'[25]

After the war had ended and Malcolm was free to leave the US navy, Wittgenstein wrote to him: 'I hope you'll come to Cambridge before I make up my mind to resign the absurd job of a prof. of philosophy. It is a kind of living death.'[26] By October, he was back in Cambridge lecturing and could not wait for the term to end so that he could return to Swansea. In December, he told Malcolm, 'I'm in Swansea again over Christmas and probably over New Year. The weather's foul, but I enjoy not being in Cambridge. I know quite a number of people here whom I like. I seem to find it more easy to get along with them here than in England. I feel much more often like smiling, e.g. when I walk in the street, or when I see children, etc.'[27]

The final version of what is now *Philosophical Investigations*, Part I, was prepared during the Michaelmas (autumn) and Lent (spring) terms of 1945–6. From the typescript he had dictated during the summer, he selected about 400 remarks to add to the work he had done in Swansea in 1944, and, after some rearrangement and renumbering, this produced the 693 numbered paragraphs of which the work now consists.

It was during that academic year too that Wittgenstein met and fell in love with Ben Richards, who was then a 21-year-old student of medicine. Following the death of his previous lover, Francis Skinner, in 1941, it probably came as a surprise to Wittgenstein that he was able to find love again, and it was the source of both great delight and great anxiety to him. He despaired if he hadn't heard from Richards for any length of time. 'Please write to me,' he wrote to Ben from Swansea in June 1946, 'don't delay it any longer. Please think of the feelings & thoughts I'm liable to have if I don't hear from you; don't give me a bad time; & may you have a good and happy time yourself!'[28]

In July, he sent Ben a tourist postcard to Swansea showing four views of the city with a horseshoe in the middle bearing the message: "Good luck". One of the views was of the city's Guildhall (then the civic centre, before the new one was built in 1982), a very striking building of 1934 with a tall, art deco clock tower. It is now a Grade I listed building, but Wittgenstein was unimpressed. Above it on his postcard to Ben, he wrote: 'This abomination is the joy and pride of Swansea.'[29] The following day he sent another postcard containing four views of Swansea, this time all four of them of the civic centre. 'I thought you might like to see a little more of our Civic Centre,'[30] he explained.

The following academic year, 1946–7, was to be Wittgenstein's last at Cambridge. For the previous few years his letters had abounded in statements of how much he disliked the place and how much he preferred Swansea. On 30 September 1946, the very day he arrived in Cambridge from Swansea, he wrote in his diary: 'Everything about the place repels me. The stiffness, the artificiality, the self-satisfaction of the people. The university atmosphere nauseates me.'[31] A few weeks later he wrote to Roy Fouracre, a friend from Guy's Hospital: 'I'm thinking every day of retiring from my job and taking on something else which might bring me into a more human contact with my fellow men. But what I'll do God Knows! For I'm already a pretty old codger.'[32] He was fifty-eight years old.

Compensating for the nausea of Cambridge was his love for Ben. 'All is happiness,' he wrote on 8 October, 'I could not write like this now if I had not spent the last 2 weeks with B.' Their love, he wrote, was 'a great and wonderful gift from the heavens.'[33] Again, '*Love*, that is the pearl of a great price that one holds to one's heart, that one would exchange for *nothing*, that one prizes above all else.'[34]

The summer of 1947 was to be the last that Wittgenstein spent in Swansea. He had decided that he had to not only leave Cambridge but also move abroad. 'In this country,' he wrote, 'there is no more obvious reaction for people like me than misanthropy.'[35] He was considering moving to either Ireland or Norway. In the event, he resigned as a professor after the summer, and spent most of his remaining time on earth (he died in April 1951, shortly after his sixty-second birthday) in Ireland.

One legacy of his last summer in Swansea is a photograph of Wittgenstein taken by Ben Richards at a train stop in Swansea Bay, which has become one of the most frequently used pictures of him, adorning the covers of many books by and about him. A more significant legacy of his time in Swansea, though, is *Philosophical*

Investigations. Wittgenstein did not prepare a version of the book that he considered publishable before his death in 1951, so his literary executors published the version he had prepared in 1945, which incorporates much of the work he had done in Swansea during the previous three years. It is possible to argue, then, that we owe to Swansea, to the comradeship and intellectual stimulation that Wittgenstein received from Rhees and the warm friendship he enjoyed with the Morgans and the Clements, the text of what became one of the most influential works of philosophy of the twentieth century.

Notes

1. I interviewed Rhees several times for my book, *Ludwig Wittgenstein: The Duty of Genius* (London: Jonathan Cape, 1990).
2. Rush Rhees (ed.), *Recollections of Wittgenstein* (Oxford: Oxford University Press, 1984), p. 209.
3. Cyril Barrett (ed.), *Wittgenstein: Lectures and Conversations on Aesthetics, Psychology and Religious Belief* (Oxford: Basil Blackwell, 1978), p. 28.
4. Barrett (ed.), *Lectures and Conversations*, p. 11.
5. Barrett (ed.), *Lectures and Conversations*, p. 10.
6. Barrett (ed.), *Lectures and Conversations*, p. 41.
7. Barrett (ed.), *Lectures and Conversations*, p. 42.
8. Barrett (ed.), *Lectures and Conversations*, p. 43.
9. Ludwig Wittgenstein, *Philosophical Investigations* (Oxford: Wiley-Blackwell, 2009), paragraph 122.
10. Barrett (ed.), *Lectures and Conversations*, p. 45.
11. Rhees (ed.), *Recollections*, p. 201.
12. Norman Malcolm, *Ludwig Wittgenstein: A Memoir* (Oxford: Oxford University Press, 1984), p. 93.
13. Told to me by the Revd Morgan.
14. Told to me by Rush Rhees.
15. Told to me by Mrs Clement.
16. Jamie Bill, in a talk given at the conference *Ludwig Wittgenstein: An Austrian in Swansea*, 16 June 2022.
17. Told to me by Mrs Clement.
18. Told to me by Mrs Clement.
19. Wittgenstein, *Philosophical Investigations*, p. 243e.
20. Ludwig Wittgenstein, *Philosophical Grammar* (Oxford: Blackwell, 1974), p. 375.
21. Wittgenstein to Rhees, 28 November 1944, copy of letter given to me by Rhees.
22. Wittgenstein, *Philosophical Investigations*, p. 3e.
23. Wittgenstein, *Philosophical Investigations*, p. 4e.

24 Wittgenstein to Rhees, 13 June 1945.
25 Malcolm, *A Memoir*, p. 96.
26 Malcolm, *A Memoir*, p. 98.
27 Malcolm, *A Memoir*, p. 101.
28 Wittgenstein to Richards, 28 June 1946.
29 Wittgenstein to Richards, 1 July 1946.
30 Wittgenstein to Richards 2 July 1946.
31 Ludwig Wittgenstein, MS 132, 30.9.46 (my translation).
32 Wittgenstein to Roy Fouracre, 21 October 1946, copy of letter given to me by Mrs Fouracre.
33 Wittgenstein, MS 132, 8.10.46.
34 Wittgenstein, MS 132, 26.10.46.
35 Wittgenstein, MS 134, 13.4.47.

2

The Cultural Milieu of Swansea in the 1930s and 1940s[1]

Jeff Towns

Ludwig Wittgenstein came to Swansea in 1942, primarily to visit his former student and philosophical acolyte Rush Rhees, an American academic who had secured a position in Swansea University's Department of Philosophy in 1940. But it seems Wittgenstein was also getting tired of the cold formality of the academic atmosphere in Cambridge. It is interesting to note that two of the finest Swansea writers of the period also had low opinions of, and negative responses to, Cambridge. Gower poet Vernon Watkins went from Swansea to Repton School and on to Cambridge to read Modern Languages. He could only manage one year at the university before falling out with two former Repton friends, both budding writers, Edward Upward and Christopher Isherwood, and then disagreeing violently with I. A. Richards. He left at the end of his first year and never returned. The other writer, Dylan Thomas, was a close friend of Watkins, but he too was similarly unimpressed with the University of Cambridge. Writing to Vernon in early November 1939, he told him that he had been invited to give a poetry reading to the university's English Club in December, but by the end of the month he was writing to the pacifist poet and critic, D. S. Savage, who he had hoped to meet in Cambridge, explaining to him that when he had the temerity to ask the Club for expenses;

> ... they pleaded poverty, the rogues & liars & wanted to postpone the meeting, or whatever ... Fuck them all. Sorry to miss you ...

Both Vernon Watkins and Dylan Thomas, along with a group of their mutual friends contributed to the *social milieu*; the intellectual and artistic culture that prevailed in Swansea when Wittgenstein arrived in 1942, and which requires exploring. Thomas and Watkins were at the heart of a group of young men who grew up in Swansea in the opening decades of the twentieth century. They have come to be known as 'The Kardomah Gang',[2] after the name of a popular Swansea coffee house that was part of a huge nation-wide chain they frequented. This is a piece of modern lazy journalese; they were neither a gang nor an organised group of any kind, and most all of them would decry such a description, for they were all fiercely independent. When and who coined the phrase is lost in time, but it has stuck. There remains a Kardomah café in Swansea, which is still very popular, but it is probably the sole surviving example of the original chain.

Alongside the two poets, and in no particular order, they were joined by Daniel Jones, a classical composer and polymath linguist who worked as a codebreaker at Bletchley Park during the war (together with Vernon Watkins and his future wife Gwen). Thomas describes his first meeting with Dan in his short story *The Fight*, from his 1939 collection of autobiographical short stories *Portrait of the Artist as a Young Dog*, a book that contains many stories depicting various strata of Swansea society. Alfred (Fred) Janes was a fine painter (and also an accomplished pianist) with a gentle, intelligent sense of humour. He trained at Swansea School of Art, and then went to London, to the Royal Academy School of Art. Although a wonderful portrait painter, he was enraptured by modern cubist and abstract art. Janes haunted the galleries in Cork Street, ravished by the work of Picasso and Braque, and his work was later exhibited alongside theirs. In London, he shared his shabby flat with Dylan Thomas and another Swansea artist, Mervyn Levy. Mervyn Montague Levy was from a prominent Swansea Jewish family, a young man who spoke Yiddish at home because he was the grandson of the refugee Russian Jew who had opened the first cinema in Swansea. His family sent him to a small dame school in Uplands where he learned and played alongside Dylan Thomas, and they remained close friends. Levy went to Art School in Swansea and London, and carved a lively career writing and broadcasting on art. He wrote important books on L. S. Lowry and D. H. Lawrence as an artist, and became a popular early TV artist with his own programme, teaching housewives how to paint.

The Cultural Milieu of the 1930s and 1940s

John Prichard was another writer in the Kardomah group. Although Thomas admired his work, Prichard was not widely published. His poems would appear in early numbers of *Wales* magazine alongside work by Thomas, Watkins and Fisher (*Wales* almost became the Kardomah house journal). His best book was the charming *Journey to the End of the Alphabet*, illustrated by Àsgeir Scott. Charles Fisher was the longest living member of the group – he died in 2006, aged 91. He was in Swansea Grammar School with Thomas (it was an all-boys school, so Charles cross-dressed to play Thomas's wife in a school drama production of *Strife* by Galsworthy). Later, they both left school and got jobs as cub reporters on the local paper, the *South Wales Daily Post*. After the war, Charles headed to Canada, settling in Ottawa where he became the Canadian Parliament's *Hansard* reporter, sitting daily in the chamber typing up the proceedings as they occurred. He and Dylan corresponded but they never met again. Fisher later wrote:

> There never was such thing as a Kardomah Group in the sense usually applied to people who meet to reinforce artistic or social aims they possess in common. We were far too individualistic for that. We had no manifesto to publish, no theory of art to propose. Our purpose in meeting was simply to talk and exchange news in the wittiest and most lively way we knew, which we did at great length and to some effect for a decade or so.

Other occasional 'members' were Tom Warner, another musician (French horn), Mabley Owen (Dylan would name his pet dog Mabley), Wynford Vaughan Thomas (a broadcaster and professional Welshman), Alban Leyshon (craftsman and inventor, who had a workshop in Salubrious Passage), and Swansea artist Ceri Richards. Richards was also a close friend of Watkins and Janes who introduced him to Thomas just before he died. Richards was so deeply distressed on hearing of Thomas's death that he threw himself into work producing a stunning suite of lithographs in 1965 inspired by Thomas's poems and many fine oils and watercolours, all based on images in Thomas's poems.

There were still other figures of cultural and literary merit who would interact with them on occasion. Thomas Taig was very active in Swansea Little Theatre, where he directed Thomas in a few productions, and also knew Jones and Watkins. At the time he was a lecturer in the

Wittgenstein in Swansea

Department of English at the fledgling University College of Swansea. In 1929, he wrote an interesting book, *Rhythm and Verse*,[3] which influenced Thomas and deserves to be better noticed. During the war years, he and Thomas worked on a proposed London Theatrical evening, comprising recitations of an anthology of poetry written by current Welsh writers, writing in English, but it never reached the stage. It was Taig who introduced Thomas and others in the group to Bert Trick, another remarkable autodidact who influenced a few of these lads, but was closest to Thomas, who mentions him in his Radio Play *Return Journey*:

> I went on my way into Glanbrydan Avenue[4] where Bert Trick kept a grocer's shop and in the Kitchen threatened the annihilation of the ruling classes over sandwiches and jelly and blancmange.

Dylan spoke of him as 'the Communist Grocer', and it was Bert who awakened Thomas's leftish and liberal political leanings, but he also encouraged his writings and hosted occasional evening meetings in his back-shop, where Thomas and a few others read and discussed their work and endeavoured to put the world to rights. It was Bert who took Thomas to a fascist rally held by Sir Oswald Mosley and his Blackshirts at a local cinema, where they watched other infiltrating local socialists bring the meeting to a violent end. The initial disruption was provoked by a wilful interruption by a mischievous socialist and very unusual local churchman, Leon Atkin, and it was Bert Trick who introduced Atkin to Thomas. Leon Atkin was a Welsh Methodist and Congregationalist minister, human rights activist, politician and poet. Atkin had opened the crypt of his church to tramps and down-and-outs, and he took his ministry out into the streets and pubs of Swansea. Dylan Thomas called him *'my Priest'*. The last photograph of Thomas ever taken in Swansea was of him in *The Bush*, a popular High Street pub, with Leon. Thomas had stopped off there before taking the train to London, and before flying off to New York on his last fatal trip in October 1953.

In February of 1947, the year that Ludwig Wittgenstein left Swansea, Dylan Thomas came back to his hometown specifically to research and write a radio drama documentary for the BBC about his time growing up in the city. The notebook he used on this reconnaissance is held in the Library of the University of Texas, and is evidence of just how concerned Thomas was to produce an accurate reminiscence. The dramatic device he uses is to have himself, aged in his mid-thirties, revisit his hometown and his own past; to search for his former self and depict the town as it was then, a trope made more poignant as the town was devastated by three nights of fierce German air-raids in February 1941. At one point in the drama, he provides us with a humorous but accurate account of a typical Kardomah gathering. The older Thomas, trudging through the ruined town in the snow, stops a random passer-by and questions him about his younger self and after some banter the chap suddenly recalls Young Thomas:

> PASSER-BY: Oh, *him* He owes me half a crown. I haven't seen him since the old Kardomah days ... Him and Charlie Fisher ... and Tom Warner and Fred Janes, drinking coffee-dashes and arguing the toss.
> NARRATOR: What about?
> PASSER-BY: Music and poetry and painting and politics. Einstein and Epstein, Stravinsky and Greta Garbo, death and religion, Picasso, and girls.
> NARRATOR: And then?
> PASSER-BY: Communism, symbolism, Bradman, Braque, the Watch Committee, free-love, free beer, murder, Michelangelo, Ping-pong, ambition.

After a digression, the Passer-by continues his list:

> Oh the hissing of the butt-ends in the drains of the coffee-dashes and the tinkle and the gibble-gabble of the morning young lounge lizards as they talked about Augustus John, Emil Jannings, Carnera, Dracula, Amy Johnson, Trial marriage, pocket-money, the Welsh sea, London stars, King Kong, anarchy, darts, T. S. Eliot, and girls.

And the Passer-by predicts:

> How Dan Jones was going to compose the most prodigious symphony, Fred Janes paint the most miraculously meticulous

picture, Charlie Fisher catch the poshest trout,[5.] Vernon Watkins and Young Thomas write the most boiling poems, how they would ring the bells of London and paint it like a tart.

The Narrator then becomes maudlin as he remembers:

> The Kardomah Cafe was razed to the snow, the voices of the coffee-drinkers – Poets, painters and musicians in their beginnings – lost in the willynilly flying of the years and the flakes

Return Journey was broadcast five times in 1947 on different channels, including the General Overseas Service, and it was often repeated in subsequent years and was also filmed by the BBC (by John Ormond Thomas). Douglas Cleverdon, in his monograph *The Art of Radio*, writes that Dylan Thomas had an 'unfailing instinct' for radio writing. Reflecting on *Return Journey to Swansea*, he notes that the work is 'a masterly piece of ironic evocation'.

The programme was a critical and popular success, well received by the listeners and the bigwigs in the BBC, where it must have made an impression – a couple of years later, in October 1949, the BBC commissioned another programme celebrating Swansea's rich culture, but this time in a more structured format. *The Radio Times* heralded it thus:

> *Swansea and the Arts* ... five men – three writers, a composer, and a painter – who ... will demonstrate clearly the outstanding vitality of present-day Swansea as a nursery for artistic talent. Few towns, even outside Wales, can show five sons who have achieved similar distinction in literature, music, and painting.

The programme was recorded on 6 October 1949, in a makeshift studio at The Grove, in the Uplands area (very near Thomas's family home in Cwmdonkin Drive). Thomas was to present the programme, give his own take on the subject as an introduction, and then introduce Vernon Watkins, Alfred Janes, Daniel Jones and John Prichard, who all delivered their carefully prepared contributions. The BBC programme announcer began: '[T]hree writers, a composer, and a painter, all Swansea men, will talk about their art and about Swansea'. Thomas used most of his introduction to ridicule, lambast and satirise the kind of pseudo-Welsh men who he had encountered in the louche London pubs and clubs of Soho and Fitzrovia, who tried too hard to deny their Welsh heritage: 'I know in London a Welsh hairdresser who has striven to so vehemently to abolish his accent that he sounds like a man speaking with the Elgin marbles in his mouth.' And he goes on:

> In exhibitions, concerts, cocktail parties, there they are on the horn-rimmed edges ... corsetting their voices so that no lilt or inflection of Welsh enthusiasm may exult or pop out. 'Ecktually' they say, 'I was born in Cwmbwrla,[6] but Soho's better for my gouaches.'

He then berates the 'many artists of Wales [who] stay in Wales too long, giants in the dark behind the parish pump, pygmies in the nationless sun, enviously sniping at the artists of other countries'. He ends by making a bold but not altogether profound statement: 'And too many artists of Wales spend too much time talking about the position of the artists of Wales. There is only one position for an artist anywhere: and that is, upright.' Reading this on the page, much of it seems to me to be somewhat trite, but no doubt it sounded fine and was delivered to receptive listeners. Still, it might reek of the pot calling the kettle black – anyone who has heard Dylan's recorded readings will not recall much trace of a Welsh accent; indeed, not only did his parents not allow him to speak his native tongue as they themselves did, but his father sent him to elocution classes to improve his speech and dampen down his Swansea twang. And much the same can be said of his four friends. I was fortunate to meet Mervyn Levy, Fred Janes, Dan Jones and Charles Fisher, and they all spoke fine English, almost perfect Received Pronunciation. Vernon Watkins had died just before I arrived in Swansea, but having seen films of him and heard recordings, his voice was almost comical – it was so 'posh', cut glass, positively regal! But he had been sent away to Repton School and then on to Cambridge University, so his accent is understandable – I did spend time with his wife Gwen, who had a beautiful English-speaking voice. I never met John Prichard. All the five 'artists' lived most, or all, of their lives in Swansea or in west Wales. Watkins speaks next after a laudatory introduction by Thomas:

> First of all, then, Vernon Watkins, poet and present. I think him to be the most profound and greatly accomplished Welshman writing poems in English ... He is proof against the dangers ... of mellifluous periphrasis, otiose solipsism, the too-easy spin and flow of the paid word.

And Watkins's contribution is much more considered and on message. He begins: 'I like Swansea because it is extraordinary, more extraordinary than Tibet, which was a favourite country when I was a small boy, and its inhabitants are even stranger.' He goes on to enthuse about Gower ('where I live') and then declares:

> Swansea is a town where art is alive If it became a cultural centre or a resort where art was fashionable and where it was always being discussed but never creative, it would be a town where art was dead. Such a Swansea, such a Salzburg[7] on the Tawe I cannot imagine.

As did most of this group, Watkins loved word play, especially puns (some of them bad), and he cannot resist ending with one such:

> A town speaks through its art. Most towns speak with an impediment, and there are some towns that can't speak at all, but can only snore and rattle, and make hideous mechanical noises. I like Swansea because it has a natural impediment: it speaks with the Mumbles.[8]

Thomas introduces Alfred Janes by describing the squalid flat they shared in London:

> those ginger bearded days seem full to me, now, of his apples carved in oil, his sulphurously glowing lemons, his infernal kippers ... after many Academy awards and several paintings in London galleries, he returned to Swansea to work and experiment, which were synonymous.

Janes's response focuses on and enlarges upon Thomas's famous, perhaps infamous, description of his hometown with which he opened his first self-scripted BBC broadcast from 1943, *Reminiscences of Childhood*: 'I was born in a large Welsh industrial town at the beginning of the Great War: an ugly, lovely town (or so it was and is to me) …'. Janes lists fourteen of the more extreme 'conflicts and contrasts', here is a selection:

> Salubrious Passage[9] and the new double highway through the town;
> Singleton[10] and the Slaughter house;
> Mumbles Road to [Clifton – crossed out] Constitution Hill;[11]
> Welsh flannel[12] at the Market and nylons near the Tenby;[13]
> Minchin Hole[14] and the Plaza Cinema.[15]

But the recent bombing raids still weigh heavy as Janes recalls: 'Then in the middle of it all is the brutal reminder of the most disastrous conflict we have yet experienced – the blitzed and blighted town.' It is these intriguing characteristics and contradictions that keep Janes living and working in Swansea. In his introduction to Daniel Jones, Thomas has this to say:

> He has never stopped writing music, with the possible exception of the time when, as an Intelligence officer in the war, he was occupied, so far as I know, with translating Chinese … This week, at the Swansea Festival he is conducting the London Symphony Orchestra in a performance of his First Symphony.

Jones's piece is the least positive; he sounds somewhat curmudgeonly and a tad superior, largely decrying the lack of music venues, concert halls and orchestras in the town. The saving grace is the annual music festival, '[t]he one bright gleam in the darkness'. Jones begins: 'It's easy to see why a painter should chose to live in Swansea Bay but as far as a composer is concerned, Swansea at first sight seems to offer few advantages.' He goes on to agree with his colleagues about Swansea's inspiring coastal locations and he ends on a more positive note: 'The character of Swansea is the people rather than the place, and their friendliness, humour and enthusiasm make me well content to live among them ... No wonder that I feel happier and can work better here than anywhere else.' John Prichard, the least well-known of the quintet, is the most controversial, as he focuses on the issue of the two languages of Wales. But all five were steered away from speaking and writing in Welsh by circumstance or parental choice. Though this, in conclusion, may still be an issue for some, today Wales has a thriving literature in both languages.

Thomas brings the programme to a close[16] with his own conclusion:

> To end, may I say why I like Swansea so much, why I used to work so freely and happily in it, why I like coming back to it as often as I can why I still live near it? It's because it's the most romantic town I know. And I haven't time to say anything more than that.

In the first half of the twentieth century, Swansea also offered strong cultural venues. The Glynn Vivian Art Gallery was based on the collection of the eponymous founder Richard Glynn Vivian (1835–1910), who was a local wealthy art collector and philanthropist from the Vivian family. In 1905, he offered his collection of paintings, drawings and china to Swansea Corporation, who, with his endowment, built the gallery, near the train station, to house it. Vivian laid the foundation stone on 14 May 1909, but he died at his London home on 7 June 1910, just over a year before the gallery was opened by his brother Graham. The art gallery was situated opposite the town's impressive Central Library. It was designed by Henry Holtom of Dewsbury in the Italian classical style, and had a grand opening in 1887, when the four non-consecutive terms Prime Minister, William Ewart Gladstone, visited to do the honours. The Library's endearing feature was its splendid circular reading room and reference library; a smaller version of the Reading Room in the British Museum Library, coming in at 86 feet (26 m) in diameter, with the domed top 25 feet (7.6 m) high in the centre. The collections there were based on books donated by Glynn Vivian and the books of J. Deffett Francis.[17] The collections provided a repository of source material for research on Swansea in particular and Wales in general, but were also very rich in art history and literature.

Alongside the library is Swansea School of Art. Founded in 1853, it is the oldest art school in Wales, and now possesses Wales's newest art and design faculty. Through its long existence, it has also been known as the Municipal School of Art and Crafts (1908–22) and the Swansea School of Arts and Crafts (1923–51). Swansea also has a very strong history in stained glass, which began at the art school in 1935 and is still going strong.

The town could also boast several fine theatres: the Grand Theatre on Singleton Street; the Palace Theatre on High Street; the Empire Theatre on Oxford Street; the Theatre Royal on Bank Street; and the Albert Hall. Perhaps of equal importance was the Swansea Little Theatre, which was established in 1924 in Southend, Mumbles, and was the first Little Theatre in Wales. The theatre company presented plays in many venues, and established itself as the foremost non-professional English-language theatre company in Wales. In the early 1930s, Dylan Thomas became an important member of the troupe after first reviewing plays by the Little Theatre for *South Wales Evening Post*. In 1932, he appeared with the group for a production of Noel Coward's *Hay Fever*, taking the role of Simon. A local critic wrote: 'Equally well done was Simon's part by D. M. Thomas.' The theatre itself was described as being 'based in Mumbles [...] close to congenial pubs',[18] and these pubs proved to be Thomas's downfall. After appearing in some dozen plays, his habit of skipping out of rehearsals to a nearby pub for a pint or a nip led to him having a fierce row with the director during the final dress rehearsal, and Thomas walked out leaving them without a leading man. Before this, however, he had been in the audience at one truly remarkable production by the Swansea Little Theatre, which made the local papers – and prompted a poem from Thomas, which he mentions in his radio piece *Return Journey*: 'Young Thomas ... you know; used to have poems printed in the *Herald of Wales*; there was one about of an open-air performance of Electra in Mrs Bertie Perkins Garden in Sketty ...'. On 5 and 6 July 1933, the company did indeed stage two performance of Sophocles's *Electra* in the garden of Mrs Alys Bertie Perkins. It was produced by Thomas Taig (an early influence on Thomas, and another of Swansea's university and Kardomah alumnus). Daniel Jones wrote and performed the music on 'Harp and Drums'. Dylan Thomas attended one performance, and we have in an eyewitness published account by Ethel Ross (Alfred Janes's future sister-in-law):[19] 'I remember seeing him, slightly apart from the audience leaning up against a tree, a cigarette hanging from his lips. He looked extremely bored.' But looks obviously deceived, because the play was the inspiration for a long eight stanza poem which was printed in the *Herald Of Wales* a few days later, and has entered Thomas's canon. It begins:

> A woman wails her dead among the trees,
> Under the green roof grieves the living;
> The living sun lanterns the dying skies,
> Lamenting falls. Pity Electra's loving

Both Daniel Jones and Dylan Thomas were regular contributors to the *Swansea Grammar School Magazine*. Thomas went on to become the editor and wrote various items including poems and stories, but he also contributed two remarkable, precocious prose essays, one in 1929 on *Modern Poetry*, and, in 1930, *The Films*, dealing with cinema. So just before his fifteenth birthday, he wrote a detailed survey of recent poetry, making confident references to Joyce and Graves and in his cinema piece he exhibited a sound understanding of this relatively new art form discussing D. W. Griffith and Zukar. Vernon Watkins describes going with Thomas to the cinema in the Uplands and they both must have been entranced by the litany of richly hyperbolic names that Swansea's many cinemas could boast – The Elysium, The Anima, The Castle, The Gem, The Maxine, The Olympic, The Oxford Electric Theatre, The Regent and The Rialto – but they were all dwarfed by the magnificent Plaza Cinema, which opened on Valentine's Day 1931 on the Kingsway. It became huge competition for all the other cinemas with its plush interior, its 3,020 seats, and its grand Christie organ.

Although not as plentiful as cinemas and theatres, Swansea could also boast a few good bookshops. Morgan and Higgs was the main new booksellers, but A. R. Way was another, and the town had a branch of W. H. Smith on the High Street. The town also boasted a legendary second-hand bookshop, Ralph's Bookshop.[20] Ralph Wishart, known locally as 'Ralph the Books', was the 'honorary' bookseller of the Kardomah Boys. Dylan Thomas was a regular customer, selling his review copies and buying detective fiction, Crompton's *Just William* books and poetry. The shop features in Thomas's radio broadcast *Return Journey*, when the young Thomas encounters a minister, and asks him if he knows the shop. The churchman replies:

The Cultural Milieu of the 1930s and 1940s

A bookshop. Yes, I knew it well ... a young man like you ... used to rub shoulders with me by the shelves in the back corner ... You see, poetry and theology was next door to each other. He was swimming out of his depth in a flood of words, and I was toiling up high mountains of biblical exegesis. Believed nothing he did ... My pleasure was to find ... a second-hand copy of The Collected Sermons of Christmas Evans.[21] His pleasure was to read at me like the bull of Basan[22] some Babylonian lines from a man he called Ezra Pound. Tried to shock me he did, but I was not shocked.

A concluding significant Swansea cultural edifice must be Swansea Museum, built for the Royal Institution of South Wales in 1841. It is the oldest museum in Wales, and was, as Dylan Thomas so eloquently described it in his 1943 BBC Welsh Home Service broadcast, *Reminiscences of Childhood*, 'the museum which should have been *in* a museum'.

The Royal Institution of South Wales (RISW), was made up of a group of art and science enthusiasts, drawn mainly from the wealthier middle classes but with philosophical and philanthropic interests. The museum is housed in a Grade-2 listed building that was commissioned by the RISW, built in the neo classical style, and completed in 1841. The building was designed to house the RISW's array of collections which ranged across natural history, local history, art and ceramics, industry, physical sciences and photography, as well as providing research and learning facilities, and a fine library. It also had an original Egyptian mummy, and a stuffed African elephant in the foyer.

Although Swansea offered this rich cultural landscape it is also worth noticing that many of this group looked beyond Swansea and Wales to engage with a wider cultural world. Dylan Thomas joined Janes and Mervyn Levy in London in 1934, where he quickly became known and respected in literary circles. He met T. S. Eliot as a poet and as the editor at Faber & Faber, and he had meetings and drinks with him. Eliot just missed out on publishing Thomas, but Eliot did publish Vernon Watkins's first half dozen books. Edith Sitwell was very supportive of him and his work. Thomas also met with the 1930s poets Auden, Spender, MacNeice and C. Day Lewis (Thomas's friend, the South African poet Roy Campbell, referred to them collectively as 'MacSpaunday'). Thomas

Wittgenstein in Swansea

was also involved in the seismic 1936 Surrealist Exhibition at London's New Burlington Galleries. He was present when Salvador Dalí delivered a lecture whilst wearing a deep-sea diving suit, a stunt that almost backfired when the crazy surrealist could not remove the heavy brass helmet and began to suffocate; only swift intervention by the young poet David Gascoyne, who arrived with a spanner just in time to release him, averted disaster. Thomas added his own impromptu performance to the bizarre event by crawling around the floor on all fours proffering members of the crowd a cup of boiled string, asking 'How do you like it, weak or strong?' He would return later to join Paul Éluard and other surrealist poets for a reading. Thomas became friends with one of the exhibition organisers, the Surrealist artist Roland Penrose, whose wife the photographer Lee Miller would take some fine photographs of Thomas. He later joined with them in a performance of Picasso's only play, *Desire Caught by the Tail*, when it was staged at the Institute of Contemporary Arts. In the 1930s, Thomas also published poetry and prose in the London-based surrealist magazine *Contemporary Poetry and Prose*, edited by Roger Roughton. In 1936, he also contributed a short story and two poems to issue 25 of Eugene Jolas's celebrated literary periodical *transition*, alongside Kafka's *Metamorphosis*.[23] Other contributors included Paul Klee, Piet Mondrian, Louis Aragon, and the magazine included an account of Dada art. Later, in the early 1950s, while in America Thomas and his wife Caitlin would stay with the surrealists Max Ernst and Dorothea Tanning at their desert hideaway in the Arizona desert, near Sedona. In 1953, Thomas met with Igor Stravinsky in Boston to discuss writing the libretto for a new opera being planned by Stravinsky – but sadly, the project never came to fruition as Thomas died only a few months after their meeting.

Just as Thomas reached out to Europe and America, so the nations responded to his work. His early books were published in America from 1939, and translated and published in French, German and Italian during his lifetime. In 1947, he spent three months in Italy, writing and engaging with Italian poets including Eugenio Montale, a left-wing writer who would go on to win the Nobel Prize for Literature in 1975. A few years later, Thomas was in Prague for a conference of Czech socialist writers, where he re-engaged with Jiri Mucha, the son of the great Art Nouveau artist Alphonse Mucha, having first met Jiri Mucha in London during the war years.

The Cultural Milieu of the 1930s and 1940s

Vernon Watkins also travelled in Europe, making early visits to Germany – Nuremberg in 1931, for example – travels that were of great importance for him, and which led to much of his free time during the Second World War being spent on translating Heine's *The North Sea* (Watkins was in the Royal Air Force Military Police, stationed at Bletchley Park), and the German writers Novalis, Goethe and Rilke. When *The North Sea* was eventually published in America by James Laughlin's New Directions in 1951 (Faber issued a UK edition in 1955), it was extremely well received. Watkins went on to become celebrated as a fine translator of European poetry, publishing poems from French, Italian, Hungarian and Spanish. The critic Kathleen Raine commented that 'Watkins is a poet of European stature and as such will come to be known'. In 1965, Watkins was visited at his Gower home by Pablo Neruda, the Chilean politician and poet who went on to win the Nobel Prize for Literature. Watkins never engaged with philosophy directly, but was deeply influenced by Kierkegaard, and it was to his writings that he turned for this kind of conceptual engagement – part philosophy, part Christian thinking. Later in his life, having retired from his work at the bank, Watkins joined the staff at the university in Swansea as a kind of writer in residence. He was affiliated to the English Department, but also engaged with Erich Heller, the Professor of German, who is best known for his book *The Disinherited Mind*.[24] Heller wrote mainly on Nietzsche and Heidegger, but he wrote as well on Wittgenstein and contributed the chapter 'Vorwort zum *Tractatus logico-Philosophicus*'[25] to a German collection of essays on Wittgenstein.

All the above seems to me to suggest that Watkins would have been the perfect Kardomah boy with whom Wittgenstein could engage. Watkins was the most cerebral of the group, a deep thinker, and a compassionate man. He loved walking and bathing on Gower, where he lived above the sea at Pennard. Watkins spoke fluent German, with some knowledge of other eastern European languages – and he was extremely well read, especially in poetry.

As far as we know, no such meeting ever occurred. Nevertheless, Wittgenstein himself very quickly became highly content in Swansea. On his first visit, he stayed with Rush Rhees on Bryn Road, just off the sea-front and above the St Helen's Cricket and Rugby ground. He left in 1943, and when he returned in 1944 he took rooms with Mrs Mann, just above Mumbles in a house on Langland Road. He gleefully wrote to Rhees: 'Am I Glad To Be Here!' The house overlooked Underhill Park, but better still if he came out of the front door and turned right up the hill, he could then quickly descend to Rotherslade Bay, which was backed by a range of beach shops, cafes and a dance hall built into the cliff face. Up above was the Osborne, a respectable Edwardian hotel. Wittgenstein could sit and watch waves crash around the huge rocky outcrop close to the beach, as did the Impressionist artist Alfred Sisley, who had stayed in the Osborne for his honeymoon in 1897 (painting at least eleven views around the bay, one of which is his view of the rock known as Donkey Rock (now in the National Museum of Wales in Cardiff). Wittgenstein soon settled in and wrote to his friend Norman Malcolm:

> The weather is foul but I enjoy not being in Cambridge I know quite a number of people here whom I like. I seem to find it more easy to get along with them here than in England. I feel much more often like smiling, e.g. when I walk in the street, or when I see children, etc.

Wittgenstein seems to be of the same opinion as Daniel Jones: 'The character of Swansea is the people rather than the place, and their friendliness, humour and enthusiasm make me well content to live among them.' In 1946, Wittgenstein wrote to Ben Richards of his love of Gower: 'But today was beautiful. I went to Langland Bay by bus & then walked along the cliffs to Caswell & to Pull [sic] Du. I wish you were here with me.' Gabriel Citron writes: 'Many of Wittgenstein's and Rhees's philosophical conversations seem to have taken place while they were walking along the Gower Peninsula or sitting in a local park in Swansea.'[26] In 1947, Wittgenstein is still enjoying his stay, writing again to Ben Richards:

> The weather here is changeable but not too bad. I go out a fair amount & often I enjoy it (though with you I'd enjoy it more). I also work & not too badly, so far. I like the air here it's altogether different than in Cambridge.

Wittgenstein even endeavoured to persuade his friend and colleague Rush Rhees to remain in Swansea, at a point when he was considering leaving:

I was glad to hear that they had the sense to offer you an appointment again at Swansea. I wish to God you'd take it!! I don't know, of course, what your special reasons are for wanting to leave Swansea, but please weigh them damn carefully. I should, for personal reasons, hate you to leave Swansea.

However, Wittgenstein did not approve of everything Swansea has to offer. In 1946, he sends Ben Richards a postcard depicting multiple views of Swansea's grand Civic Centre Building, but it was not to his taste as he scrawled across the face of the card: 'This abomination is joy and pride of Swansea'. And indeed it was. Opened in 1934 by the Duke of Kent, it was designed by the Welsh architect Sir Percy Thomas in a somewhat Brutalist neoclassical style, but it was probably the very Germanic Art Deco fixtures and fittings that irked Wittgenstein. However, a Swansea mayor and local dignitary, Alderman Edward Harris, Mayor, emblazoned the cover of his 1934 history *Swansea: Its Port and Trade and their Development* with a stylised depiction of the building and a copy of the book was gifted to every junior school child in Swansea.

Even after Wittgenstein had left Swansea in 1947, never to return, it seems he always remembered it warmly – in August 1949, he was writing again to Rhees from Ithaca: 'There are some nice walks here, though nothing compared with the Gower coast. Nature here doesn't look as <u>natural</u> as in Wales.' After his brief sojourn in Swansea, Wittgenstein seems to have been smitten with *hiraeth*, the almost untranslatable Welsh word that describes a deep nostalgic, wistful love and longing for a significant place, but a feeling tinged with sadness and loss. The same feeling often comes out in Thomas's writings about Swansea, surmised in his 1943 radio broadcast *Reminiscences of Childhood*:

> And I fly over the trees and chimneys of my town, over the dockyards, skimming the masts and funnels ... over the trees of the everlasting park ... over the yellow seashore and the stone-chasing dogs and the old men and the singing sea. The memories of childhood have no order, and no end.

In a 1938 letter to Charles Fisher, Thomas writes:

Swansea is still the best place, tell Fred he's right ...When somebody else's ship comes home I'll set up in Swansea in a neat villa full of and pianos and lawn-mowers and dumb-bells and canvases for all of us ...

Then in 1939 Thomas writes to Bert Trick:

I'm strong and sentimental for the town and people, for long virulent Sundays with you and scrapbooks and strawberry jelly at the end, for readings and roarings with all the grand boys.

To conclude, two synchronicities of note. In his biography of Wittgenstein, Ray Monk writes: 'Before he left for Newcastle Wittgenstein spent some time in Swansea with Rush Rhees. There he resumed the conversations he had the previous summer about Freud.' Indeed, Freud and his work seems to have been a recurring topic in the conversations of these two philosophers, and one wonders whether they were aware that the neurologist and psychoanalyst Ernest Jones was born in the north Gower village of Gowerton, and grew up in Swansea, attending the same school as Thomas and his Kardomah friends – and that although he moved away to London and Europe to pursue his education and profession, he was always proud of his Welsh origins. Jones became a member of the Welsh Nationalist Party, Plaid Cymru, and he had a particular love for Gower, which he had explored extensively in his youth. Following the purchase of a holiday cottage in Llanmadoc, this area became a regular holiday retreat for the Jones family. He was instrumental in helping secure its status in 1956 as the first region of the UK designated an Area of Outstanding Natural Beauty. Jones was the first English-speaking practitioner of psychoanalysis, and became its leading exponent in the English-speaking world. As a lifelong friend and colleague of Sigmund Freud, he became his official biographer, and the translator and editor of his major works. Although he died in London where his funeral was held, Jones's ashes were returned to Gower, and are interred next to his daughter's grave in Llanmadoc. Jones performed much the same role for Freud as Rush Rhees did for Wittgenstein. When Rhees died in 1989, he too was buried in Swansea, in Oystermouth Cemetery, Mumbles.

The Cultural Milieu of the 1930s and 1940s

One further intriguing synchronicity. From Christmas 1944 until the summer of 1947, whenever he was in Swansea, Wittgenstein lodged very happily in Cwmdonkin Terrace in Swansea's Uplands. First, he stayed with the Methodist minister Revd Wynford Morgan, who lived at 2 Cwmdonkin Terrace. Although they argued about religion, the two men got on well, and Mrs Morgan was an attentive host. Living next door in number one was the Clement family. Mrs Clement in particular took a liking to the somewhat eccentric philosopher, and invited him for weekly Sunday lunch with her and her husband, and their two daughters Joan and Barbara. Wittgenstein eventually moved in and became their lodger.

Whilst lodging on Cwmdonkin Terrace, Wittgenstein would have looked directly down Cwmdonkin Drive, where, just fifty yards down, was a row of terraced semi-detached houses lining one side of the road climbing up from the Uplands. The newly-built number 5 had been purchased from the builder in 1914 by David John Thomas, a Carmarthenshire man, who (having gained a first-class honours degree in Literature from Aberystwyth University) had moved into Swansea, staying with his young wife Florrie's family. Florrie's family also hailed from rural Carmarthenshire, but had moved into a terraced house in Delhi Street, in the heart of Swansea's east-side, a working-class area close to the thriving dockyards. D. J. Thomas had started a career in teaching, and was ambitious. He and Florrie had an eight-year-old daughter, Nancy, but Florrie was again pregnant. D.J. (as he was known) would soon become head of English at the respectable Swansea Grammar School, climbing the social ladder, and they scraped together £350 to buy a 99-year lease on a brand new four-bedroomed semi-detached house with bay windows on Cwmdonkin Drive. They had not long settled in before, on 27 October 1914, Florrie gave birth to a son in the upstairs front bedroom. They named him Dylan Marlais Thomas (a name loaded with Celtic resonance), and he would grow up to become a famous (or was it infamous?) poet of international repute. Dylan would live at this house in Swansea until 1935, when he moved to London, and for the rest of his short life would be mostly itinerant (he died in New York in 1953, aged 39).

By the time Wittgenstein moved to the terrace in 1944, D. J. Thomas and Florrie had moved to the Gower village of Bishopston, but their literary son would have been only too well known in the neighbourhood.

31

Dylan Thomas was never shy of publicity, and often made the local press for various reasons – and once he left for London, he made the national papers too. It is hard to think that the Morgans and the Clements might not have pointed out the house where he was born and raised, and told their intellectual lodger something about Thomas. In 1940, Thomas's book of semi-autobiographical short stories, *Portrait of the Artist as a Young Dog*, was published by J. M. Dent & Sons. All of the stories were set in Swansea or rural Carmarthenshire. The book was well received and reviewed in local and national press, but a few years later the most sensational events in Thomas's life occurred. To escape from the London blitz, Thomas had moved with his wife and young daughter Aeronwy to New Quay, Cardiganshire, where they were living in a cliff-top wooden bungalow named Majoda – which in turn gave its name to the notorious *Majoda Incident*.

On the night of 6 March 1945, Captain William Killick, a Special Operations Executive (SOE) Commando and Dylan's neighbour and erstwhile drinking chum, appeared with a Sten gun and hand grenade, firing into the bungalow in which Dylan and his family were residing. Three friends were also present at the time. Killick entered the bungalow brandishing the grenade, and Dylan showed unexpected bravery and restraint in gently talking to and calming the deranged soldier, until the local constabulary arrived. Luckily, there were no casualties. The ferment led to a court case in Lampeter, which was covered by the major newspapers. Killick had recently returned from active service in Greece, much of it behind enemy lines, and he was most likely suffering post-traumatic stress disorder and venting his spleen following tensions with Dylan – which included the relationship between Dylan and the Captain's wife, Vera, with whom Dylan had grown up in Swansea (he was also best man at their wedding). Thomas testified at the trial, but tried to protect Killick, who was acquitted. One can easily imagine this being a topic of conversation at dining and pub tables around the Uplands, and Wittgenstein may have been aware of this tale.

In the same year, two of Thomas's most famous Swansea-based radio scripts, *Reminiscences of Childhood* and *Memories of Christmas*, were broadcast. In all, Thomas wrote and broadcast nineteen scripts on the BBC between 1943 and 1947, proving to be somewhat ubiquitous during the 1940s.

The Cultural Milieu of the 1930s and 1940s

In addition, when D.J. and Florrie moved from Cwmdonkin Drive, the new occupant, W. Emlyn Davies, was also a teacher, musician and a gifted calligrapher – and a passionate admirer of Dylan Thomas's poems, which he painstakingly rendered in intricate coloured calligrams later to be published. In 1946, Emlyn sent Thomas his artwork based on *The Ballad of the Long- Legged Bait*, and he received a very warm letter of thanks in return from Thomas. In his introduction to his own book, Davies writes that he was commissioned to make a 'larger version on vellum ... commissioned by the College Bookshop, of the University of Swansea, as the first memorial to the poet in his own town'. Emlyn also fabricated a very unusual wrought-iron gate, which incorporated the house-number into the design. It's hard to imagine that either the Revd Morgan or Mr and Mrs Clement would not mention their erstwhile famous literary near neighbour to their educated and academic lodger; nor that every time Wittgenstein would leave the terrace and head down the hill towards the university, his curiosity would not be intrigued by the gate to Number 5.

Notes

1. Ludwig Wittgenstein arrived in Swansea in 1942; a Swansea that, despite the recent devastating blitz, was a cultural and literary hotbed, due substantially to the activities of Dylan Thomas and the Kardomah Gang in earlier years. This chapter explains how the artistic and natural environment of Swansea would have been beneficial to the shaping of some of Wittgenstein's thinking and writing.
2. Kardomah Cafés were a chain of coffee shops in England, Wales and a few in Paris, popular from the early 1900s until the 1960s. They featured live entertainment provided by string quartets. The original Swansea branch was on High Street, formally known as 'The Kardomah Exhibition Cafe & Tea Rooms'. It moved to Castle Street in 1908, where these chaps met; it was built on the site of the former Congregational chapel, where Thomas's parents were married in 1903. Thomas referred to it in a letter to Charles Fisher as 'the Kardomah my home sweet homah'.
3. Taig also wrote a good article in the Summer 1968 issue of the *Anglo Welsh Review*, 'Swansea Between the Wars', with much on the Kardomah boys.
4. Sited on the cusp between Uplands and Brynmill.
5. Fisher lived up to his name and was a keen and skilful angler. He wrote a fishing column for the *Swansea Post* with his by-line, *Blue Dun* (a classic dry fly pattern that was originated to imitate young Mayflies).
6. Cwmbwrla was a deprived, rough, and run-down suburb on the town's east side.

Wittgenstein in Swansea

7   The city where, in 1918, Wittgenstein finally finished the book later published as *Tractatus Logico-Philosophicus*.
8   A village to the west of the town, and the gateway to Gower beaches, it was once a thriving fishing village with oyster beds.
9   A small Georgian covered passageway that led from busy Wind Street across to the town beaches. I ran my Dylan's Bookstore there for forty years – it was a wonderful address for a bookshop.
10 Swansea's splendid coastal park, which surrounds the university. The 250 acres were once part of the Vivian family estate.
11 A notorious extremely steep cobbled road, which climbs from Walter Road to the houses up above. It has a twenty degree gradient.
12 Penclawdd 'Cockle Women' would stall out in the market hall wrapped in shawls and skirts made of thick traditional Welsh flannel.
13 The Tenby was a rough and louche pub of ill-repute on Walter Road, at the bottom of Constitution Hill.
14 Minchin Hole, the largest cave on Gower, is located at the base of a spectacular ravine in the steep cliffs west of Pwll-Du, which Wittgenstein visited, as Alfred Schmidt informed us. Sediments and animal bones have been found in Minchin Hole and there have been various finds from the Celtic Iron Age and Roman periods.
15 The Plaza Cinema, the largest cinema to be erected in Wales, was a grand and imposing state of the art cinema, with seating for 3,000. It was built on Swansea's Kingsway, and it opened on 14 February 1931.
16 The BBC was still not done with Swansea, and this group and returned to it in the early days of television. In April 1953 (Thomas would die just a little over six months later in New York City), Thomas, Watkins, Jones and Janes reconvened in a Cardiff studio and endeavoured to restage *Swansea and the Arts* for television, as *Home Town Swansea*. They used a Swansea producer, D. J. TV Thomas, and a quintessential Swansea Welsh presenter, Wynford Vaughan Thomas. The format was Dylan in the studio looking at Janes, with portraits of Watkins and Jones, whereupon they would appear and engage with Thomas. Sadly, the programme has not survived, but a draft of the script is in The Harry Ransom Library at Texas, and it was printed in *Texas Quarterly* (Winter 1961). Vernon Watkins made the transcription, and added his comments, stating that the programme was 'devised by Dylan Thomas with the producer'.
17 John Deffett Francis (1815–1901) was a Swansea portrait painter and art collector. He is particularly well known for his portraits of Queen Victoria and Prime Minster Robert Peel, and the bequests of his personal library and art collection to Swansea Library. Overall, the collection of artefacts that Francis collected and donated to Swansea between 1876 and his death totalled 7,000 books and 2,000 pictures and engravings.
18 In a 1934, letter to his first serious girlfriend, Pamela Hansford Johnson, Thomas describes a typical evening: 'first I call at The Marine, then

The Antelope and then The Mermaid. If there is no rehearsal, I continue to commune with these two legendary creatures.'
19 Ethel Ross, *Dylan Thomas and the Amateur Theatre* (Swansea: Swansea Little Theatre, 1979), published in aid of the Little Theatre's new Dylan Thomas Theatre in Gloucester Place.
20 As a young man, Ralph worked for the town's main new bookshop, Morgan & Higgs, but he left and started his own business in Alexandra Road, near Swansea's High Street train station. The front part of his shop operated as a newsagent, with the books crammed into a room behind. He employed both his sister and brother as assistants, but their bibliographic knowledge was seriously limited. Ralph later moved to bigger, better premises on Dillwyn Street in the centre of Swansea.
21 Christmas Evans (1766–1838) was a Welsh nonconformist, described as 'the greatest preacher that the Baptists ever had'. Thomas warmed to him for his eccentric appearance; he is written of thus: 'In spite of his early disadvantages and personal disfigurement (he had lost an eye in a youthful brawl), he was a remarkably powerful preacher that was said to have been 7 feet tall.'
22 'Many bulls encircle me, strong bulls of Bashan surround me; they open wide their mouths at me, like a ravening and roaring lion.' Psalm 22 v 12/13.
23 Kafka also featured on the cover and inside the 1939 issue 6/7 of *Wales* magazine, which contained two unpublished fragments by Kafka. Dylan Thomas is listed as co-editor, and also contributed two poems; two other Swansea poets and Kardomah boys, Vernon Watkins and John Prichard, also contributed.
24 Erich Heller, *The Disinherited Mind. Essays In Modern German Literature And Thought* (London: Bowes & Bowes, 1952).
25 Erich Heller, 'Vorwort zum *Tractatus logico-philosophicus*', in Ludwig Wittgenstein, *Schriften: Beiheft; mit Beiträgen von Ingeborg Bachmann* (Frankfurt am Main: Suhrkamp, 1960).
26 'Wittgenstein's Philosophical Conversations with Rush Rhees (1939–50): From the Notes of Rush Rhees', edited by Gabriel Citron, published in *Mind*, 124/493 (January 2015).

3

The Place of Swansea on the Road to Philosophical Investigations

Jonathan Smith

Introduction

From his return to philosophy in 1929 to his death in 1951, it was Wittgenstein's intention to publish a book, or books, that explained his new philosophy. This much is clear from his correspondence with friends and colleagues, when he regularly writes of progress, or lack of it, on a work he usually called his 'book', though his concept of what this entailed changed over time. He struggled long and hard to produce a work that satisfied his intentions, but, though Wittgenstein came close to publication on more than one occasion, publication ultimately fell to his literary heirs. *Philosophical Investigations*, the closest approximation to Wittgenstein's 'book', was published in 1953 from two of the most finished typescripts in the archive of material that he left them. Further publications were to follow.

Much of the difficulty that Wittgenstein found in publishing his work centred around the interrelated roles of his philosophical method and his writing process. His writing process involved producing philosophical remarks, anywhere between a sentence and a few paragraphs long. These he originally intended to arrange and join together (he uses the evocative word 'weld')[1] in order to produce a sequential text. However, he grew to realise that the best he could manage would be a series of remarks arranged as best suited him. That he failed to do so was more down to the difficulty of the task than to his lack of effort. Wittgenstein's cognitive style was such that he would approach a given problem from a number of aspects, making the construction of a perfectly arranged linear text which retained the complex, nuanced meaning its author intended impossible. As early as April 1932, he admitted to his friend W. H. Watson his doubts as to whether he could mould his ideas into a publishable shape:' I'm growing more and more doubtful as to the publication of my own work, that is, of what I have been writing in the last 3 or 4 years. Somehow, I may not have the power of condensing it and getting it into a publishable shape ...'.[2] This long attempt to create the text of a book that would satisfy his exacting standards falls into several phases.

Wittgenstein's struggle to write his book lasted over thirty years and took place in a number of locations. Though the nature of Wittgenstein's process was central to his difficulties, there is also clear evidence that he found some places more congenial to writing than others and that this had a distinct effect on the progress of his work. In trying to locate Swansea within this struggle, I wish to look at three of these locations – Cambridge, Skjolden and Swansea – and evaluate what they offered to Wittgenstein as writer, in terms of the material, and also in the abstract. I would like to consider the concepts of 'space' and 'place' and how these may have had a positive or negative affect on Wittgenstein. The concept of 'space' refers to the physical – location, geography, etc. – while that of 'place' is less definable, a feeling one gets about a place, its cultural identity, etc. Equally important in understanding how they might influence Wittgenstein is the way in which space and place relate to the self. The sense of place – the feeling one gets about a place or a type of place – develops in childhood and becomes a fundamental component of the way that most people understand who they are.[3] Aspects of place contribute to our feelings of security and belonging or conversely to feelings of unsettledness and outsidership. Both place and space also control what we are able and unable to do – 'People are always in space and spaces constrain and enable'.[4]

Cambridge and its rejection

In January 1929, Wittgenstein returned to Cambridge with a view to devoting himself full-time to philosophy once more. As an academic space, Cambridge had developed over many years with a view to supporting education and research and as such offered much in material terms to aid Wittgenstein in his goal. Indeed, with Russell, Keynes, Moore, and Littlewood willing to help, his particular support group was extremely powerful. To support him financially in his research,[5] Trinity College first awarded a research scholarship with the backing of Russell and Littlewood, and then in 1930 elected him to a Senior Research Fellowship which ran until 1936. The College also offered accommodation, Wittgenstein settling on a set of rooms at a slight remove from the social centre of the college. It also offered collegiate facilities such as communal dining, a senior common room, though Wittgenstein would rarely make use of them, while the University's Moral Sciences Club offered a forum for philosophical debate. One of the most attractive aspects that Cambridge offered Wittgenstein was a pool of academics who might prove to be critical readers of his work, who might help him perfect his ideas and bring his project to fruition. Before the War he turned to Russell for assistance, but on his return to Cambridge he looked to a new generation of scholars with whom to discuss his work. Foremost amongst these were Frank Ramsey, the Cambridge prodigy who made significant contributions in mathematics, economics, and philosophy, before his untimely death in 1930 and Piero Sraffa, an Italian economist whom Keynes had encouraged to come to Britain after his criticism of Fascist policy had roused the ire of Mussolini.

 The single most important stimulus of Wittgenstein's full-time return to philosophy and to Cambridge was Ramsey's criticism of aspects of the *Tractatus*. Ramsey knew the work well as he had translated the *Tractatus* into English as a teenager and had met to discuss the work with Wittgenstein throughout the 1920s. The two men first met in Puchberg in 1923, when they worked through the *Tractatus* page-by-page, and in the subsequent years these discussions continued, in person or by mail. Though there was a hiatus after an awkward meeting in Sussex in 1925, a reconciliation between the two men was engineered by Keynes soon after Wittgenstein arrived back in Cambridge. During 1929, the two men met several times a week to discuss philosophy. Ramsey was one of the few Cambridge academics who truly understood the *Tractatus* and who had the mental stamina to discuss philosophy with Wittgenstein – the older Keynes, Russell and Moore repeatedly complained how exhausting it was to them.

Ramsey's role as stimulating critic is acknowledged in an introduction written by Wittgenstein in 1944, which was used as the introduction to the *Investigations* by his executors: 'I was helped to realise these mistakes – to a degree which I am myself hardly able to estimate – by the criticism which my ideas encountered from Frank Ramsey.'[6]

When Ramsey died in January 1930, the role of trusted critic was assumed by Sraffa. The two men met regularly to discuss, *inter alia*, philosophical matters throughout the 1930s, though Sraffa often found the exercise enervating and periodically refused to meet with Wittgenstein. On the occasions when this happened, Wittgenstein tried to mend the situation by diagnosing the problems between them – he wanted, or needed, Sraffa's intellectual input. According to Rush Rhees, Wittgenstein credited Sraffa with introducing to Wittgenstein an 'anthropological' way of looking at problems[7], suggesting a methodological and conceptual influence, and said that discussions with Sraffa left him feeling like a tree completely shorn of its branches. Indeed, Sraffa received the ultimate accolade from Wittgenstein his introduction to the Philosophical Investigations, where he admits he owed more to Sraffa's criticism even than to Ramsey's. 'Even more than to this – always powerful and assured – criticism, I am indebted to that which a teacher of this University, Mr. P Sraffa, for many years unceasingly applied to my thoughts. It is to this stimulus that I owe the most fruitful ideas of this book.'[8]

If Cambridge provided the two most important critical readers who had a positive effect on the development of Wittgenstein's thought, he found moulding his ideas into publishable form there more difficult. Writing to G. E. Moore in his role as the Editor of *Mind*, he put the matter quite succinctly: 'That which is retarding the publication of my work, the difficulty of presenting it in a clear and coherent form, *a fortiori* prevents me from stating my thoughts within the space of a letter'[9] Wittgenstein's first substantial attempt to produce something for publication was in 1933 when he produced a document that has become known as 'The Big Typescript'[10] during one of his periodic trips to Vienna. True to Wittgenstein's process, this typescript was based on others that had themselves been constructed from material taken from his notebooks from the period 1929 to 1933. Wittgenstein's dissatisfaction with the text, seen in the many substantial manuscript amendments to the typescript which he began almost immediately, is

On the Road to Philosophical Investigations

confirmed in a letter to his friend Watson. 'Thanks for your letter. It reached me in Vienna where I was busy dictating 800 pages of my bloody Philosophy. They contain all I want to say but very badly said and I have now begun to rewrite the whole business'. He subsequently made two further attempts to partially amend the text, the first in late 1933 and early 1934, and another towards the end of the latter year, but neither proved satisfactory. Though it became a useful repository of remarks for later use, the Big Typescript as the text for a book was essentially dead. Instead, he undertook a new project, dictating in the academic year 1934/35 a text which would become known as The Brown Book to his students Alice Ambrose and Francis Skinner, to which he would return later.

The problems Wittgenstein encountered in producing a publishable text in Cambridge were not simply a product of his philosophical approach and cognitive style, but also with what Cambridge provided – good or bad – in terms of fulfilling his needs as a writer. For all the advantages for study offered by a university city, there is clear evidence that from early days he found aspects of Cambridge a hindrance. He felt there were too many distractions to be able to concentrate on his works and, despite making several friends, he also felt an antipathy towards Cambridge academic society in general. In 1913, he announced to David Pinsent that he felt he ought to:

> [e]xile himself and live away from everyone he knows – say in Norway. That he should live alone and by himself – a hermit's life – and do nothing but work on Logic. His reasons for this are very queer to me – but no doubt are very real for him: firstly he feels he will do infinitely more and better work in such circumstances, than at Cambridge, where, he says, his constant liability to interruption and distractions (such as concerts) is an awful hindrance. Secondly, he feels that he has no right to live in an antipathetic world (and of course to him very few people are sympathetic) – a world where he perpetually finds himself feeling contempt for others, and irritating others by his nervous temperament – without some justification for that contempt etc.; such as being a really great man and having done really great work.[11]

Looking back in 1937 on the previous seven years, Wittgenstein wrote, '[i]n Cambridge I could teach, but not write'.[12] We should note Wittgenstein's use of the word 'write', rather than 'think': he had little problem producing new philosophical ideas when he was in Cambridge, only in shaping them into a text that he felt adequately expressed his ideas. We should also note that he contrasts teaching with writing as if the former hindered the latter (a situation familiar to academics today). In January 1930, he had accepted a probationary lectureship offered to him by the Faculty of Moral Sciences, which was soon formalised, and thereafter he taught regular courses in Cambridge. His appointment at this time helped make him financially secure, another example of Cambridge providing the material, but it brought with it other responsibilities. His lectures famously took the form of him wrestling with philosophical ideas in real time, but contrary to their appearance they took a lot of preparation. Though the subjects that he covered in his lectures were wider than in his own writing, the process of lecturing necessarily forced Wittgenstein into thinking about how best to communicate his ideas. As Jim Klagge puts it, '[t]hey gave him countless opportunities, or forced upon him countless occasions, to articulate his ideas'.[13] However, rather than having a positive effect on his writing, lecturing came at a price in the considerable time and effort that he expended in preparing his lectures. More specifically, he found that preparing the lectures in English disturbed the train of his thought when writing in his native language.

Skjolden and the return to Cambridge

Wittgenstein's Senior Research Fellowship at Trinity lapsed in 1936. Now he had the opportunity to put into practice the idea that he had mentioned to Pinsent over twenty years before. He had a ready-made retreat. During his visit to Norway in 1913, he set about building a small house in Skjolden on Sognefjord a little away from the main village with a view to using it as a place to complete the work on logic that was exercising him at the time. Here it was that he retired in 1936, with the express intention of completing his work, spending a year and a half, and only making the occasional visit to Vienna and Cambridge. At first, he pursued his intention of writing a German version of the Brown Book. He had dictated the original to two of his students in

Cambridge, a method intended to concentrate the power of the mind in composition rather than the materiality of writing. This was occasionally used as a means of breaking through 'writer's block' – Maurice Dobb had offered to act as amanuensis to Piero Sraffa when the latter was having trouble writing his Cambridge lectures. However, after producing nearly 200 pages of manuscript,[14] he decided that his work was 'completely worthless'.[15] Cambridge had provided students all too willing to take dictation, but once again, the fact that he communicated to them in English seemed to prove a problem. He explained in a letter to G. E. Moore 'I found it all, or nearly all, boring and artificial. For having the English version before me had cramped my thinking ... I have therefore decided to start all over again and not to let my thoughts be guided by anything but themselves.'[16]

This abrupt end to his work on the Brown Book did not prove fatal to Wittgenstein's work in Skjolden, but instead sent it off in an exciting new direction. Between November 1936 and May the following year, he reworked his ideas into a manuscript,[17] with the title 'Philosophische Untersuchungen' – Philosophical Investigations – the first text that is recognisable as being an early version of the book published under that name in 1953. He had the text typed up and worked on a sequel,[18] which substantially dealt with mathematical subjects. The results pleased him sufficiently to approach Cambridge University Press in 1938 with a view to publication. Though Wittgenstein soon had second thoughts about this, it is apparent that his time in Skjolden was ultimately positive. Writing to G E Moore in autumn 1936, he praised the quiet of the place, but also the effect the scenery had on him: 'I do believe it was the right thing for me to come here, thank God. I can't imagine that I could have worked anywhere as I do here. It's the quiet and, perhaps, the *wonderful* scenery; I mean its quiet seriousness.'[19] It sounds very much as if the sense of place that Skolden evoked in Wittgenstein was a positive influence on his writing, even if it took a little time to have an effect. He would subsequently choose the similar locations of Swansea and the west of Ireland as locations to work on his book. Like Skjolden, both gave easy access to wild countryside with rocky coastlines and expanses of water.

Wittgenstein returned to Cambridge in 1938. He might never have returned at all, were it not for the Anschluss and his subsequent desire to obtain British citizenship, and we can imagine that it must have been a difficult decision given his ambivalent relationship with Cambridge. His homeland was closed off to him – Sraffa persuaded him that if he returned there he would probably not be able to leave – and Norway and much of the rest of Europe became so the following year. He confirmed his decision by accepting the Chair of Philosophy at Cambridge, and was elected a Fellow of Trinity for a second time in 1939. For the first part of the war, Wittgenstein fulfilled his university duties, though he was frustrated at not being able to contribute to the war effort in a practical way. In 1941, he obtained a job as a porter at Guy's Hospital in London, and thence moved to Newcastle in 1943 to assist in work on the treatment of shock. During this period, he did not give up thinking about philosophy as his notebooks reveal. He also revised the draft that he had produced in Norway and even offered it to Cambridge University Press, again successfully. However, by the time the publishers replied in the affirmative, Wittgenstein, not for the first time, changed his mind, and when his work in Newcastle was done, he turned again to editing and augmenting his text for publication.

Swansea

Wittgenstein's decision to return to writing his book while the war was still going on left him with a quandary: he found Cambridge unsuitable for the purpose of writing and he was unable yet to return to Norway. In their place, he chose Swansea as the location to make his latest attempt at preparing his work for publication, gaining permission to be excused from his professorial duties, which were already on hold for his war work, until the end of the academic year. Wittgenstein had visited Swansea occasionally throughout the previous years, his connection with the city being through the American philosopher Rush Rhees, who made Swansea his home for much of his professional life. Rhees had attended Wittgenstein's lectures at Cambridge in 1936, and a friendship developed between the two men, Wittgenstein coming to regard Rhees as 'an excellent man, [who had] a real talent for philosophy too'.[20] On his visits he enjoyed discussing philosophy with Rhees, either in Cwmdonkin Park, or, better still, while walking in the Gower peninsula that bordered the city to the west. So, when Wittgenstein chose it as a suitable place to edit his work, he did it knowing the city well.

On the Road to Philosophical Investigations

Wittgenstein stayed in Swansea from March to September 1944, devoting as much time as possible to working on his book. At first, he continued his work on the philosophy of mathematics, which was intended to follow on from the revision of the typescript produced in Norway. However, towards the end of his sojourn in the south of Wales he made the striking decision to remove this mathematical section from his book. Instead, he replaced it with a discussion of psychological subjects such as his private language arguments, imagining, consciousness etc., beginning a manuscript on these subjects in mid-August.[21] This was typed up either in Swansea or Cambridge.[22] So, after his visit to Swansea, Wittgenstein's book looked quite different to how he previously perceived it. This 'Intermediate Version' has been reconstructed by von Wright,[23] and consists of a reworked version of the first of his Norwegian typescripts,[24] a few remarks from his second Norwegian typescript, followed by a considerable section taken from the new material produced in Swansea. What is remarkable is that despite replacing the mathematical section of his work with one that deals with psychological subjects, the new material follows perfectly from the reasoning in his earlier text to which it was conjoined. The importance of this decision is hard to overestimate. It fundamentally changed the nature of the work published as *Philosophical Investigations*, it marked a permanent move by Wittgenstein away from the subject that had first attracted him to philosophy, and it forces us to look on the text forming the earlier part of the *Investigations* from a different perspective. As Baker and Hacker point out,[25] for Wittgenstein there was a fundamental similarity in the methodology of philosophical investigations in the philosophies of mathematics and of psychology. It is this similarity that enabled the new text composed in Swansea to smoothly replace that on the philosophy of mathematics.

What stimulated Wittgenstein to make such a change is unclear. We might surmise that it was Rhees, whose opinions Wittgenstein respected and with whom he had been discussing, *inter alia*, aspects of the philosophy of psychology.[26] Yet, while he chose Rhees as one of his literary executors, he did not name him as an influence along with Ramsey and Sraffa in the introduction he wrote shortly after his 1944 Swansea visit, which he surely would have done had he influenced such a fundamental change in the nature of the work. Yet is seems clear that the final decision to alter the scope of his book in the way he did seems to have come in Swansea, as the fact that he introduced this change more than halfway through his stay confirms that he did not arrive there already intending to make it.

Even if we cannot say that the intellectual community in Swansea influenced Wittgenstein in making this radical change in the nature and structure of *Philosophical Investigations*, it is not necessary to do so in order to see Swansea's effect on Wittgenstein and his work. Given the fact that he chose Swansea as a location to seriously pick up the struggle of writing his 'book' that had been interrupted by his desire to contribute in some way to the war effort, we can safely surmise that there was something about the place that he found congenial to writing. Part of this may have been the act of going away to think and that one of the positives of Swansea was that it was 'not-Cambridge'. We have after all seen how he was eager to leave Cambridge and all its distractions when his Trinity Research Fellowship ended; whatever the place offered him in terms of the University and all that entailed. On that occasion, he left for a lone life surrounded by the natural beauty of the fjords, where he was able to make great strides in setting out the early remarks of *Philosophical Investigations*. In Swansea he found something similar, for though he was not alone, always lodging with others, he had access to nature. Another attractive aspect of the place for Wittgenstein was that he also found the locals more congenial than the academics he mostly encountered at Cambridge. And the fact that this 'nervous' man was able to leave behind 'antithetical' Cambridge may also have contributed to his ability to write: 'The weather's foul, but I enjoy not being in Cambridge. I know a number of people here whom I like,' he wrote, 'I seem to find it more easy to get along with them here than in England',[27] which contrasts quite markedly with his depiction of his Cambridge colleagues.

One of the joys of academic life is that academics are not necessarily tied to one place in order to do their work – an office, factory, boat, for example. Contractual requirements aside, they are free to wander with their thoughts. Wittgenstein carried pocket notebooks with him in order to record his thoughts wherever he was. There is ample evidence from *Phaedrus*[28] onwards of the importance of a change of place in influencing our thinking. Often this takes the form of a reconnection with nature, a move from the town to wilder environments which stimulates our thinking. A change of place also gives an opportunity for a change of perspective and an opportunity to look back on a body of work and set off in new directions. It is, surely, no coincidence that the radical changes Wittgenstein made in constructing his 'book' – the rejection of the Brown Book project and the replacement of the section on the foundations of mathematics – happened while away from Cambridge. It is also no coincidence that on both occasions he did not arrive at Skjolden and Swansea ready to make such important changes but made the decision to do so having been in those locations for some time.

Metaphorical landscapes

Wittgenstein used striking geographical metaphors and similes when describing his approach to philosophy. In the introduction to the *Investigations*, he writes:

> my thoughts soon grew feeble if I tried to force them along a single track against their natural inclination. – And this was, of course, connected with the very nature of the investigation. For it compels us to travel criss-crossing every direction over a wide field of thought. – The philosophical remarks in this book are, as it were, a number of sketches of landscapes which were made in the course of these long and meandering journeys.
> The same or almost the same points were always being approached afresh from different directions, and new sketches made.[29]

Spatial metaphors are commonplace in the worlds of the academic and the writer. We speak of a 'field' of study, of arguments 'going too far' or 'going off track', but metaphors do have a connection, however distant, to the material, otherwise they would never have evolved:[30] 'One major feature of spatial metaphors is simply that they do ultimately allude to some concrete, material "reality", be it ordinary physical space or commonsensical understandings of social proximity or distance between individuals.'[31] Wittgenstein's metaphor in his introduction is evocative of mapping a walk or walks in the country, where, if one wishes, one is able to journey where one will, traversing the countryside in every direction and approaching a particular point in the landscape from different directions. This contrasts distinctly with life in a city such as Cambridge. Here, rather than a right to roam there are boundaries everywhere dividing public spaces from private ones and routes across the city between these spaces are busy with people and strictly prescribed. Though Wittgenstein's metaphor relates to the failure of his original plan for his book and having to settle for an alternative way of arranging his thoughts, it is essentially about the nature of investigation. It is interesting to speculate whether it is not simply an attempt to explain his approach in his philosophical investigations, but also has its roots in the greater cognitive freedom and wider perspective he found in wilder regions such as Swansea, Skjolden and Ireland in comparison with Cambridge.

Conclusion

Swansea offered Wittgenstein much. He enjoyed visiting to discuss philosophy with his friend Rush Rhees, he loved walking in the beautiful surroundings of the Gower peninsula, and he enjoyed the warmth and honesty of the locals. It was a place that put a smile on his face. It was also a place that he chose to spend six months, trying to finally bring the book that he had begun working on in 1929 to fruition. Though he was ultimately unsuccessful in this intention, it was in Swansea that he made considerable progress, dramatically changing the nature of the work and producing a considerable amount of text that was included in *Philosophical Investigations*. There is no indication that this successful period came about through the direct influence of Swansea academic circles. There is, however, much to suggest that Wittgenstein found in Swansea a congenial place that enabled him in his writing, and which shared a family resemblance with other places to which he retreated.

Notes

1 Ludwig Wittgenstein, *Philosophische Untersuchungen: Philosophical Investigations* (London: Wiley-Blackwell, 2009), p. 3.
2 Letter from Wittgenstein to Watson, 8 April 1932, in Brian McGuinness, *Wittgenstein in Cambridge: Letters and Documents 1911–1951* (London: Wiley-Blackwell, 2012), p. 199.
3 See Gordon Jack, 'Place Matters: The Significance of Place Attachment for Children's Well-Being', *British Journal of Social Work*, 40 (2010), 755–71.

4 Robert D. Sack, 'The Power of Place and Space', *Geographical Review*, 83/3 (1993), 329.
5 Though born into an extremely rich family, Wittgenstein had given away his inheritance after the First World War.
6 Wittgenstein, *Philosophische Untersuchungen*, p. 4.
7 Wittgenstein, *Philosophische Untersuchungen*, p. 4.
8 Wittgenstein, *Philosophische Untersuchungen*, p. 4.
9 Letter from Wittgenstein to The Editor of *Mind*, 27 May 1933, in McGuinness, *Wittgenstein in Cambridge*, p. 210.
10 TS 213. References to items in Wittgenstein's Nachlass are given according to von Wright's catalogue of the papers.
11 Entry from Pinsent's diary, 24 September 1913, quoted in Ray Monk, *Ludwig Wittgenstein: The Duty of Genius* (London, Melbourne, Sydney, Auckland, Johannesburg: Vintage, 1991), p 89.
12 MS 115, pp. 118–292.
13 James C. Klagge, 'The Wittgenstein Lectures, Revisited', *Nordic Wittgenstein Review*, 8/1–2 (2019), 11–82.
14 MS 115, pp. 118–292.
15 MS 115, p. 292.
16 Letter from Wittgenstein to G. E. Moore, 20 November [1936], in McGuinness, *Wittgenstein in Cambridge*, p. 257.
17 MS 142.
18 TSS 220 and 221 respectively.
19 Letter from Wittgenstein to G. E. Moore, in McGuinness, *Wittgenstein in Cambridge*, p. 255.
20 Letter from Wittgenstein to Norman Malcolm, 7 December 1943, in McGuinness, *Wittgenstein in Cambridge*, p. 309.
21 MS 129.
22 TS 241.
23 A copy of von Wright's typescript of this intermediate version is held in Trinity College Library, Cambridge.
24 TS 239.
25 Gordon Baker and Peter Hacker, *Wittgenstein: Rules, Grammar and Necessity* (London: Wiley-Blackwell, 2009), pp. 3–21.
26 Gabriel Citron, 'Wittgenstein's Philosophical Conversations with Rush Rhees (1939–50): from the Notes of Rush Rhees', *Mind*, 124 (2015), 1–71.
27 Letter from Wittgenstein to Norman Malcolm, 15 December 1945, in McGuinness, *Wittgenstein in Cambridge*, p. 392.
28 Nedra Reynolds, *Geographies of Writing: Inhabiting Places and Encountering Difference* (Carbondale: Southern Illinois University Press, 2004), p. 1.
29 Wittgenstein, *Philosophische Untersuchungen*, p. 3.
30 Reynolds, *Geographies of Writing*, p. 13.
31 Ilana Friedrich Silber, 'Space, Fields, Boundaries: The Rise of Spatial Metaphors in Contemporary Sociological Theory', *Social Research*, 62/2 (1995), 346.

4

'It's good to be away from Cambridge & to be here, & among friendly people'[1]

Wittgenstein's letters to Ben Richards and his philosophical work in Swansea

Alfred Schmidt

Between summer 1942 and summer 1947 Wittgenstein spent most of his holidays – Easter, Summer, Christmas – in Swansea (see Appendix 1: Wittgenstein's sojourns at Swansea). It is evident that it was Rush Rhees's presence in Swansea[2] that first made this place attractive for Wittgenstein. Wittgenstein held Rhees in high esteem as a friend and philosophical interlocutor.[3] Soon he developed a deep relationship with the city, the surrounding landscape where he made long walks, as well as with the people. As had been the case in Skjolden, Norway, many years before, Wittgenstein found the atmosphere in Swansea very suitable and fruitful for his philosophical work. He was more and more convinced that he was unable to continue his philosophical work (and to finish his book the *Philosophical Investigations*) in Cambridge. This was the reason he finally quit his chair at Cambridge University by the end of 1947 and went to Ireland. His special appreciation of Swansea is reflected in his letters to Ben Richards, which were written from there between August 1946 and July 1947.

The Wittgenstein–Richards correspondence

The recently published correspondence between Ludwig Wittgenstein and Ben Richards,[4] held by the Austrian National Library, is probably the most extensive collection of letters of Wittgenstein we know about – and one of the most personal and intimate. All in all, it consists of 374 pieces, including postcards and some telegrams; around 270 letters are written by Ludwig Wittgenstein, with about 100 by Ben Richards.

Ben Richards died in 1995. That same year, the Austrian National Library acquired 150 letters from Ludwig Wittgenstein to Ben Richards from his wife Tara. At that time, we did not know of any further correspondence. The Austrian National Library letters date from August 1947 to a few days before Wittgenstein's death on 29 April 1951. At Ben Richards's testamentary request, the letters remained closed to the public until 2020. When I started to work on the editing of these letters, Miranda Richards (Ben and Tara Richards's daughter) informed me that further letters from the correspondence of Wittgenstein with her father were in her possession. Namely, an additional 100-plus letters from Ludwig Wittgenstein to her father, as well as about 90 counter-letters, from the period July 1946 to April 1951, along with greeting cards, telegrams, and photographs. In 2021, the Austrian National Library was finally able to acquire the second part of the Wittgenstein–Richards correspondence, which had been hitherto unknown. There is no indication as to why this division was made – possibly by Ben Richards himself.

Wittgenstein's letters to Ben Richards are not only valuable biographical sources on the last period of his life, but they also express an emotional closeness and affinity to Richards that probably cannot be found in any other known correspondence of Wittgenstein. They are touching, often desperate love letters that leave no doubt that Ben Richards was Wittgenstein's closest friend in these last years of his life, probably the greatest love of his life.

Ben (Robert Benedict Oliver) Richards, born on 23 June 1924, came from a family of London doctors. His father, William Arthur Richards, was a general practitioner in Uxbridge, a suburb northwest of London. His mother, Noel Richards (née Olivier, 1892–1969), worked as a paediatrician at Westminster Hospital. Raised in a left-liberal home – together with her three older sisters Margery, Brynhild, and Daphne – she was a very dazzling figure.[5] Her father, Sydney Olivier, was one of the leading people in the Socialist Fabian Society in England and a close friend of H. G. Wells and G. B. Shaw. He spent the years 1907 to 1913 with his family as English Governor of the Crown Colony of Jamaica. Virginia

Woolf called the circle of friends around the English poet Rupert Brooke (1887–1915) and the four Olivier sisters 'Neo-Pagans' because of their nature-loving, permissive lifestyle. For example, they used to swim naked in the rivers on the summer camps. Brooke, who became a national idol after his early death in the First World War, fell passionately in love with Noel when she was only fifteen years old. Along with her three sisters, she was also close to the Bloomsbury circle around Virginia Woolf and the Apostles. An interesting detail is that Wittgenstein also frequented these circles around this time, which was during his first stay in Cambridge from 1911–13. Until the 1930s, Noel Richards was also close friends with the psychoanalyst James Strachey (1887–1967), the brother of the writer Lytton Strachey. James Strachey, together with Ben Richards's eldest sister Angela, later edited the first English translation of Sigmund Freud's writings. Wittgenstein also wrote several letters to Angela and met her a few times during his period in Oxford in 1950.

Ben Richards began studying medicine at King's College, Cambridge in November 1942. In June 1945, he obtained his Bachelor's degree in the first part of the Natural Sciences Tripos. In 1946, he changed to Moral Sciences (Section Psychology) and passed his MB (Medicinae Baccalaureus) examinations in 1949/50. Later, he practised for many years as a specialist in orthopaedics and rheumatology at Watford General Hospital, Hertfordshire, England. Richards was a keen mountaineer and was also passionate about music. He played the viola in a string ensemble and sang in various choirs. His correspondence with Georg Henrik von Wright after Wittgenstein's death shows his lifelong interest in philosophy. Richards died on 22 January 1995, leaving his wife Tara, to whom he had been married since 1976, and his daughter Miranda.

Ludwig Wittgenstein met the medical student Ben Richards in the autumn of 1945, when Richards had attended one of Wittgenstein's philosophical lectures in Cambridge. The following passionate love affair with this man, thirty-five years younger than himself, had a decisive influence on Wittgenstein's subsequent years up until the end of his life. There are no written records of the first months of their acquaintance. In July 1946 the preserved correspondence commences. It is also at this time that Richards's name first appears in Wittgenstein's manuscripts. Wittgenstein notes a desperate lament about his passionate feelings, which he feels unable to cope with:

I am terribly depressed. Quite unclear about my future. My love affair with Richards has quite debilitated me. It has held me down, like madness almost, for the last 9 months. It is as if I have been running after a phenomenon with all my strength; sometimes with the hope of catching it, more often still in fear or despair. But I can't reproach myself, i.e. I don't blame myself. Was it good, was it bad? I don't know. I will only say: it was a terrible doom.⁶

Wittgenstein's letters to Ben Richards from Swansea

The whole summer holidays in 1946, from 28 June to 30 September, Wittgenstein spent in Swansea. In his second letter to Ben Richards from Swansea, dated 1 July, he attached a picture postcard from Swansea, showing the Civic Centre, and used an arrow to note the image in the upper left corner: 'This abomination is the joy & pride of Swansea.' One day later he sent another postcard of the same building to Richards and wrote ironically on the backside: 'I thought that you might like to see a little more of our Civic Centre.'

The Swansea Guildhall, opened in 1934, with its 48 metre-high clock tower designed by Sir Percy Thomas in a neoclassical style,

Figure 1: Postcard attached to Wittgenstein's letter to Ben Richards from 1 July 1946 (ANL: Autogr. 1840/2-1 HAN)

Letters to Ben Richards and Philosophical Work in Swansea

Figure 2: Postcard Wittgenstein to Ben Richards from
2 July 1946 (ANL: Autogr. 1840/3-1 HAN)

obviously didn't meet Wittgenstein's taste. It is well known that he was a very critical, and sensible, observer of architecture and had himself built a house for his sister Margaret Stonborough in Vienna between 1926–8. In a famous passage from a 1931 manuscript, he compares the work of an architect with that of a philosopher: 'Die Arbeit an der Philosophie ist – wie vielfach die Arbeit in der Architektur – eigentlich mehr die || eine Arbeit an Einem selbst. An der eignen Auffassung. Daran, wie man die Dinge sieht. (Und was man von ihnen verlangt.)'.[7]

Wittgenstein's letter to Richards a few weeks later (28 July 1946) is more sympathetic towards his holiday resort and shows him in harmony with his environment.[8]

℅ Rev. Morgan
2 Cwmdonkin Terrace
Swansea
28.7.46

My dear Ben,

I've been for a lot of very lovely walks lately, many of them quite new to me. I'm doing a moderate amount of work and I hope I'll be doing more and more as time goes on. I sometimes think that perhaps I'll publish soon after all.

It's good to be away from Cambridge and to be here, and among friendly people. The weather is very changeable; rain almost every day, but part of the day fine. – I think of you a great deal. God bless you, always!

With love

Ludwig

I hope you have good weather! L.L.

Taking walks was essential for Wittgenstein's ability to undertake philosophical work. It seems that the movement of his thoughts and the movement of his legs were interconnected in a sublime way. He used to take small notebooks with him writing down his ideas as they may suddenly appear. Ray Monk tells us this illuminating story about his time in Red Cross, Ireland, some month later in winter 1948:

> He took his notebook with him on his walks around Red Cross and would often work outdoors. A neighbour of the Kingstons' [sic], who often saw Wittgenstein out on his favourite walk, reports that he once passed him sitting in a ditch, writing furiously, oblivious of anything going on around him. This is presumably one of those occasions when, as he told Drury, his ideas came so quickly that he felt as if his pen were being guided.[9]

And in a very late letter to Richards from 27 February 1951, Wittgenstein writes: 'I occasionally try to think about a certain problem & I find that my thoughts don't move. I can't handle a problem anymore; just as I can't go for a walk.'[10]

Wittgenstein longest sojourn in Swansea was in 1944. From March to July he stayed in Mrs Mann's house near Langland Bay, Mumbles, then afterwards until September in Rhees's in Brynmill. In the Christmas holidays of 1944, he moved to the house of Revd Wynford Morgan, 2 Cwmdonkin Terrace, Uplands, with an impressive view over the spacious Swansea Bay. Ray Monk, referring to verbal information from Rhees, reports the following anecdote: 'When Morgan asked Wittgenstein if he believed in God, he replied, "Yes I do, but the difference between what you believe and what I believe may be infinite."'[11]

Letters to Ben Richards and Philosophical Work in Swansea

Wittgenstein's letter to Richards from July 1946 also shows that his work was entering its final stage, and he was keen to publish his opus magnum – the *Philosophical Investigations* – soon, though this did not happen until after his death, as we know.[12] Wittgenstein's letter from 6 September 1946 includes a touching, intimate passage in the postscript that reflects his feelings towards Ben.

2 Cwmdonkin Terrace
Swansea
6.9.46.

... The weather has been better last two days. Not far from Swansea there's a place where lots of horses & foals are grazing. The foals are lovely and so tame one can get near them, pat them, etc. The other day when I talked to one of them, I found myself using the same words I often use when I talk to you. That's a fact, Love Ludwig

Wittgenstein, while stroking some tame foals on his walks around Swansea, remembers that he uses the same terms of endearment for Ben. A few days later, Ben Richards visited Wittgenstein in Swansea for two weeks (12–30 September 1946). Except for a few days in Exeter, together with Maurice O'Connor Drury in July 1946, this was their first long holiday together.

Also, during winter, Wittgenstein loved to take longer walks around Swansea, as he describes in a letter from 24 December 1946:

2 Cwmdonkin Terrace
Swansea
24.12.46.

My dear Ben,
   This is chiefly to say that I am thinking of you a very great deal. – Thank you for the X-mas card. We've had awful weather here until last night: first terribly cold, so that I felt really wretched, and then rain. But today was beautiful. I went to Langland Bay by bus & then walked along the cliffs to Caswell & and on to Pull [sic] Du[13]. I wished you were with me. – By the way, if anyone asks you "How are you?"

answer him: "Thank you, fine! We eat crunchy Ryvita as our daily bread." –
I hope I'll hear from you soon!
God bless you!

With love, always
Ludwig

From Ben Richards's Christmas 1946 letter to Wittgenstein, we learn that he sent him a photo camera as a Christmas present. The letter also shows his obvious drawing talent.

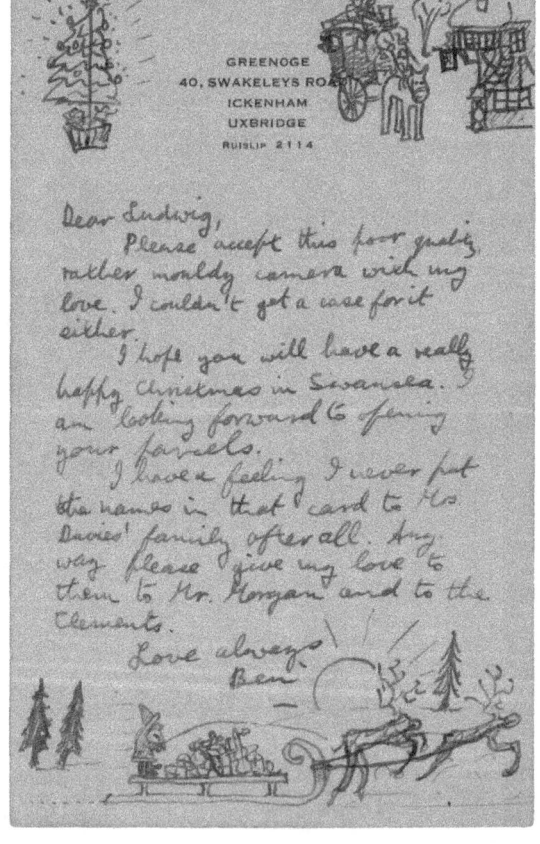

Figure 3: Letter from Ben Richards to Ludwig Wittgenstein, Christmas 1946 (ANL: Autogr. 1844/28-1 HAN)

Wittgenstein was, without doubt, happy with this present and answered a few days later:[14]

My dear Ben, O. H.,

I just now got your lovely present, it's <u>much</u> too nice for me! Thanks! and thanks for your Xmas letter. (You did write the names on the card you sent to Hugh Davies. He & his parents were most delighted with the theatre.) To come back to your letter: you say that you're looking forward to opening my parcels. Well now you know that they contained junk, but my heart went with it. ...

    With love, always

           Ludwig

This is the first snapshot I took with your camera. It was a pretty terrifying experience!

                                      L.L.

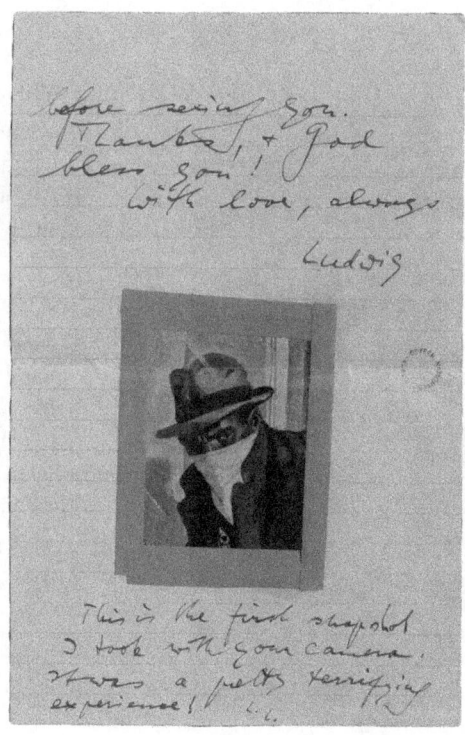

With Richards's present, Wittgenstein immediately began to take snapshopts of his host and neighbours in Swansea and sent them to Richards. A few days later he wrote to his friend:

> 2 Cwmdonkin Terr.
> Swansea
> 31.12.46.
>
> My dear Ben,
>   Thanks for your letter. ...
>   I took my first photos today and have used up the roll of film you sent me. The first two pictures are no good. I know because I had trouble with the finder. One of the finders doesn't work, I think it's been damaged on the transport. The upright one works. I took Mrs. Morgan & Morgan and Mrs. Clement. This is all just a preparation for taking you from all possible angles. – ...

These photos have survived and are now in the Nedo archives, Cambridge.[15]

The summer of 1947 was the last period Wittgenstein spent in Swansea. During Richards's visit in July the famous double portrait, which Wittgenstein and Richards took of each other, was made. It is probable that these photos were taken with the camera which Wittgenstein received from Ben Richards at Christmas 1946. The photographs were taken in front of the back wall of the – now defunct – train shelter at Brynmill Railway Station, Mumbles Road on the Swansea and Mumbles line.[16] Wittgenstein later comments on them in a letter from Rosro from 5 May 1948:

Thanks for the photos. I've kept two: the one of you in profile and mine standing against the wall and not smiling. The smiling one is hellish, the ones of me in the Fellows' Garden are just nasty, and on the full-face ones of you look like an actor educated at King's College. The two decent ones need cutting, perhaps circular, very close to the head.

Wittgenstein had a passion for retrospective cropping of photos, as can be especially seen from his personal photo album.[17] Wittgenstein's last letter to Richards from Swansea written on 17 July expresses his deep connection with his home of choice: he sensed a difference in the air here than in the artificial academic atmosphere of Cambridge.

1, Cwmdonkin Terrace
Swansea

17/7/47

Dear Ben, d. h. !

Thanks for your letter, & please write to me <u>often</u>. If you want me to feel happy & well, and to work decently, do it; God bless you, always. – The weather here is changeable but not too bad and I go out a fair amount and often and often enjoy it (though with you I'd enjoy it more). I also work and not too badly, so far. I like the air here, it's altogether different than in Cambridge.

Wittgenstein's philosophical work at Swansea[18]

We can assume that a substantial part of the *Philosophical Investigations* (PI, part I), as they were published posthumously by his executors in 1953, were written in Swansea. After completing his wartime contribution in a medical research team in Newcastle, Wittgenstein returned to Cambridge in February 1944, and was granted a longer research leave by the University of Cambridge. He retired to Swansea from mid-March until September 1944, with the firm intention to complete his book – the PI. To the so called *Urfassung* of the PI, which he had written in Skjolden 1936/37 containing the first

189 paragraphs,[19] he added a large number of newly written remarks in 1944,[20] and expanded the work to about twice its original size. In Swansea, Wittgenstein wrote most of the central passages on rule-following and – logically connected to this – the private language argument and inner experience.[21] For this so-called 'Intermediate draft' of the PI (the typescript of which is lost, but has been reconstructed by von Wright), he wrote several drafts of a preface in Cambridge in January 1945.[22]

The next decisive revision of the PI took place to a large extent in Swansea in the summer of 1945. Largely based on the manuscripts 129 and 130, most of which were written in Swansea (and older material), Wittgenstein dictated typescript 228 ('Bemerkungen I' and revised as "Bemerkungen II", TS 230) consisting of almost 700 remarks, of which he finally choose about 400, and incorporated them into the intermediate draft of the PI. The provisional final version of the PI emerged in the form of TS 227, though Wittgenstein made further handwritten edits within the next years. In summary, it is no exaggeration to say that the PI (part I) were essentially created in Skjolden and Swansea.

Besides that, from summer 1946 onwards, Wittgenstein was also working on a series of manuscripts, starting from MS 130, which he continued in Ireland. These focused on problems within the philosophy of psychology. They were partly included in the so-called part II of the PI, which today is considered an independent text: *Philosophy of Psychology. A Fragment* (MS 144, TS 234 (lost)).[23]

Endnote

All manuscripts by Wittgenstein are quoted according to the online edition of the Wittgenstein Archives at the University of Bergen:

Wittgenstein, Ludwig, *Interactive Dynamic Presentation (IDP) of Ludwig Wittgenstein's philosophical Nachlass* [http://wittgenstein online.no/]. Edited by the Wittgenstein Archives at the University of Bergen under the direction of Alois Pichler. (Bergen: Wittgenstein Archives at the University of Bergen, 2016–).

Letters to Ben Richards and Philosophical Work in Swansea

Correspondence to and from Wittgenstein is quoted according to the online edition:

Wittgenstein, Ludwig, *Gesamtbriefwechsel/Complete* Correspondence (2nd Release) (201), Innsbrucker Electronic Edition. Monika Seekircher et al. (Hrsg.) (Charlottesville, Virginia, USA: InteLex Corporation, 2011).

Appendix 1: Wittgenstein's sojourns at Swansea

Time	Wittgenstein's lodgings in Swansea (source in brackets the source for that)	Manuscripts, written in Swansea	Letters L.W. to Ben Richards from Swansea
1942			
July	Rush Rhees, 96 Bryn Rd (Monk 1990, p. 437)		
1943			
Easter (approx. 13–20.4.)	Rhees (L.W. letter to Rhees 1.4. ('Could I stay somewhere near you'; to Rosa Rand 19.4.)		
August	Rhees (letter from R. Rand to L.W., 16.8.1943)		
Christmas– January 1944	Rhees (R. Rhees to L.W., 30.1.1944 ('I keep remembering your visit here at Christmas time, and I'm constantly grateful to you for coming.')		
1944			
March–June	Mrs Mann, 10 Langland Road, Mumbles (L.W. to Rowland Hutt, 17.3., 20.4.)	MS 124 (p. 96 ff) MS 129; Ts 241a,b, 242	
July– September	Rhees, 96 Bryn Rd. (L.W. to Rowland Hutt, 3.8.; 3.9.)		
Christmas and New Year	Rev. Morgan, 2 Cwmdonkin Terrace (L.W. to R. Hutt, 28.12.)		

Wittgenstein in Swansea

Time	Wittgenstein's lodgings in Swansea (source in brackets the source for that)	Manuscripts, written in Swansea	Letters L.W. to Ben Richards from Swansea
1945			
Easter	Revd Morgan (L.W. to Jean Rhees, 8.4.)		
Summer	Rhees (L.W.to R. Hutt, 3.8. ('My address in Swansea will be c/o Rhees 96, Bryn Rd.'), L.W. to Malcolm 20.8.; L.W. to Hutt 8.9.)	TS 228(?)	
Christmas and New Year	Revd Morgan, (L.W. to Malcolm, 15.12.)		
1946			
Easter	Revd Morgan (L.W. to Malcolm, 25.4.; L.W. to R. Rhees, 20.4.)		
Summer (28. 6.–30.9.)	Revd Morgan (L.W. to Richards)	MS 130 (p. 185 ff) MS 131 MS 132 (p. 1-85)	28.6.; 1.7.; 2.7.; 20.7.; 24.7.; 28.7.; 3.8.; 15.8.; 21.8.; 31.8.; 6.9.; 12.9.
12.9.–30.09	Visit of Ben Richards in Swansea		
Christmas and New Year (21.12.–12.1.47)	Revd Morgan (L.W. to A. Rebni, 21.12.)	MS 133 (p. 46 ff)	24.12.; 28.12.; 31.12.; 7.1.47; 10.1.47
1947			
Easter (1.4.–14.4.)	Fam. Clement, 1 Cwmdonkin Terrace (L.W. to Richards 1.4.)	MS 134 (p.81 ff)	1.4.; 10.4.; 4.4.;
Summer	Fam. Clement (L.W. to Helene Salzer 22.7.)	MS 135	8.7.; 17.7.; 27.7.
July	Visit of Ben Richards		

Notes

1. Ludwig Wittgenstein, letter to Ben Richards, Swansea, 28 July 1946 (Austrian National Library, Autogr. 1840/5-1 HAN)
2. Rush Rhees regularly attended Wittgenstein's lectures from 1936 on, and became one of his favourite students. From 1940–66, Rhees taught at Swansea University.
3. On 1 April 1944, Wittgenstein wrote to Rhees:

   Dear Rhees, There is a possibility of my coming to Swansea on April 13th or 14th and staying until April 19th or 20th. Supposing I could come, would it suit you? Could I stay somewhere near you, and would you like to have discussions with me?? If, for whatever reason, my visit doesn't suit you just now, please don't for a moment hesitate to say so. I'd only come – if I can – if it happens to be the right thing for you, too, and if it's all right with Mrs.. ...

4. A publication of the whole correspondence, edited by the author if this chapter, appeared in spring 2023: Ludwig Wittgenstein, *'I think of you with love constantly' Der Briefwechsel zwischen Ludwig Wittgensteins und Ben Richards 1946–1951*, hrsg. von Alfred Schmidt unter Mitarbeit von Gabriel Citron (Innsbruck: Haymon, 2023).
5. See Sarah Watling: *Noble savages: The Olivier sisters: Four lives in seven fragments* (Oxford: Oxford University Press, 2019).
6. MS 130, p. 185, entry from 22 July 1946.
7. 'The work on philosophy – like much of the work in architecture – is actually more a work on oneself. On one's own perception. On how one sees things. (And what one demands of them.)'. (MS 112, 24r).
8. Already in his letter to Norman Malcolm from 15 December 1945, Wittgenstein had expressed the same positive feelings towards his holiday residence:

   I'm in Swansea again over Christmas and probably over New Year. The weather's foul. but I enjoy not being in Cambridge. I know quite a number of people here whom I like. I seem to find it more easy to get along with them here than in England. I feel much more often like smiling, e.g. when I walk in the street, or when I see children, etc.

9. Ray Monk, *Wittgenstein. The Duty of Genius* (London: Jonathan Cape, 1990), p. 521.
10. ANL, Autogr. 1900/33-6 HAN.
11. See Monk, *Wittgenstein*, p. 463.
12. See the last section in this chapter, 'Wittgenstein's philosophical work at Swansea'.
13. Pwll Du is a small village on the coast, some 8 km west of Swansea University's Singleton Campus.

14 December 1946; ANL: Autogr. 1840/20-1 HAN.
15 In an exhibition in the Leopoldmuseum, Vienna, these photographs were shown recently (12 November 2021–6 March 2022): *Ludwig Wittgenstein. Photography as analytical practice*, ed. Verena Gamper and Hans-Peter Wipplinger (Köln: Verlag der Buchhandlung Walther und Franz König, 2021), esp. p. 153.
16 I am grateful to Alan Sandry, editor of this volume, for this reference.
17 See: *Ludwig Wittgenstein. Photography as analytical practice*, pp. 114–39.
18 See Alois Pichler, *Wittgensteins Philosophische Untersuchungen: Zur textgenese von §§1–4* (Bergen: University of Bergen, 1997), chapter 1; Ludwig Wittgenstein, *Philosophische Untersuchungen: Kritisch-genetische Edition*, ed. Joachim Schulte in collaboration with Heikki Nyman, Eike von Savigny and Georg Henrik von Wright (Frankfurt am Main: Suhrkamp, 2001), pp. 12–30; Ludwig Wittgenstein, *Philosophische Untersuchungen. Philosophical Investigations. Philosophie der Psychologie- ein Fragment* (PI; PPF), the German text with an English translation by G.E. Anscomb, P. M. S. Hacker and Joachim Schulte (Oxford: Wiley-Blackwell, 2009), pp. xviii–xxii; Georg Henrik Von Wright, 'The Origin and Composition of the Philosophical Investigations', in G. H. von Wright, *Wittgenstein* (Oxford: Blackwell, 1982), pp. 113–36.
19 MS 142 / TS 220 and revised draft TS 239.
20 From TS 141,142 a.o.
21 §§198–421.
22 MS 128, 129, TS 227, Ts 243, MS 130.
23 *Philosophy of Psychology. A Fragment* (MS 144, TS 234 (lost).

5

The 'Swansea School'

Mario von der Ruhr

I. Introduction

In one of his last philosophical writings, a paper entitled 'Can We Understand Ourselves?', the eminent philosopher and former Wittgenstein trustee Peter Winch writes:

> An apparently very important part of European popular culture is a consuming interest in professional football. I do not merely not share this popular passion; it is so alien to me that I do not feel I *understand* what most of my fellows feel for it. It is not that I do not know what to expect of them, or that I am unaware of the background to the sport or even totally blind to the beauties of genuine skill in it. Nevertheless – ich kann mich in sie nicht finden.[1]

The quotation is salient, not only for what it reveals about Winch's personal reaction to a familiar feature of popular culture, but for the way in which, for him, that *autobiographical* response gave rise to, or became intertwined with, *philosophical* reflection on the notion of understanding. What such reflection shows, according to Winch, is not merely that the line between what is and what is not 'alien' is quite indeterminate, but that certain aspects of one's own culture may be even *more* alien than cultural manifestations that are temporally or geographically remote. As he goes on to say:

I see no reason why a contemporary historical scholar might not feel himself more at home in the world of medieval alchemy than in that of twentieth century professional football.[2]

As anyone familiar with Winch's philosophical oeuvre will confirm, the question of what is involved in *understanding* – a language, a culture, other human beings, oneself – was one of its enduring concerns. The issue surfaces not only in his fine book on the French philosopher Simone Weil,[3] where it is connected with questions about rootedness, human flourishing, and spiritual growth, but in the collection of essays published under the title *Trying to Make Sense*,[4] in his seminal paper, 'On Understanding a Primitive Society',[5] and his ground-breaking *The Idea of a Social Science and its Relation to Philosophy*.[6] The latter was written during his time at Swansea (1951–64), where he first taught philosophy to students working in social administration, and where his colleague Roy Holland edited the prestigious Routledge series *Studies in Philosophical Psychology*, for which the book was subsequently commissioned. Just how significant the Swansea years were for Winch, both philosophically and personally, comes out in a poignant letter to Wittgenstein's friend Rush Rhees, penned well over a decade after Winch's departure from Wales, on 31 August 1976:

> I feel moved to try to say something about my relations with you over the years: about this hopeless inadequacy I have felt in myself to live up to and respond to what you have offered ... The extent to which I have been able to find in philosophy something from which I could draw nourishment is due to an overwhelming extent to my contact with you, and especially to the years of our discussions in Swansea.[7]

Given Rush Rhees's influence on Winch's philosophical development, the congenial intellectual *milieu* in which he found himself at Swansea, and indeed Ludwig Wittgenstein's own connection with Dylan Thomas's 'ugly, lovely town' – Ray Monk's biography of the Austrian philosopher devotes an entire chapter to it[8] – it is worth recalling the fortuitous combination of circumstances that brought Rhees and Wittgenstein to Swansea and eventually led to the formation of the 'Swansea School' of philosophy.[9]

II. Rhees, Wittgenstein, and Philosophy at Swansea

Rhees is commonly described as a former student of Wittgenstein who subsequently became one of his literary executors – the others being Elizabeth Anscombe and Georg Henrik von Wright – as well as an editor and commentator on his work. Though factually accurate, the epithet 'student' is nevertheless misleading and requires an explanatory addendum. Unlike the majority of students who attended Cambridge in the 1930s, including Elizabeth Anscombe, Desmond Lee and Frank Ramsey, Rush Rhees was no longer in his late teens when he began to frequent Wittgenstein's lectures in 1936, but a mature and intellectually independent, 31-year-old philosopher with an academic background that placed him at least a decade ahead of his peers.

Having begun his university education at the University of Rochester/USA in 1922, he had already completed with high distinction a four-year MA programme in *Mental Philosophy* under the supervision of the well-known Kant scholar Norman Kemp Smith, worked as an assistant lecturer at Manchester for four years, spent a year in Innsbruck studying with the Franz Brentano expert Alfred Kastil, and been enrolled on a PhD programme with Cambridge philosopher G. E. Moore for three years. Nor was Rhees among the caravan of intellectual voyeurs who would rush to Wittgenstein's seminars at the earliest opportunity. According to Ray Monk, 'he had, at first, been put off attending Wittgenstein's lectures by the mannerisms of his students', and only overcame his misgivings in February 1936, though he continued to attend all lectures of the academic session thereafter.[10] It is telling that, while Rhees's initial encounter with Wittgenstein was relatively brief – the latter's research fellowship expired at the end of the Easter term and was followed by an extended period of travel, including to France, Ireland, and Norway – it already laid the foundation for a lifelong friendship between the two thinkers.

In 1937, while Wittgenstein was working in Skjolden, Norway, Rhees briefly returned to Manchester to replace the Aristotle scholar J. L. Stocks (1882–1937), who had accepted a post as vice-chancellor of Liverpool University, but was still unsure about the future direction of his life. His uncertainty was not so much the result of Wittgenstein's advice to friends and students that, unless they were able to manufacture their own 'oxygen', as it were, they should leave academia and find a job elsewhere,[11] though Rhees certainly took the suggestion seriously. Rather, he wondered whether the role of a lecturer really suited him, especially since he hadn't published anything and doubted that he ever would. However, when he first wondered out loud whether he shouldn't go into welding instead, even Wittgenstein thought the proposal foolish and the work itself 'too impersonal'.[12] But when, a few months later, Rhees told him that he had taken on a welding job in a factory, after all, Wittgenstein was more agreeable. 'I like the idea of your doing work in a factory', he wrote to Rhees on 5 April 1940, 'You'll get better & better I have no doubt, if you can stick.'[13]

Unfortunately, Rhees soon discovered that he was, in fact, 'a duffer in a machine shop', as he had never had the proper kind of apprenticeship for this line of work. Perhaps Wittgenstein's initial reaction to his welding plans had been right all along, and he would do better in a job that was less 'impersonal'?[14] Meanwhile, a temporary deputy lectureship had been advertised at Swansea, mainly to cover for Karl Britton (1909–83) and W. B. Gallie (1912–98), who had been drafted into war service. Rhees decided to apply, and when the Foundation Professor of Philosophy at Swansea, the humanist thinker A. E. Heath (1887–1961), offered him the post, he accepted – though 'not right off the bat'.[15] After much hesitation and internal agonising, he also conveyed his decision to Wittgenstein, on 31 December 1940: 'I was rather afraid to see you', he confessed, 'because I thought you would be disgusted with me for taking this job here.'[16] As for changing his job, he explained:

> My welding kept on being bad, and I thought (not so stupidly either) that it probably would never develop into anything decent ... [S]uch training as I had had was in the academic and pedagogical line ... It seemed then that I might be more useful if I were in some job in which the training I had got (?) might help.[17]

Not that the Swansea appointment brought Rhees the settled existence he had been hoping for. Almost thirty-five years old, he was still only a 'temporary assistant lecturer' – or adjunct faculty – whose contract would terminate in June 1941. He also felt that, even with his teaching experience, he might fail to live up to what would be demanded of him:

The business about my training making me fitted for this kind of job is plain rubbish. And I don't know how much good I should do anyone if I were better ... There's not much point in trying to make long term plans. But I suppose that if I'm alive and not in government service after June, I may make a stab at getting back into welding again.[18]

Fortunately for Swansea, Rhees did not have another go at welding. Not only was his initial appointment extended beyond June 1941, but a permanent post created for him in 1944. Even so, Rhees continued to be plagued by self-doubt and, in the summer of 1946, again found himself on the brink of quitting. Wittgenstein did his best to dissuade him:

> I don't know, of course, what your special reasons are for wanting to leave Swansea, but please weigh them damn carefully. I should, for personal reasons, hate you to leave Swansea. Our talks & discussions have done me good. Don't stupidly throw away an opportunity of doing some good. Your derogatory remarks about your philosophical abilities & success are so much rubbish. You are all right. And I mean just that: nothing more & nothing less. Philosophical influences much worse than yours & mine are spreading rapidly, & it's important that you should stay at your job ... – Don't misunderstand me. I'm not trying to appear wise. I'm just as silly as you are. But that doesn't make you any less silly.[19]

To ensure that Rhees would think 'damn carefully' about leaving Swansea, Wittgenstein concluded his letter with the exhortation, 'P.S. Read this letter again from the beginning.' Rhees must have taken it to heart, as he not only ended up staying at University College of Swansea – as it was then called – until his retirement in 1966, but continued to have weekly discussions with other members of the Philosophy Department until his death in 1989. Conversation in the Socratic spirit, i.e., one in which the interlocutor was committed to following the argument wherever it might lead, was essential to Rhees's whole way of being. 'Discussion,' he remarked during his last stay in hospital, 'is my only medicine. When that is finished, so am I.'[20] In order to promote this kind of discussion, Rhees also founded The Philosophical Society, launched not long after he had taken up his post as temporary lecturer. As his former student D. Z. Phillips recalls:

> The Philosophical Society played an important part in philosophy at Swansea. Founded by Rhees in 1940, it has met weekly ever since. Before my time, Wittgenstein attended it during his frequent visits for discussions with Rhees. Visiting speakers would sometimes advance general theories about language, knowledge, belief or morality. These would come under heavy attack, sometimes with an unnecessary ferocity, which, I must confess, I enjoyed, along with other students, at the time.[21]

The 'ferocity' with which guest speakers might find themselves attacked was not motivated by personal dislike or aloofness, however, but by the demands of philosophy as a rigorous intellectual discipline:

> To do philosophy, a man must be able not only to see questions where those not given to philosophy see none, but also to look on these questions in a particular way. Not wanting to dismiss the questions, nor to 'get rid of them' through any sort of answer, or to show that they are a sort of needless worry to be put out of mind.[22]

True to his own admonition, Rhees played a pivotal role in the Philosophical Society's proceedings:

> Until retirement, Rhees dominated its discussions. He would almost always ask the first question, a question which took one to the heart of the paper being discussed. Often, a general theory propounded by a speaker would be seen to collapse once the question was asked. Rhees would show great patience with any question, however simplistic, if the questions were genuine, but his reactions to sham and pretence could be fierce. After discussions, it was not at all unusual for the person giving the paper, or for someone who had made a particular contribution to the discussion, to receive long typed letters from Rhees which were philosophical papers in themselves.[23]

That Rhees went to such lengths testifies to the seriousness with which he approached philosophical debate. It also reveals something about the ethical dimension of thinking: it was important not to fall into confusion, whether in philosophy or in other areas of life where understanding was at stake, and the endeavour always involved an effort of will. 'Work on philosophy', Wittgenstein once remarked, 'is really more work on oneself. On one's own conception. On how one sees things.'[24] Similarly for Rhees:

> The difficulties of philosophy have in certain ways the character of moral difficulties. This is what Wittgenstein implies when he says that in philosophy one has to struggle constantly against a resistance within oneself, which is a resistance of *will*. One is unwilling to let certain ways of thinking go.[25]

For Wittgenstein and Rhees, these ways of thinking included philosophical theories – e.g., of rationality, knowledge, morality, aesthetic appreciation, religious belief, the relation between mental and physical phenomena, language, meaning, etc., whose 'craving for generality' was precisely what led the philosopher astray:

> Philosophers constantly see the method of science before their eyes, and are irresistibly tempted to ask and answer questions in the way science does. This tendency ... leads the philosopher into complete darkness. I want to say here that it can never be our job to reduce anything to anything, or to explain anything ... Instead of 'craving for generality' I could also have said 'the contemptuous attitude towards the particular case'.[26]

Rhees himself tried to counter that natural but pernicious attitude by urging his students to heed the meaning of 'E.G.', which he would write – in giant print – on the blackboard at the beginning of every class he taught. Like Wittgenstein, Rhees believed that 'there is something more like an internal connexion between what you are engaged on in philosophy, and the sort of life you lead', that 'we should be surprised to find anyone who was a serious philosopher and was at the same time a playboy or man about town', and that 'devotion to philosophy goes together with a certain asceticism in one's life, and a certain humility'.²⁷ Given this shared conception of philosophy, it is not surprising that Wittgenstein was also looking forward to meeting up with Rhees in Swansea. He first visited him in 1942, partly in order to recover from a gall-stone operation, but also because Rhees was one of the few people whose philosophical judgment he trusted and whom he regarded as his equal in discussion.²⁸ In addition, he greatly enjoyed his walks with Rhees along the Gower coast and was greatly taken with the Welsh people:

> I know quite a number of people here whom I like. I seem to find it more easy to get along with them here than in England. I feel much more often like smiling, e.g. when I walk in the street, or when I see children, etc.²⁹

During the period 1942–7, Wittgenstein returned to Swansea on a regular basis and found the atmosphere there incomparably more congenial than at Cambridge. Indeed, only a year after his initial visit, he told his former student Norman Malcolm, 'I very rarely come to Cambridge now, about once every three months', adding that he had even given up his rooms in College there.³⁰ Even when his work – on the manuscript of the posthumously published *Philosophical Investigations* – wasn't going well, and various health issues made him feel 'jumpy and bad tempered', he was enjoying his absence from Cambridge and could still crack jokes about the sudden shortage in Britain of his favourite American detective magazines:

> I can only hope Lord Keynes will make this quite clear in Washington. For I say: if the USA won't give us detective mags we can't give them philosophy, & so America will be the loser in the end. See?³¹

However, after what was to be his last visit to Swansea – in the spring of 1947 – Wittgenstein was pessimistic about returning to Wales anytime soon. Suffering from protracted insomnia and feeling seriously out of sorts, he already forewarned Rhees in a letter dated 20 August 1948, 'Unless something very unexpected happens, I shall not come to Swansea in the near future.'³² In a subsequent note from Dublin, he also had to admit that, much though he loved the town and its surroundings, 'Swansea has the great disadvantage of being so very hilly. It's beautiful, but I can't climb hills these days.'[33] But even though Wittgenstein could not visit Swansea again, he continued to stay in touch with Rhees, who, since their first encounter in Cambridge twelve years previously, had become a close friend. Ray Monk rightly draws attention to Rhees's 'incomparable knowledge of Wittgenstein's work and his many insights into both Wittgenstein's personality and his philosophy',[34] and there is no doubt that much of this privileged insight was due to the philosophers' discussions in Swansea. As Rhees himself recalls:

> Wittgenstein did go through the *Investigations* with me – some parts of it several times – before it was published. And although such understanding of it as I have has come more since his death, I should have understood less if I had not heard him read it and had him discuss it with me.[35]

Convinced that growth in understanding depended at least as much on the interlocutors' personalities or characters as it did on their intellectual abilities, Rhees did what he could to mould Swansea's philosophy department in the light of these desiderata. In 1951, the year of Wittgenstein's death, he first appointed Roy Holland, then Peter Winch (1951–64) and J. R. Jones (1952–70). Before he retired in 1966, Rhees also recruited Ilham Dilman (1961–97), Cora Diamond (1961–2), and his former student D. Z. Phillips (1965–2006), who was to become the world's leading 'Wittgensteinian' philosopher of religion. Other – and equally influential – members of the Swansea School, who joined the department after Rhees's retirement, were H. O. Mounce (1969–99), R. W. Beardsmore (1969–97) and Ieuan Lloyd (1990–2005), with whom he shared an abiding interest in the philosophy of education. While the backgrounds and research specialisations of these appointees differed widely, they nevertheless agreed about what kinds of issues mattered in philosophy and how these ought to be tackled, and it is precisely their kinship with Wittgenstein's own outlook that ultimately warrants the term 'Swansea School'. It should be noted, however, that its members did not coin the description themselves. Reminiscing on his philosophical training in the early days of Swansea's philosophy department, D. Z. Phillips writes:

The labels *Swansea School of Philosophy*, or *Swansea Wittgensteinians*, were not given to themselves by Swansea's philosophers. They are labels given by others, sometimes in agreement, sometimes in disagreement, but sometimes in anger and hostility, not least by philosophers who are themselves influenced by Wittgenstein.[36]

Phillips also points out that, in the early 1950s, after Winch and Holland had arrived from Oxford, one could not really have spoken of a 'school', but that this had changed by the mid-1960s:

> By the time my teachers departed, the description 'Swansea School' had arrived, and was even applied to them thereafter, and to İlham Dilman, H. O. Mounce, R. W. Beardsmore and myself.[37]

Contrary to what might have been expected, Phillips and his fellow students did not encounter Wittgenstein through an explicit discussion of his work, but rather 'through *the way* [they heard] a whole range of topics being discussed'.[38] Among other things, that way of philosophising eschewed technical jargon and grand theories, whether in an analysis of the relation between language and the world, reflections on epistemological issues, elucidations of moral or aesthetic phenomena, or expositions of religious concepts. The School's aversion to convoluting syntax and obfuscating phraseology nevertheless went hand in hand with the view that philosophy was a difficult subject, and that one would be doing it a serious disservice by making it more digestible, even to the generally educated reader. On the contrary: '[t]he day when philosophy becomes a popular subject', Peter Winch insisted, 'is the day for the philosopher to consider where he took the wrong turning',[39] and what is striking about the character of the Swansea School's output is that it remains faithful to Winch's admonition without becoming inaccessible to non-professional philosophers.

III. The Swansea School, Literature, and Tarzan

The need for attention to 'the particular case' also underlies the School's interest in *literature* as a distinctive mode of understanding, not least in the realm of moral phenomena. One thinks here of Peter Winch's fine discussion of Herman Melville's *Billy Budd* (in *Ethics & Action*, 1972), Roy Holland's reflections on Joseph Conrad (in *Against Empiricism*, 1980), İlham Dilman's work on Dostoyevsky (*Raskolnikov's Rebirth*, 2000), H. O. Mounce's book on Tolstoy (*Tolstoy on Aesthetics*, 2001), R. W. Beardsmore's *Art and Morality* (1971), and indeed D. Z. Phillips's philosophical exploration of contemporary fiction in *From Fantasy to Faith* (2006).

What is perhaps not so widely known is that, in the 1950s, various members of the Swansea School, including D. Z. Phillips and Peter Winch, also met and socialised with the novelist Kingsley Amis (1922–95), who taught in Swansea's English department between 1949 and 1961, and, during that time, wrote four novels, viz. *Lucky Jim* (1954), *That Uncertain Feeling* (1955) – subsequently made into a film that featured various Swansea locations – *I Like It Here* (1958), and *Take a Girl Like You* (1960). In a humorous anecdote from his student days at Swansea (1952–8), D. Z. Phillips recalls how, one day, Peter Winch and Kingsley Amis went to the Albert Hall Cinema to watch a *Tarzan* movie together.[40] The experience was as memorable as it was embarrassing:

> The initial shock to the system came when Tarzan made his first appearance, swinging as usual from tree to tree. There was no call! Amis was furious. How could you have a Tarzan without a call ... So incensed was Amis at this aesthetic and dramatic blunder that, when Tarzan swung for the third or fourth time, he decided to supply the call from the circle. One could hardly say it was expected, and no one applauded it. Perhaps Amis thought it was better than nothing. In any case, the result was that we had the usher's torch on us: 'I must ask you to be quiet. There are people trying to enjoy the film.'[41]

However, the movie soon presented another problem, as it featured a (wicked) tribe whose members seemed to know only one word, viz. 'opa':[42]

> Winch and Amis began discussing, too loudly, I admit, whether it made sense to have a language with only one word in it ...

More alarmed by the loudness of the discussion than anything else, I cannot recall its details. Having had the torch on us once I did not want it on us again. But on us again it came: 'This is the second time I've asked you to be quiet. I shan't ask you again.'[43]

As the film was reaching its climax and a beautiful young woman was about to be sacrificed to the wicked tribe's Gorilla God, a heated exchange ensued between the tribal chief and an equally wicked white man, who fancied her for himself. As Phillips recounts:

> The Chief said: 'God want woman', to which the other fellow replied, 'If God want woman, why not me want woman?' At which point Amis said loudly from our circle seats, 'You must admit he's got a damn good point there.' The torch was on us again: 'Gentlemen, I must ask you to leave. So we did.[44]

It was the only time in his life that Phillips was ever thrown out of a cinema.

IV. The Swansea School and Religion

The School's attitude towards religion was by no means monolithic and is consequently more difficult to describe. On the one hand, its members certainly agreed with D. Z. Phillips that the philosopher must take religious belief seriously and cannot simply dismiss it as irrational, superstitious, or nonsensical: 'He may want to oppose it, proclaim it or simply note it as a serious point of view, but he cannot dismiss it as a product of confusion.'[45] On the other hand, the personal beliefs of the School spanned the whole spectrum from atheism (R. W. Beardsmore) to orthodox Christianity (H. O. Mounce, Ieuan Lloyd), with Rhees, Phillips and Winch probably coming closest to Wittgenstein's own views, i.e. deeply sympathetic to a religious perspective on life, somewhat sceptical of institutionalised religion and clerical hierarchy, orthodox with respect to *some* aspects of the Christian tradition (e.g., the concepts of sin, atonement and redemption, the nature of God), but also 'heretical' in regard to others (e.g., the miraculous, the incarnation, the resurrection, immortality).

It is worth noting here that, through Rush Rhees, the French philosopher Simone Weil (1909–43) exerted almost as strong an influence on the Swansea School's engagement with religion as did Wittgenstein, even when their spiritual sensibilities were pulling them in quite different directions. As H. O. Mounce recalls:

> Rhees was deeply impressed by the writings of Simone Weil and familiar with them from the time they first appeared. Until middle age, he was a militant atheist. He held, in the manner of Nietzsche, that religion was both false and servile. By the 1950s, his attitude had entirely changed. It is not clear how this change came about. It may have been the influence of Simone Weil that led to this change of attitude. But I suspect that it was his change of attitude that led him to Simone Weil.[46]

D. Z. Phillips himself did not realise the extent of Rhees's reflections on religion until he edited the latter's *On Religion and Philosophy*,[47] which he now regards as 'one of the most important collections of essays in twentieth century philosophy of religion'; in fact, he thinks that 'there has [not] been anything comparable of its kind since Kierkegaard'.[48]

These accolades demonstrate once again that, far from being an expounder of Wittgenstein's work, Rhees was a highly original thinker in his own right, whose unexpectedly large (16,000-page) Nachlass ranges widely in its subject matter and includes not only Greek philosophy, philosophical logic, and the philosophy of mathematics, but moral philosophy, political philosophy, philosophy of religion, aesthetics, Wittgenstein, and the writings of Simone Weil. Thanks to D. Z. Phillips's dedication – and an astonishing photographic memory – another seven volumes could be published from the Rhees archives during the period 1997–2004 alone.[49] For Phillips himself, this intense engagement with his former teacher's writings was as significant as editing Wittgenstein's work had been for Rhees:

> Editing the work of Rush Rhees, something I would not have thought, in my wildest dreams, I would be doing, has taken me back to what he was trying to teach me in those early Swansea years, hopefully, with greater understanding.[50]

As Phillips also points out in a special issue of *Philosophical Investigation*, published on the fiftieth anniversary of Wittgenstein's death, Rhees's admiration for the latter's work was by no means uncritical:

> Rhees came to be critical of certain aspects of Wittgenstein's thought as early as four years after the publication of the *Investigations*, and probably earlier. He thought he had let the analogy between language and games run away with him, but wanted to develop further the important notion of 'a form of life'.[51]

That Rhees's engagement with Wittgenstein's work goes well beyond expository commentary is already evident in his well-known paper, 'Wittgenstein's Builders',[52] which he wrote when he was still teaching at Swansea, but the posthumously published *Wittgenstein and the Possibility of Discourse*[53] is equally revelatory of his intellectual independence and philosophical depth. Even so, D. Z. Phillips cannot help wondering in his Introduction to the book how it will be received. His speculation ends on a pessimistic note:

> [It] will be ignored by many, since an interest in Wittgenstein hardly occupies centre-stage in contemporary philosophy. That the book is more than a commentary on Wittgenstein will not matter. It calls for a style of reflection at variance with mainstream philosophy.[54]

Phillips's sober but accurate assessment of the Swansea School's relation to 'mainstream' philosophy – unlike Henri Bergson's 1913 lectures at Columbia University, Rhees's seminars on Wittgenstein had never caused a major traffic jam, even on Mumbles Road – applies equally to the reception of his own work in the philosophy of religion, whether it concerns his critical analysis of such concepts as prayer, belief in a bodily resurrection, personal immortality, or the so-called problem of evil. Well aware that most philosophers of religion would react to his analyses with incomprehension, he nevertheless continued to reject the notion of the resurrection, for example, as an 'ultimate safety valve in the sky that redeems all afflictions',[55] just as much as a belief in immortality that, on close inspection, amounted to little more than 'a transcendentalized version of "See you later"'.[56] In his last book, *The Problem of Evil and the Problem of God*,[57] published not long before his sudden death (in 2006), he rightly attacks the attempt to justify human suffering, even suffering in extremis, by reference to a greater good in the eschaton. For Phillips, this religious utilitarianism is not merely unconvincing; it also trivialises the existence of evil itself. The absurdity and moral bankruptcy of the proposal is illustrated by this analogy: 'To rescue sufferings from degradation by employing cost-benefit analysis is like rescuing a prostitute from degradation by telling her to charge higher fees.'[58] As Phillips sees it, the philosopher's task here – as in other areas of discourse – is simply that of trying to understand and to show that 'nonsense remains nonsense even if we associate God's name with it'.[59]

I began my observations about the Swansea School by talking about one of its early representatives (Peter Winch) and finished with comments on one of its last (D. Z. Phillips). Of the original members, only H. O. Mounce remains, and he deserves a special mention here, not only for his fine – and now standard – work on Wittgenstein's *Tractatus*,[60] but for having acted from 2006 until 2020 as the editor-in-chief of the journal *Philosophical Investigations* and ensured that Wittgenstein's legacy would be transmitted to a new generation of philosophers. As Peter Hacker has rightly observed, '[e]mpirical knowledge can be bequeathed, but philosophical understanding has to be achieved anew by each generation'.[61] It is because the Swansea School has played such a significant role in recovering and promoting that understanding that its memory deserves to be kept alive.

Notes

1 Peter Winch, 'Can We Understand Ourselves?', in *Philosophical Investigations*, 20/3 (1997), 10. The German phrase alludes to Wittgenstein's remark, 'We cannot find our feet with them.' See *Philosophical Investigations*, 2nd edn, trans. G. E. M. Anscombe (Oxford: Blackwell, 1958), Part II, p. 225.
2 Winch, 'Can We Understand Ourselves?', p. 6.
3 Peter Winch, *Simone Weil – The Just Balance* (Cambridge: Cambridge University Press, 1989).
4 Peter Winch, *Trying to Make Sense* (Oxford: Wiley-Blackwell, 1987).

5 Peter Winch, 'Understanding a Primitive Society', *American Philosophical Quarterly*, 1/4 (1964), 307–24.
6 Peter Winch, *The Idea of a Social Science and its Relation to Philosophy* (London: Routledge, 2007).
7 Unpublished letter to Rush Rhees, 31 August 1976.
8 Ray Monk, *Wittgenstein: The Duty of Genius* (London/New York: Penguin, 1990), pp. 458–70.
9 For a more detailed overview of the 'Swansea School', see my 'Wittgenstein, Rhees, and the Swansea School', in John Edelman (ed.), *Sense and Reality – Essays out of Swansea* (Frankfurt: Ontos, 2009), pp. 219–35.
10 Ray Monk, *Wittgenstein: The Duty of Genius* (London: Vintage, 1990), p. 357.
11 Monk, *Wittgenstein*, p. 334.
12 Letter to Wittgenstein, 30 December 1940. *Briefwechsel. Innsbrucker elektronische Ausgabe*. M. Seekircher, B. McGuinness, A. Unterkircher (InteLex: Charlottesville/VA, 2004).
13 Letter to Wittgenstein, 5 April 1940. *Briefwechsel*.
14 Letter to Wittgenstein, 5 April 1940. *Briefwechsel*.
15 Letter to Wittgenstein, 31 December 1940. *Briefwechsel*.
16 Letter to Wittgenstein, 31 December 1940. *Briefwechsel*.
17 Letter to Wittgenstein, 31 December 1940. *Briefwechsel*.
18 Letter to Wittgenstein, 31 December 1940. *Briefwechsel*.
19 Letter from Wittgenstein, 21 May 1946. *Briefwechsel*.
20 Rush Rhees, *Wittgenstein and the Possibility of Discourse*, 2nd edn, ed. D. Z. Phillips (Oxford: Blackwell, 2006), p. 274.
21 D. Z. Phillips, 'On Wittgenstein', *Philosophical Investigations*, 24/2 (2001), 148–9.
22 Rhees, *Wittgenstein and the Possibility of Discourse*, p. xiii.
23 See Rhees, *Wittgenstein and the Possibility of Discourse*, pp. 273–4.
24 Ludwig Wittgenstein, *Culture and Value*, ed. G. H. von Wright, trans. Peter Winch (Oxford: Oxford University Press, 1998), p. 24.
25 Rhees, *Wittgenstein and the Possibility of Discourse*, p. xii.
26 Ludwig Wittgenstein, *Blue & Brown Books* (Oxford: Oxford University Press, 1969), 2nd edn, p. 18.
27 Rhees, *Wittgenstein and the Possibility of Discourse*, p. xii.
28 Monk, *Wittgenstein: The Duty of Genius*, p. 437.
29 Letter to Norman Malcolm, 15 December 1945, quoted in Monk, *Wittgenstein: The Duty of Genius*, p. 459.
30 Letter to Norman Malcolm, 11 September 1943. *Briefwechsel*.
31 Letter to Norman Malcolm, 8 September 1945. *Briefwechsel*.
32 Letter to Rush Rhees, 20 August 1948. *Briefwechsel*.
33 Letter to Rush Rhees, 11 June 1949. *Briefwechsel*.
34 Monk, *Wittgenstein: The Duty of Genius*, p. xii.
35 'On Wittgenstein', *Philosophical Investigations*, p. 153.
36 'On Wittgenstein', *Philosophical Investigations*, p. 147.

37 'On Wittgenstein', *Philosophical Investigations*, p. 147.
38 'On Wittgenstein', *Philosophical Investigations*, p. 148.
39 Peter Winch, *The Idea of a Social Science and its Relation to Philosophy* (London: Routledge, 2008), p. 2.
40 Phillips does not provide the title of the movie, but it may have been *Tarzan and the Lost Safari* (1957).
41 D. Z. Phillips, 'Calling in on Tarzan', p. 1. Unpublished handwritten manuscript.
42 Phillips, 'Calling in on Tarzan', p. 2.
43 Phillips, 'Calling in on Tarzan', p. 3.
44 Phillips, 'Calling in on Tarzan', pp. 3–4.
45 D. Z. Phillips, *Religion Without Explanation* (Oxford: Blackwell, 1976), p. 189.
46 H. O. Mounce, 'On the Differences Between Rush Rhees and Simone Weil', *Philosophical Investigations*, 43/1–2 (2020), p. 71.
47 'On Wittgenstein', *Philosophical Investigations*, pp. 149–50.
48 From an unpublished typescript of D. Z. Phillips's revised Introduction to Rhees (1997). Unfortunately, Phillips died before a new edition of the book could be published.
49 *On Religion and Philosophy* (1997); *Wittgenstein and the Possibility of Discourse* (1998/2006); *Moral Questions* (1999); *Discussions of Simone Weil* (1999); *Wittgenstein's 'On Certainty'* (2002); *In Dialogue with the Greeks Volume 1: The Presocratics and Reality* (2004); and *In Dialogue with the Greeks Volume 2: Plato and Dialectic* (2004).
50 'On Wittgenstein', *Philosophical Investigations*, p. 151.
51 'On Wittgenstein', *Philosophical Investigations*, p. 14.
52 Rush Rhees, 'Wittgenstein's Builders', *Proceedings of the Aristotelian Society* (1959/60), 171–86.
53 Rush Rhees, *Wittgenstein and the Possibility of Discourse*, ed. D. Z. Phillips (Oxford: Blackwell, 2006), 2nd edn.
54 Rhees, *Wittgenstein and the Possibility of Discourse*, pp. xlii–xliii.
55 Phillips, *The Problem of Evil*, p. 271.
56 D. Z. Phillips, 'Dislocating the Soul', in D. Z. Phillips (ed.), *Can Religion Be Explained Away?* (London: Macmillan, 1996), p. 247.
57 D. Z. Phillips, *The Problem of Evil and the Problem of God* (London: SCM Press, 2004).
58 Phillips, *The Problem of Evil*, p. 71.
59 D. Z. Phillips, 'Wittgenstein and Religion: Some Fashionable Criticisms', in Kai Nielsen and D. Z. Phillips (eds), *Wittgensteinian Fideism?* (London: SCM Press, 1995), p. 48.
60 H. O. Mounce, *Wittgenstein's Tractatus: An Introduction* (Oxford: Wiley-Blackwell, 1981).
61 Peter Hacker, 'On Wittgenstein', *Philosophical Investigations*, 24:2 (2001), p. 130.

6

J. R. Jones and Wittgenstein: Resisting the Demise of the Welsh-language 'Neighbourhood'

Huw Williams

A juxtaposition of the common Welsh refrain 'Cenedl heb iaith, cenedl heb galon' ('A nation without its language is a nation without a heart'), and Wittgenstein's famous declaration 'the limits of my language means the limits of my world', is a fruitful if potentially fraught place to begin this essay. Regardless, it is entirely apt in my view for reflecting on the legacy of Wittgenstein in what we might refer to as his second home. Today, a debate continues to unfold around the negative impact of seasonal residents on community and language in Wales, but it is fair to suggest that the Austrian is one visitor who left a positive and lasting legacy.

In much the same way as other chapters in this volume disclose how his personal relationships and interactions in Swansea were deeply meaningful, and speak to an elective affinity between person and place, this chapter discloses a similar affinity between his thought and the intellectual, spiritual and social issues facing Wales during the halcyon days of the Swansea School. The aim is to show how Wittgenstein's later philosophy, developed in part through his interlocutions in Swansea, provided a philosophical context within which the most powerful response to the crisis of the Welsh language – *y Gymraeg* – emerged.

The narrative proceeds in the main with reference to one of the School's members, namely J. R. Jones (J.R. henceforth, as he was known in the Welsh intellectual community, where Joneses were all too common). By the time J.R. had established himself in Swansea, Cymru (Wales) had reached a societal crossroads, with warnings of the untimely death of its native language becoming ever louder, and ever more imploring. This was within the wider context of the perceived cultural malaise of the western world, typified by concerns around secularisation and the ravages of modernity, in the shadow of the two world wars, and expressed in the work of a number of influential thinkers of that period.

In such a context, faced with an existential crisis, Welsh appeals to the importance of language – and motifs and slogans such as the one at the opening of this chapter – were coined or amplified with ever-increasing urgency. Such appeals and claims, however, require articulation and argumentation, and this is where they connect with Wittgenstein's later philosophy of language, and where its basic presuppositions became salient. The analysis of how J.R.'s Welsh-language tracts on language and society emerged through his engagement with Wittgenstein's philosophy is related largely through the reflections of his colleague D. Z. Phillips (likewise D.Z. henceforth). The story, however, is not a straightforward one of Wittgenstein simply presenting the basis for the articulation and argumentation of J.R.'s ideas; it is rather how his philosophy was part of the broader intellectual backdrop that influenced J.R. and D.Z., and can be considered one (albeit crucial) element of a wider array of intellectual debates, in which the disarticulation of religious life in Wales was also a crucial factor.

Yr Argyfwng Gwacter Ystyr – The Descent of Wales

This disarticulation and the deep existential questions it raised are captured most notably – and notoriously – in J.R.'s pamphlet published in 1964,[1] in which he coined the phrase 'Argyfwng Gwacter Ystyr' (the 'Crisis of Meaninglessness'), articulating an analysis of the Welsh condition through ideas arising in Paul Tillich's book *The Courage to Be*[2] – specifically the idea of the anxiety of meaninglessness. The phrase continues to reverberate today, and the visceral manner in which it conveyed a world 'empty' of meaning reflects very effectively the deep anxieties felt in Wales by many at the time. For the uninitiated, a somewhat short and schematic version of the backstory is set out here in order to establish the relevance of the wider historical context.

J. R. Jones and Wittgenstein

In broad terms, the Welsh were a stateless nation whose identity had historically been defined to a great extent by their religion and language – and their interdependence. Indeed they played a key part in a number of our creation myths, although myths often rooted in historical fact. The *Brythoniaid* (Ancient Britons), Celtic tribes connected by their shared language, had been Romanised and Christanised, before they were gradually pushed to the western peripheries of an island that had once been largely their own, by the pagan hordes of the Angles, Jutes and Saxons. They considered themselves to be guardians of the faith and one of God's chosen people, fighting to defend Christendom, and as they lost ground, compressed into the modern-day territory of Wales by the sixth and seventh century, they began to call themselves Cymry – roughly equating to compatriots – and so began to form the 'ethnie' that would be the basis for the modern Welsh nation. Their sense of fate as one of God's chosen people, and their basis as a group defined linguistically, is symbolically reflected in the refrain 'iaith y nefoedd' ('the language of heaven') used to describe Cymraeg (the Welsh language). The centrality of this fusion of Christianity and Cymraeg as the basis of identity persisted over time. It was reified in the comparatively early translation of the Bible into Welsh in 1588, as a Protestant reformation with meaning took hold under Elizabeth I. By this time Wales, after a period of colonisation by the Norman state between 1282 and 1536, had been annexed by England in Henry VIII's Acts of Union. This was the act of a Tudor family who made much of their Welsh heritage. The Welsh language, however, had been squeezed out of public life by those Acts of Union, which had banned it from the state's institutions. The subsequent translation of the Bible under Elizabeth, therefore, and the use of Welsh in worship would later be heralded as the saviour of the language.

The deep fusion of language and religion took on its modern manifestation in the religious awakening precipitated by a revival led by the Methodists – primarily Calvinist – in the eighteenth century. Although nominally within the Church, the methods of the so-called 'jumpers' – with their energetic evangelical open-air sermons and appeal to emotion through iconic hymns – were thoroughly nonconformist, and by the nineteenth century they had formally split from the Church and forged a querulous yet incredibly effective alliance with the 'old' dissenters – Baptists and Independents – to transform Wales into a thoroughgoing nonconformist nation. They were joined also by the more recently established, and politically radical Unitarianism, and the broadly progressive and aspirational culture of this movement allied with the liberal politics of the nineteenth century leading to a so-called 'Rebirth of a Nation'.[3] Whilst the movement was in no way ideologically unified with respect to the place of the language within it, by the turn of the twentieth century the language had reached a historical zenith with a million speakers, and many deeply embedded within this wider religious culture. It was short-lived, however, as a combination of the world wars, depression-induced migration, and the increasing influence of anti-Welsh language ideology combined to precipitate a radical decline in the number of speakers from around half the population in 1911 to around a quarter in 1961.

Whilst intellectuals such as J.R. were not blind to the material realities that were driving this collapse, it was understandably ideology that became the subject of their response, not least because any attempt at arresting the decline required a recognition that the language was of value. This was not an argument that was easily made to a population who had for centuries seen their language subjected to numerous tropes, and practically marginalised within the burgeoning English and then British state, a process deepened and intensified with the expansion of the state in the nineteenth century. This was most famously manifested in the so-called 'Treason' of the Blue Books, a report on the educational state of Wales and which connected poverty, ignorance and even immorality with the language. These processes laid the ideological groundwork for a linguistic turn where parents ceased to pass on the language to their children. Particularly in the industrialised south, which saw huge immigration especially at the turn of the twentieth century, Cymraeg saw a dramatic decline. The truth is that the nonconformist culture did not always act as a bulwark; many in the movement imbibed this ideology and set out to prove themselves as refined Brits, and even saw language death as part of God's providential plan, and in this regard it was the Christian God and not the language that remained society's predominant deity.

It was likewise true, however, that many of its Chapels remained at the heart of Welsh-language life and sustained it spiritually and intellectually as a key institution. For those attempting to defend the importance of the language to the people, the now rising force that would soon eclipse nonconformism as the regulating culture of many Welsh communities – socialism – was eyed with increasing suspicion. This was particularly the case after the early advocates of Labourism in Wales, who viewed the socialist project through a national lense and were advocates for the language, were displaced by a generation intent on following the road to British socialism.[4] In fact, when Plaid Cymru, the nationalist party, was established in 1925, among its members were some who had migrated from the Labour Party. In the post-Second World War environment, however, Labourism would be regarded as the main enemy of the Welsh language, with its emphasis on class politics, universalism and solidarity – which broadly painted the politics of language as a distraction if not retardant of the working-class cause.

It was in the face of this universalism and new-found pride in a victorious Britain that the language faced a crisis, as even the Welsh-language heartlands faced a slow decline in numbers and crucially density of Welsh-speakers, which could maintain it as the default language. The issues came to a head in the late 1950s with the infamous fate of Tryweryn, a valley in north-east Wales that was one of these rarer Welsh-language communities. The English city of Liverpool (ironically known as the 'Capital of North Wales' because of the preponderance of Welsh people who lived there historically) needed a new water supply and the most convenient site was the valley, despite the fact it was home to the village of Capel Celyn and its surrounding rural community. Opposition from nationalists and even the Welsh Labour MPs in the Westminster parliament could not save it and the drowning of the valley in 1965, and its martyrdom became the stimulus for both deep soul-searching on the part of the Cymry and a counter-movement, with the formation of Cymdeithas yr Iaith Gymraeg (The Welsh Language Society) that would reject the parliamentarianism of Plaid Cymru and begin on the path of civil disobedience among students and the younger generation.

A watershed moment came with a 1962 radio lecture by the founding president of Plaid Cymru, the divisive but brilliant figure of Saunders Lewis, who delivered a talk that both prophesied the death of the language whilst provoking a popular response by declaring, in opposition to his party, that it was 'trwy ddulliau chwyldro yn unig' ('through revolutionary means only') that the language could be saved from extinction. For older generations, including D.Z. and the older

J.R., the dislocation of Welsh-speaking communities coincided with the crisis of non-conformity, and whilst many in the language movement were happy to embrace a new politics shorn of any Christian impulse, for them and others the two could not be yet be disaggregated. In this context we see in the case of D.Z. that his embrace of Wittgenstein's philosophy allowed him to articulate a philosophy of religion that provided a meaningful response to the empiricist attack on God that spoke directly to his own community's crisis of faith (and whose mainstream largely rejected his vision).

Likewise, it allowed him to articulate arguments in support of the Welsh language, but it was in the figure of his senior colleague J.R. that these would take shape in a manner that directly impacted on the revolutionary language politics of 1960s Wales, and which infused the movement with an unparalleled intellectual vigour. Indeed, Saunders Lewis himself later declared that it was in J.R.'s writings that the 'Treasures of Wales's Nationalism' were to be found,[5] while D.Z. would in hindsight state that J.R. was 'the main philosophical inspiration of Cymdeithas yr Iaith'.[6] Before turning to J.R.'s inspiration and his linguistic nationalism, we can return to his *Argyfwng Gwacter Ystyr* as a tract that both established him as a leading intellectual figure and crystallised the sense of civilisational crisis that engulfed parts of Welsh society at that time, and that provided the backdrop for the ensuing political activity.

Broadly speaking, Jones was wrestling with the death of God and its implications for society. According to the Tillich-inspired analysis, two tendencies had nailed God in the coffin – first was the tendency to regard God as an object among objects, and second was the critical intellect released, ironically, by the protest of the reformation. Where the figure of God takes on an objectivity and personification that posits His existence in its typical sense, this opens the door for the question of proof, of where one can find evidence for this claim. This is then the death knell for God, in a society that has become thoroughly empirical in its outlook as an outgrowth of the questioning, critical spirit fostered by the Protestant reformation. In the same way that Marx believed capitalism creates its own grave-diggers, so Jones asserts that the key to its own demise was to be found in the essence of the Protestant faith. That is to say, it laid the basis for the modern critical spirit that questioned, and would become the basis for the scientific, empirical mind.

J. R. Jones and Wittgenstein

When applied to the question of the existence of God, if that figure is held to be an object among objects and no empirical evidence is forthcoming, there is only one likely outcome. J.R. notes that whilst existential anxiety existed previously in Christian society, this was an anxiety fixated on the wrath of God and the possibility of eternal damnation, which was so effectively mobilised in Wales during its revivals. However, in a society where such a God is no longer in existence, it is affected by anxiety of another form (one of three described by Tillich), namely the anxiety that there is no meaning to existence. In his tract, J.R. attempts to respond to the crisis by articulating another Tillichian, existentialist motif of God more attuned to the modern worldview, namely as the 'ground of being' – an idea of God that moves us beyond the idea of an object or person. It is seldom noted that this has obvious parallels with the single most important inspiration for Welsh nonconformism, Morgan Llwyd, whose Puritan writings during the mid-seventeenth century were inspired by the German mystic Jakub Boehme and his neoplatonic idea of the 'One'. As with his colleague D.Z., however, J.R.'s attempts to rethink Christian belief were met with a mixture of disdain and fear, in a Christian community whose most muscular response to the crisis came in the shape of an evangelical movement that favoured returning to Calvinist orthodoxy.

Although J.R. in this period wrote other tracts, arguing for the place of the nation and its language within the Christian tradition, by the mid 1960s his writing had taken on a more overtly political tone, where the assumption of Christian belief as a foundation for a cultural, linguistic nationalism was no longer prevalent – even if the rhetoric, adorned with Biblical verses and stories, continued to appeal to that tradition, and if one were so inclined one might assume a Christian foundation from the text. Indeed part of the scepticism from the Christian community towards J.R. was that those earlier tracts, and their focus on a more removed and impersonal God, seemed to open a space for the understanding of language and culture as the ultimate source of everyday meaning in our mortal existence on the planet. Whilst this might chime with a younger generation and those adopting the more secular spirit of the times – and could allow J.R. to present a linguistic nationalism where God's presence was largely felt not articulated, or was even extraneous enough to be cast aside for those who chose – for his critics, he was simply guilty of killing God by other means.

J. R. Jones and Wittgenstein

For J.R. to become such a significant figure in Welsh public life was not always something that may have been anticipated by his contemporaries; and, as we will see from the accounts of his intellectual development, it is argued that his confrontation with Wittgenstein, in the figure of Rush Rhees, played a key role. J.R. had treaded the path of other contemporaries such D.Z. and Meredydd Evans, in studying philosophy in the University of Wales as part of their presumed pathway into the nonconformist ministry. J.R. hailed from Pwllheli in north-west Wales, in the Welsh-speaking heartland of Pen Llŷn, a still largely monoglot Welsh community. His father died when he was still a young boy, and his family faced economic hardship, which meant a career as a minister promised much. As with the others, however, he found himself in possession of a unique talent for philosophy, which persuaded him that an academic career beckoned. Having studied as an undergraduate at Aberystwyth at the end of the 1920s, he went on to study at Oxford before later returning to 'the College by the Sea' as a member of staff. In Aberystwyth, he would be schooled in the British Empiricist tradition that was finally taking hold, in spite of the challenge it embodied to the faith of some of its Welsh disciples. J.R soon made a name for himself, and gained a good deal of recognition for his work on established themes in analytic philosophy – such as universals, and the question of identity. In 1952, there came an offer that would place him on a very different philosophical pathway, to take up a personal chair at Swansea.

The rest, as they say, is history, inasmuch as J.R. was thrust into an environment where a new school of philosophy was quickly flowering under the towering figure of Rhees. By the start of the 1960s, J.R. had developed from a very well-respected analytical English-language philosopher into a figure hailed as a 'prophet' in his homeland. One trigger, it is said, for his conversion, was a sabbatical spent in 1960 in the United States. His experience there left a profound mark on him (not unlike the father of modern Welsh nationalism Michael D. Jones's own experience in Ohio in the 1840s). J.R. was deeply troubled by what he regarded as the vacuity of American culture, the lack of roots, and the sense in which a people devoid of genuine meaning devoted themselves to material pursuits. It is suggested that on his return this is the lense through which he viewed his native Wales, where in his mind his people were quickly losing their rootedness with the descent of organised religion and the attrition of the Welsh language. One can imagine how in this context the spectre of Tryweryn would have been a harbinger of civilisational collapse, and why J.R. therefore responded with such urgency.

This was hardly a transformation, however. J.R. had long been a lay preacher, and was familiar with delivering some fire and brimstone from the pulpit, and so what we witness in the 1960s is an allying of his spiritual fervour, philosophical acumen and nationalist commitment into a rhetorical force that, if not irresistible, was certainly arresting for all those who shared his sympathies. Two or even three J.R.'s are sometimes spoken of – the preacher, the philosopher, and the prophet. Anecdotes tell of how, for some, never the twain or three would meet –they could not recognise the one J.R. in the other – but, more than anything perhaps, this tells of the apartness of the ivory tower. Certainly, when they became confluent in his later years, the results were unique; and, in understanding the role of Wittgenstein in this, we can turn to two others who were at the Swansea School as students at the end of the 1950s. They were D.Z. and Walford Gealy, the latter who would go on to a career in the extramural department at Aberystwyth University.

A starker contrast could not be drawn in terms of their understanding of J.R.'s development in the Swansea School. Gealy paints a picture of a tragic figure, beset by self-doubt, who in being thrust from the stronghold of Empiricism in Aberystwyth to the 'philosophical revolution' in Swansea lost all confidence and philosophical direction, something that was accompanied not by a search for understanding in the matter of his Christian faith, but rather by a complete disenchantment. Gealy points to his empiricist fellow travellers in Aberystwyth, such as Richard Aaron, who remained faithful both to their philosophical school and their religious creed, suggesting that J.R.'s weakness was an over-developed sense of intellectual humility that led him to be tossed between different philosophical and theological positions. Indeed, Gealy identifies this pattern before his arrival at Swansea, noting the commitment to scientism in the differing forms of Marxism and Logical Positivism. Rather than an inquisitive and open intellect, Gealy describes this as an often harmful tendency to vacillation that, faced with the emerging Wittgensteinian school, led to a form of academic breakdown. 'From Aberystwyth where J.R. was entirely comfortable at an intellectual level, he was thrown into the Lion's Den of the philosophical revolution that was beginning in Swansea.'[7] There, Gealy relates how, at the weekly, fiery meetings of the Philosophy Society, 'the saddest thing of all was to see the poor professor, with his head in his hands between his legs, almost without articulating one word from his mouth, in the same way from week to week. The new philosophy was so new to him he was frightened to say a thing!'[8] Gealy cites the impact in terms of J.R.'s output – eight papers were published by him in the three years preceding his appointment in journals such as *Mind, Philosophy, Philosophical Studies* and *Analysis*, but after his move he published only four more papers at the so-called 'highest' level. Gealy describes it as a process of having to re-learn philosophy, and divesting himself of his previous presuppositions, and, he notes, 'to his eternal credit, he succeeded'. But what was the result of what Gealy described as this successful nightmare? 'It appears to me,' states Gealy, 'that from the beginning of the 1960s he gave up on his serious philosophical work.'[9] That Gealy should ascribe such a verdict to his work in Welsh is itself fascinating, and is suggestive of all those assumptions and presumptions that continue with respect to what qualifies as philosophy proper. It is all the more interesting given the value that Gealy saw in his work, in as much as he celebrates the fact that J.R. inspired Cymdeithas yr Iaith (as the main activist group established in the 1960s), who inspired others. Crucially, however, it is alleged that J.R., in 'articulating the profundity of his feelings of love for his country and his people, lost control of that cold feelinglessness, neutrality of the philosophical discipline'. Crucially, in demonstrating that if J.R. had understood the philosophical revolution he had not quite joined it, Gealy notes that he regressed into the bad habits of the old philosophical world by advocating forms of logical essentialism in his political philosophy. From the perspective of an orthodox Wittgensteinian, the work of the late, Welsh J. R. Jones was a confusion of philosophical and theological influences that resulted in a body of work that (whilst inspiring his people) could not be considered a serious contribution to the business of philosophy.

Before considering D.Z.'s very different interpretation, it is worth considering another contrasting view of J.R.'s evolution (rather than regression) from another Swansea philosopher. In an insightful chapter discussing key concepts in J.R.'s later political, Welsh-language tracts, Steve Edwards takes the view that the distinguishing feature of this body of work is precisely the language through which J.R. expresses his idea. That is to say, without of course diminishing the idea that J.R. had been on a philosophical journey, a key to understanding this later work is that J.R. adopts a different philosophical methodology, through the use of his mother tongue. Whilst in the English language he had occupied the space of the anglophone, analytical philosopher, in Edwards's view once J.R. converted to writing in Welsh he had crossed the rubicon into what is typically considered a Continental style of philosophy. To this end, Edwards addresses J.R.'s use of the idea of narrative identity and his key concept of 'cydymdreddiad' ('interpenetration', of land and language) in a comparative context, analysing and understanding these ideas with reference to Ricoeur, MacIntyre and the work of Merleau-Ponty. He summaries by saying that J.R. 'felt more free in Welsh as he did not have to philosophise in accordance with the same restrictions, namely the narrow restrictions of analytic philosophy ... Cartesian restrictions are at play in his English work, but in Welsh J.R. worked in the field of anthropological philosophy – the tradition of Heidegger rather than Descartes.'[10] It may be no coincidence in terms of his assessment that Edwards himself had moved to Swansea from England, learning Welsh in later life (to the extent that he was able to contribute essays to the publications of the Urdd Athronyddol, the academic society established by Richard Aaron and others for the discussion and promotion of philosophy through the medium of Welsh, to which J.R. had contributed since the 1930s). As a philosopher who had crossed the linguistic divide, Edwards's awareness of the liminality of this position, with a self-conscious awareness of the consequences of immersing oneself in another linguistic world, would have been more sensitive to the consequences than the native Welsh-speakers educated philosophically in English, who switched codes as effortlessly and unthinkingly as an amphibian passes from land to water. To Edwards, it made perfect sense that this different linguistic lifeworld (which different external influences, such as psychoanalysis, penetrated more profoundly) should be the basis for a different philosophical style and approach. As we will see, this would chime with J.R.'s own account of linguistic relativity and the nature of what he would term linguistic microcosms – 'bychanfydoedd'.

Whilst Edwards's account bears some similarity with Gealy in drawing a clear distinction between J.R.'s English-language and Welsh-language work, D.Z. takes an interesting and I would suggest insightful approach to the question – and in some ways we might regard him as being the best positioned to provide such an account as both a student and colleague of J.R., as he returned as a member of staff to Swansea in the late 1960s and would have worked alongside J.R. for some three years until the latter's untimely death. Indeed, in his book length account of J.R., the same admiration that Gealy expresses for the person is evident, but while Gealy regarded the later work as a product of philosophical confusion, D.Z. describes it as a matter of progression that was in fact influenced in a positive and productive manner by his engagement with Wittgensteinian philosophy. Indeed, there is enough in D.Z.'s account to allow us to potentially regard J.R. as a part of the Swansea School proper, even if he was on the margins and involved in his own very personal philosophical project.

D.Z.'s insight into J.R.'s development as a thinker is evident in as much as he traces a nuanced philosophical evolution in the face of new challenges. In this context, the towering figure of Rhees is judged to be a formative influence. While it might be overstating the case to suggest he took J.R. under his wing (this would be to diminish J.R.'s status as a philosopher), it seems fair to assert that he provided a guiding hand. There was undoubtedly mutual respect, and it would have been difficult for any philosopher, regardless of their status and prowess, to ignore or dismiss the advances of one of the foremost twentieth-century philosophers. It was also the case that, according to J.R.'s daughter, Rush Rhees boarded in their house for some time.

According to D.Z., the manner in which Rhees's influence exerted itself on J.R.'s thinking was that his empiricist philosophy (which we might in a very schematic sense describe as an approach that takes the individual in isolation in the first instance) should be inflected by the more communitarian (for want of a better word) approach of Wittgenstein. That is to say, because Wittgenstein places the focus on language as the means through which human life is mediated and through which meaning is brought into our world, it is naturally a philosophical perspective that inclines to look at the collective – the linguistic community. The individual is in this sense regarded as relational and constituted through those linguistic interactions with others.

J. R. Jones and Wittgenstein

Indeed, this is an idea that Edwards suggests in different terms, in his argument that J.R.'s Welsh-language work rejects the notion of the Cartesian self – and that instead of reflecting on the self as something that is atomised from everything else, it is rather considered as an integral part of the linguistic community and even the land (a concept to which we will return). The satisfying phrase that D.Z. uses to describe this is the centrality of 'the human neighbourhood' to Wittgenstein's philosophy – through this realisation or acceptance of the idea of the centrality of this neighbourhood to our everyday life, J.R. was able to develop new ways of thinking.[11]

Thinking around these matters did not involve a clean break for J.R. In terms of his oeuvre and the themes he had focused on in his work previous to Swansea – especially with regard to the nature of the self – these were questions around identity and inter-relations that remained consistent, but that could now be approached from this new perspective. However, and this is where the nature of the times and J.R.'s social context becomes crucial, the issues that faced J.R.'s own 'human neighbourhood' at the time related to its existential crisis, and the possibility that it might unravel within a generation. In this way, a perspective inspired by or informed by this Wittgensteinian philosophy was on far more fertile and promising terrain for J.R. in order to get to grips with the social issues that were emerging in the 1950s, and coming to a head by the end of the decade. Neither does it seem unfair to suggest that, although Wittgenstein was in some ways an anglophone philosopher who came into the subject through the analytic tradition, his philosophy offered a more capacious view of the world that could offer a bridge to some of the other influences of the period that J.R. was exposed to. Tillich was another Germanic thinker expressing himself in the anglophone world; Simone Weil raised questions and issues around the need for roots in a style that would have been entirely alien to the empiricist tradition; and, in wrestling with the issue of language, although Wittgenstein himself might dispute the claim, there were obvious connections between a philosophy of language that emphasised context and its defining influence on our lives, and the work of a philosopher such as Herder.

This distinctive philosophy of language is something that D.Z. himself discusses in a later paper named 'Pam Achub Iaith?' ('Why Save a Language?').[12] In it, he argues that the Wittgensteinian view of language is in direct contrast and offers a powerful critique of the empiricist view of language, as represented in the philosophy of John Locke. This was a limited but powerful foray into the politics of language by D.Z., who, as we know, applied Wittgenstein's philosophy to that other great social issue of the time, the empiricist challenge to religion and the Christian faith (this was the other main way in which Wittgenstein left a positive legacy in terms of his 'second home', although again the wider Welsh public sphere was less engaged with D.Z.'s philosophy than it might have been). The crux of D.Z.'s argument foreshadows the distinction that Charles Taylor situated centrally in his recent, definitive work on the philosophy of language, *The Language Animal*.[13] D.Z. elicits the limits of the empiricist view of language as a means to label an external world that is ontologically distinct and in a sense prior to language. Thus, language is restricted to a means of communication between people in relating their individual experience of the world to each other – this is the 'descriptive' function of language that Taylor relates to the tradition of Hobbes, Locke and Condorcet. D.Z., however, argues that Wittgenstein's view of language, what Taylor would describe as 'constitutive', demonstrates that language is more fundamental to human life and in fact creates rather than merely describes our world. It is through language and our linguistic community that the world is constituted and made intelligible – and so, rather, a language embodies or signifies a 'ffurf ar fyw' ('a form of being'). This creative aspect of language, and the way in which it continually generates new meanings and horizons, is the vast linguistic landscape that Taylor argues those in Locke's tradition cannot account for or understand.

In D.Z.'s own development or interpretation of the Wittgensteinian view of language, we see the progress of his earlier idea that certain language games (or what we might call meta-language games) constitute what he describes as a 'byd-darlun' ('world-image'). This is the term he uses to discuss the empiricist view of the world and the Christian view in his early work on religion in *Athronyddu am Grefydd*.[14] He saw the disarticulation of the Christian faith as a process where that particular language game, or world-image, was fraying and disintegrating both in the face of changes in societal practice that underpinned the game, but also in the challenge emerging from another world-image with which (despite the efforts of some empiricist philosophers) it could not co-exist. Whilst in this context certain language games are seen as lenses through which the world is understood, in the later paper D.Z. suggests that a particular language (Welsh, English, etc.) can in and of itself be understood as a unique means through which life is lived and understood. It is confused to suppose that one will find the same form of being in one language and the other, and so every language is to be considered a unique phenomenon. In this context, D.Z. suggests it would be terrible to compare languages as if they were companies competing in the market. To be blind to the impulse to save a language – to save a form of being – is a matter of lacking respect, and this is an all too common attitude. In articulating the idea of what the death of a language constitutes, D.Z. states that, in J.R.'s terms, this is the loss of a 'bychanfyd ieithyddol' ('linguistic microcosm'), and in so doing relates it directly to the view of Rhees and Wittgenstein on language. To this idea and J.R.'s wider political thought we now turn.

The Spirit's Cradle

In his iconic book, *Prydeindod*,[15] published in 1966, J.R. presents his political philosophy in its most complete form (if not fully developed – as a few interesting aspects emerge in his later writings, partly in response to critics). Politically, the main intention of the work is to analyse and reveal how the British state is precipitating the erosion of the Welsh language and how, in this way, it constitutes a mortal threat to Cymru (Wales). On a philosophical level, the purpose is to offer a normative interpretation of the essence of nationhood and nationality; that is to say, how we should define those elements that make a nation a nation, and how we should understand how a nation relates to human existence, and manifests itself through nationality in our everyday lives. In the context of this discussion, we can set aside for a moment the criticism of Britishness, focusing on these conceptual elements that coalesce around the central theme of the 'bychanfyd' (whilst noting that the critique is rooted in the idea that Britain can never offer a genuine home for the Welsh-speaking person).

In the first instance, more fundamental than the concept of a nation for J.R. is the concept of a people. In contemporary terminology, J.R.'s 'nation' would be understood in terms of the 'nation-state', because for him a nation is a people (or, it is sometimes suggested, peoples) who have secured a state for themselves. The people are in this way instantiated in the state, which forms as it were a protective carapace around them, and the logic of the state is to act in the interests of its people, and specifically to maintain its identity and separateness. The state has a very important role in this respect to ensure that the people maintain a level of self-awareness with respect to who they are, above all through the promotion of historical consciousness and protecting its unique 'bychanfyd(oedd)'. A modern people cannot be truly confident that its identity can be maintained, without the particular ability that a state has to preserve and reproduce national memory (an earlier paper by Jones on the idea of the nation articulated such processes in a manner that clearly prefigured Michael Billig's concept of banal nationalism).[16]

It is difficult to do justice to J.R.'s idea of a people concisely, but to understand it at all requires a grasp of the concept of 'cydymdreiddiad' – the interpenetration of language and land – and which leads us back to the idea of the 'bychanfyd ieithyddol' ('linguistic lifeword'). J. R. Jones understands a people as a group with a particular characteristic – and that characteristic is constituted by the language they speak, and the land on which they live. And yet, it is not these bare elements that are the most fundamentally important, but the connection between them. For J.R., it is the *interpenetration* between the land and the language that takes place over an extensive historical period that characterises what distinguishes a people. It is worth emphasising how simple and arguably elegant J.R.'s concepts of people and nation are in one regard. That is to say, there are no complex and prolonged discussions about the various presumed characteristics of the contemporary nation such as economy, religion, mythology, law, the press, and vague subjective aspects and so on. J.R.'s philosophical intention is to identify what is essential and sufficient for a people and a nation; and, for him, language, land and state are the fundamental trinity.

Likewise however, we must also recognise the complexity of the central concept of the interpenetration of language and land, which is vitally important in terms of the essential nature of a people and their nation. This historical interpenetration in its most concrete and obvious form is manifested in the names of places and localities, and in its objective and practical form in the linguistic community that speaks the language; its most fundamental and important presence is its existence in the spirit (understood in broad terms in J.R.'s writing as our consciousness or mental life): that site where the interpenetration is experienced subjectively by a people. In the same manner as expressed by D.Z., for J.R. the language is a form of life, but in his hands this idea takes on a more expansive and deeper metaphysical quality through a materialist emphasis, which is expressed by the idea of a historical process of amassing meaning and substance, through the intimate relationship with the physical locale, its attributes and proclivities.

J.R. attempts to articulate the full extent of its significance in relation to its connection with the human condition, by arguing that far from being simply a means of communication, language and the microcosm it embodies are where the deepest needs of the human personality are played out. This comes to the fore in one of his earlier Welsh-language writings on Christianity and nationality in 1961,[17] which is in a basic sense an attempt to give an account of the nation as something that has a place 'in the will, and therefore in God's plan' – in contrast with other Christians who view the nation as thwarting the universal ends of humanity. He begins the discussion with reference to one of his other main philosophical influences, Simone Weil, and her own analysis of the basic needs of humanity. He builds on her work, or perhaps responds somewhat critically to it, by suggesting that the basic need of 'nourishment' for human beings, as described by Weil, should be regarded as secondary to the more fundamental 'need for a world'. J.R. says: 'In short, the scope of man's experience – the theatre of his life – must be a world. It is a prerogative of man that he must have this whole world as a nursery.'[18]

J.R.'s emphasis on this need for a *place* is deeply connected to his understanding of the state of existence, and its basic duality in body and spirit. He says of it:

> Our life has two frames ... the frame of space and the frame of time. Our body is placed under definite limitations within these, namely within its length and width in space, and between the poles of its birth and death in time. But ... our spirit breaks out of this enclosure and is cognizant of the infinity of these two frames.[19]

According to J.R., our existence is one that has been characterised by the physical and the spiritual (or in those more prosaic terms, our mental life, or consciousness) – and space and time set boundaries on them. What is characteristic of the second characteristic (and which suggests the 'mental' or 'conscious' that J.R. has in mind) is that it can 'break out' of these frames. That is, the spiritual in the case of humanity has the ability to break free from the present in space and time, and look backwards and forwards, and indeed regard itself as subject. This is what J.R. claims is the 'self-transcending' nature of spirit and humanity which characterises our potential for freedom. However, this ability to break through the boundaries of time and commune with the infinite element does not necessarily represent emancipation.

Quite the opposite, in fact, for this is the path to restlessness and anxiety J.R. suggests, because as a result of this self-transcendence, 'the human spirit is on a kind of wandering in a world without borders, a world where further possibilities beyond all borders echo'.[20] Of necessity, then, because of the spirit's ability to transcend itself and be aware of the infinity of space and time, it comes face to face with a crisis: 'it is constantly threatened, as it were, by the terror of nothingness', as if it were 'always on the verge of discovering that existence has no meaning'.[21] This is the essence of the human condition, then, one that is defined by the needs of the spirit to pacify or calm itself.

In the text *Troedle* (1970; the title translates as 'foothold'), J.R. comes close to suggesting that the spirit is the entirety of, or at least the essence of man's existence, taking priority entirely over the physical: 'But since man is "spirit", and that he must, in order to meet its need for a place, seek more than the space that is directly in the neighbourhood of his body, his "need for a dwelling place" must be understood as a "need for a microcosm".'[22] More specifically than pacifying the spirit, the challenge that faces and needs to be answered (if we want to be at home in the world) is to ensure an existence that not only, and of necessity, offers a space and place for the body, but that offers a home for the spirit.

And so, although we in our embodied form require a place to live, that is not sufficient for the spirit. The human being, as spirit embodied, requires a dwelling in the world that offers a combination of the geographical and the spiritual to furnish it. And where will such a dwelling be?

At bottom, this will be a terrestrial or geographical habitat. But its geographical aspects will be reconciled with human aspects. The network of man's intercourse with others is mediated through the bulk of his network of hills and valleys and rocks and trees. And the most important medium of human intercourse is Language; not any language, of course, but the mother tongue of the land.[23]

The lands bound themselves 'with our old language until it imbued it with such meaning that render it the spirit's cradle, in the empty dwelling of space'.[24] The answer, therefore, to the terrible state of being that threatens to empty our lives of any substance or meaning is to grasp the spiritual element that can offer us this meaning. Man gropes for 'an eternal track in which he can stand consciously ... an eternal track in his memory'.[25] In other words, 'it is the need for a microcosm, for a world assembled out of the endless oceans of the possibilities of existence'.[26]

In J.R.'s words, therefore, while we can understand a 'bychanfyd' (linguistic microcosm) as the product of a language historically interpenetrated with the land, and therefore as a discrete entity from one particular place on earth, it also carries with it a universal quality. That is to say, it is an instantiation of the universal – one version of humanity's being on earth, or in his words, '[i]t is a concentration of the contents of the world. And in the consciousness of the members of the microcosm this concentration will exist.'[27]

The spiritual plane is that which characterises the 'bychanfyd', therefore, and its completeness in embodying 'the content of the world' is important to grasp, being essential when trying to understand why it is the nation, rather than any other entity, that instantiates it and provides the conditions for it to thrive, It will not be possible for the spirit to be at home only within the family, or a locality, or for that matter within the global society, because it is only the nation that offers the opportunity for the spirit to be at home in its self-transcendence.

> There will be no value in a microcosm, in which we seek refuge from nihility, if it were to turn into a prison with respect to the possibilities of self-transcendence of the spirit. Because by limiting these possibilities, man's abilities to create are limited. His awareness of further possibilities, in every finite situation, made him the creator of his civilisations.[28]

Instead, we must try to secure ourselves an anchor in time that is commensurate with the fullness of the spirit.

The microcosm, therefore, must be a kind of accumulation of man's creative achievements and the expansion of his spirit over the centuries. This means that he must 'familiarize himself with standing in the flow of time, within a track that will span the ages. And it is quite obvious that there is no such track for us but for the track in which we stand in our national distinctiveness, the track of our nation's age-old past.'[29] What the nation allows us as spiritual beings is to recognise who we are in the 'environment of the Ages', providing us to with witnesses to who we are. Without this historical awareness, civilisation in J.R.'s opinion cannot exist.

In the same way as we see it is spirit that characterises man, and his existence in time, we see that it is in history, through time, that a people (in this case y Cymry) characterises itself as a vessel for the microcosm: 'From the point of view of space, Cymru is but a slice on the face of the earth, but in the dimension of time it is a concentration of the world – a compilation of the achievements of the human spirit down the centuries.'[30] It has a material existence, but it is what happened upon it, through it, and in connection with it, that is responsible for its identity: 'On this piece of earth the centuries distilled, out of the material of the spirit's achievements, an incomparable microcosm, carrying with it its own incomparable memory.'[31] Of course, that which is the vessel for this memory, and what defines the microcosm, is the language. And because it is in the language that the nation stands, losing it would be 'losing one concentration of the world which (like all others, of course) is incomparable and irreplaceable'.[32] It in these terms that J.R. attempts to articulate to us the seemingly prosaic idea conveyed to us by D.Z. in saying that to lose a language is to lose a form of life. We will return in conclusion to the question of whether this philosophy of language can in any sense be regarded Wittgensteinian, but it is first worth elucidating briefly the political ramifications of J.R.'s thinking.

In the first instance, J.R.'s taxonomy of the nation is the basis for his critique of Britishness. Analytically, his account denies the idea of a British people, because a people, as we have noted, is constituted at a formative level by the interpenetration of its language with the land. In this sense, the British Isles are home to a patchwork of peoples, including the English, whose own language has historically interpenetrated with a certain geographical territory. However, where the English succeeded and where the Cymry (and the Cornish, and the Scottish Gaels for that matter) failed was in securing a permanent state for themselves. We can therefore speak of the English nation, as in their case there has been the formative triple-tie between language, land and state. And it is not only that the other peoples failed to secure themselves as a nation; the fateful development for the Cymry is that they, as with other peoples, were tied to a state that was not their own. Instead they were annexed as part of the English state, whose logic is to conserve and promote the English language microcosm; the historical process therefore has been one that has arrested and stultified, or actively thwarted, the reproduction of the Cymry over time. It is no mistake, therefore, that the Welsh language is in decline, because this is a function of the logic of the English state. Britishness, however, is a particularly invidious ideology in J.R.'s view, because it has created the false belief that the British state (which is in fact the English state enlarged) has been administered in the interests of the Cymry as well. Politically, therefore, J.R.'s critique serves as a basis for calling for resistance, and for the Cymry to understand and acknowledge that they are being choked out of existence.

In this respect, J.R.'s account has further ramifications that merit comment as we reach our conclusion. Firstly, we see that J.R. identifies the essence of the Cymry, or of any people, in their language microcosm, and in particular in its formative significance. That is to say, regardless of the contemporary situation of a language, it is its central role in the forming of a people that is of fundamental significance and which carries the separateness of a people up to today. On the functional level, that is in the day-to-day activity of those who are members of the people, the efficacy of this historical interpenetration can vary, and obviously, according to J.R.'s account, it is those peoples who have assured themselves states that will have best maintained their linguistic integrity. In the case of the Cymry, J.R. at this time is clearly persuaded, along with his contemporaries, that they could be facing their last days, in the sense that the active interpenetration of land and language may soon come to an end at a functional level. He points more than once towards the Cornish in order to illustrate the fate that awaits – a shell of a historical people who have been assimilated entirely by the English and exist only in the most attenuated of senses and largely as a historical memory. When the language atrophies and then disappears at the functional level, J.R. claims, Cymru will no longer exist. Intriguingly he says *Wales* will persist, but this will not be the same entity; this will be a people with a historical memory of their distinctiveness and some measure of discrete identity, but they will not exist apart from the English; they will be fully subsumed under the British/English identity. With a form of life desisting, so a people will desist.

Another consequence of J.R.'s analysis goes to the heart of the difficulties with such a form of linguistic nationalism, and how this plays out in a population where four in five do not speak the language. Politically, this has long been an issue that Welsh nationalism has always struggled with, amid sentiments on the one hand that those who do not speak the language are not as 'fully' Welsh, and sentiments on the other that the language is a relic best dispensed with. This is particularly true of the language discourse of the 1960s, which today no doubt would be referred to as a culture war. J.R., I would suggest, was very much aware of and wary of this issue, and in one of his last tracts, *A Raid i'r Iaith ein Gwahanu? – Must the language divide us?*,[33] he attempts to bridge, or rather go beneath, the divide.

It is in some ways a defensive discussion, especially in the opening passages, because J.R. is concerned with the contemporary power dynamic that marginalised Welsh-speakers in terms of rights and practicalities; however, he is fully conscious of the need for solidarity and the role that those who do not speak Welsh play in terms of the future of the language, and therefore the people. Rather than pushing for the practical step of more 'second-language' teaching (he is very sceptical about the positive impact of learning a few words) J.R. argues that it is on the formative, and not functional level that people must be engaged. That is to say, what is fundamental for J.R. is building a historical consciousness of the formative role of the language, in creating the Cymry as a people. It is such a level of understanding that allows for the possible reconciliation of the anglophone Welsh and Welsh-speakers, not only in unifying them in their understanding of the past, but also in forming the basis for action in the future. Those who understand the critique and embrace the critique of Britishness will be in a spiritual space that will likely see them supportive of the language, and insist on its revitalisation for the next generation. Thus the linguistic microcosm can be repaired, patched up, and potentially invigorated with a new generation of speakers who will, in their new-found historical consciousness, also wish to work towards the establishing of Cymru as a nation, where an independent state serves the interest of its people.

Conclusions

The overt linguistic nationalism of J. R. Jones seemingly takes us a long way away from the philosophy of Wittgenstein. Indeed, as Gealy's critique suggests, it is questionable the extent to which Wittgenstein would have considered such political pamphlets to be philosophical, by his understanding of the term. The lion's share of the work produced by J.R. after his move to Swansea is also characterised by the melding several influences, of which here we have invoked another three, namely Herder, Weil and Tillich. These are influences that hail from a very different context than Wittgenstein, and in some senses it is impossible to square them with the work of the Viennese philosopher. As Edwards argues, one can note how in philosophising in Welsh, J.R. entered a different, anthropological form of philosophy.

Yet one can also detect the deep connections and the basis for the claim that J.R. would not have produced this most remarkable flurry of writings were it not for his collision with Rush Rhees and the Swansea School. In elucidating the idea of a language microcosm, its relationship to people and nation, J.R. expounds the idea of a form of life that D.Z. himself – very much a Wittgensteinian – claims can derive directly from this school of thought. In so doing, however, J.R. invokes profound metaphysical ideas of a kind that one suspects may have drawn Wittgenstein's ire were they to be propounded as philosophy. If we take another view of J.R.'s work, however, we may be able to square the circle, in the sense that what he arguably achieves in the most basic sense is an account of how the Cymry understand their own language and existence. In this sense, his work can be viewed from the Wittgensteinian perspective as an attempt to analyse and articulate those profound ideas that inspired the language activists of the 1960s and their sense of who they were – to make sense of a set of beliefs and ideas that were 'there, as with our life'. One can note however, that what is un-Wittgensteinian is J.R.'s apparent attempt to generalise these ideas in a schematic, essentialist theory of the nation – and this reflects an ever-present tension in his work, when it is never entirely clear to what extent J.R. truly thought these accounts were to represent a more general theory of nation and nationality.

What we may claim is that J.R.'s dialogue with Wittgenstein, mediated through Rush Rhees, changed him in ways that together with other events precipitated the most remarkable philosophical journey that produced some of the greatest texts of the Welsh language (the greatest, in my view). There is undoubtedly an elective affinity between the late work of Wittgenstein, and the meaning of the Welsh language to its speakers, which philosophically are clearly based on the same general assumptions about the value and meaning of language. Taken together with his growing interest in Herder, Weil and others, J.R. developed the tools to analyse both the 'language game' of Welsh language discourse, and the meaning of the language itself as a form of life, or a language microcosm. We can see the Wittgensteinian impact on J.R. as an emancipation from his empiricist roots, which inspired him to great heights. Gealy disagrees, but, when one reads J.R.'s Welsh-language tracts, one is reminded of that great work of art by Picasso, *Les Desmoiselles d'Avignon*, which brings together numerous disparate influences in an entirely new and original form, which in its entirety creates a unique and life-shifting body of work. There is no doubt in my mind that in response to the crisis of his time, J.R. was inspired to great heights, in no small part by his life in the Swansea School, and that this produced ideas and texts which helped to change Wales forever.

Notes

1 J. R. Jones, *Yr Argyfwng Gwacter Ystyr* (Llandybie: Llyfrau'r Dryw, 1964).
2 P. J. Tillich, *The Courage to Be* (New Haven: Yale University Press, 1952).
3 K. O. Morgan, *Rebirth of a Nation: A History of Modern Wales 1880–1980* (Oxford: Oxford University Press, 1980). For a complete history of Wales, which broadly informs the narrative set out in this chapter, refer to G. A. Williams, *When Was Wales? A History of the Welsh* (London: Penguin, 1984).
4 R. D. Griffiths, *Turning to London: Labour's Attitude to Wales 1898–1956* (Cardiff: Y Faner Goch, 1980).
5 J. S. Lewis, *Tynged yr Iaith*, 2nd edn (Talybont: Y Lolfa/Cymdeithas yr Iaith, 1972).
6 D. Z. Phillips, *J. R. Jones (Writers of Wales)* (Cardiff: University of Wales Press, 1995), p. 9.

7 W. L. Gealy, 'J. R. Jones, y Dyn a'i Athroniaeth', in E. Gwynn Matthews (ed.), *Argyfwng Hunaniaeth a Chred: Ysgrifau ar Athroniaeth J. R. Jones*, Astudiaethau Athronyddol 6 (Talybont: Y Lolfa, 2016), p. 23 [my translation].
8 Gealy, 'J. R. Jones', p. 23.
9 Gealy, 'J. R. Jones', p. 28.
10 S. D. Edwards, 'Dau Syniad Metaffisegol yr Athro J. R. Jones: Hunaniaeth a Chydymdreiddiad', in E. Gwynn Matthews (ed.), *Argyfwng Hunaniaeth a Chred: Ysgrifau ar Athroniaeth J. R. Jones*, Astudiaethau Athronyddol 6 (Talybont: Y Lolfa, 2016), p. 86 [my translation].
11 Phillips, *J. R. Jones*, pp. 14–31.
12 D. Z. Phillips, 'Pam Achub Iaith?', *Efrydiau Athronyddol*, 56 (1993), 1–12.
13 C. M. Taylor, *The Language Animal: The Full Shape of the Linguistic Human Capacity* (Cambridge, MA: Belknap Press of Harvard University Press, 2016),
14 D. Z. Phillips, *Athronyddu am Grefydd: Cyfeiriadau Newydd* (Llandysul: Gwasg Gomer, 1974).
15 J. R. Jones, *Prydeindod* (Llandybie: Llyfrau'r Dryw, 1966).
16 J. R. Jones, 'Y Syniad o Genedl', *Efrydiau Athronyddol*, 24 (1961), 3–17.
17 J. R. Jones, 'Cenedligrwydd a Chrefydd', in *Gwaedd yng Nghymru* (Pontypridd: Cyhoeddiadau Modern Cymreig Cyf., 1970 [1961]), pp. 7–16.
18 Jones, 'Cenedligrwydd a Chrefydd', p. 11.
19 Jones, 'Cenedligrwydd a Chrefydd', p. 11.
20 Jones, 'Cenedligrwydd a Chrefydd', p. 11.
21 Jones, 'Cenedligrwydd a Chrefydd', p. 11.
22 J. R. Jones, 'Troedle', *Barn*, 87 (Ionawr 1970), 61–2.
23 Jones, 'Cenedligrwydd a Chrefydd', p. 12.
24 Jones, 'Cenedligrwydd a Chrefydd', p. 13.
25 Jones, 'Cenedligrwydd a Chrefydd', p. 15.
26 Jones, 'Cenedligrwydd a Chrefydd', p. 11.
27 Jones, 'Cenedligrwydd a Chrefydd', p. 15.
28 Jones, 'Cenedligrwydd a Chrefydd', p. 13.
29 Jones, 'Cenedligrwydd a Chrefydd', p. 13.
30 Jones, 'Cenedligrwydd a Chrefydd', p. 15.
31 Jones, 'Cenedligrwydd a Chrefydd', p. 15.
32 Jones, 'Cenedligrwydd a Chrefydd', p. 15.
33 J. R. Jones, *A Raid i'r Iaith ein Gwahanu?* (Aberystwyth: Undeb Cymru Fydd, 1967).

7

Wittgenstein, Communitarianism, and Welsh Cultural-Linguistic Identity

Rhianwen Daniel

What is the relation between Wittgenstein's philosophy of language and its implications for the Welsh cultural-linguistic identity, as articulated by nationalist intellectuals whose work was the central ideological undercurrent driving twentieth century Welsh nationalism? The Welsh case presents a philosophically and socio-culturally interesting example of a systematic, densely concentrated, and salient expression of the importance of cultural roots, linguistic vitality, and the interpenetration of land and language which draws extensively on human geography, anthropology, philosophy, and economic and political thought. It can be argued that Wittgenstein's philosophy of language, which found a particular and socially engaged expression within the 'Swansea School', can be used to rationally justify and restate the relevance of the cultural-linguistic link and communitarianism which were foundational in the nationalist drive.

The Swansea School of Philosophy was characterised first and foremost by its Wittgensteinian method of inquiry. This is not to say that its members shared a uniform set of philosophical doctrines, principles, or outlooks; least of all an approach to finding 'solutions' to age-old philosophical problems. Rather, its method consisted of what can broadly be described as writing and teaching in the spirit of Wittgenstein's work. This involves converting 'disguised nonsense to something that is patent nonsense'[1] by disentangling webs of conceptual confusions and latent reasoning fallacies which arise from subtle misuses of language such as indiscriminate jargon and buzzwords, equivocations, and unwarranted assumptions and stipulations. The method's result is to dissolve rather than construct philosophical theories and quasi-scientific accounts permeated with philosophical confusion, so as to dismantle illusions and provide common sense-based reminders of how language and concepts are actually used and understood.[2] This usually restores our pre-philosophical commonsensical knowledge of what is always 'before our eyes'.[3]

Rather than being confined to the purely negative activity of deconstructing the theories and pseudo-explanations of others by exposing their latent confusions, however, the Swansea School's remit was particularly far-reaching. Wittgenstein's insistence on attending to particulars rather than succumbing to the 'craving for generality'[4] by attempting to provide reductive, generalised, quasi-scientific explanations for non-scientific phenomena (ethics, religion, aesthetics, epistemological issues etc.) was put to varied use at the department.

Perhaps the most salient area of interest here was religion. For most of the twentieth century, the philosophy of religion had fallen into disrepute due to the far-reaching influence of the 'logical positivism' of the Vienna Circle and A. J. Ayer's *Language, Truth and Logic* (1936) which denounced religious language and propositions as meaningless due to their inability to be empirically verified by means of strictly scientific methods. Consequently, the subject was all but abandoned by Anglo-American analytic philosophers and migrated/morphed into the independent fields of process theology and philosophical theology. The Wittgensteinian turn in Swansea, however, reignited the philosophy of religion as the likes of Rush Rhees, D. Z. Phillips, Peter Winch and Walford Gealy applied the Wittgensteinian method of analysing the context-dependent structure of language to shed light on various matters of relevance.

To attempt to model our understanding of religion and theology on the scientific paradigm was to commit a category error, since religion has never purported to be a fundamentally empirical matter in the first place. The God of classical monotheism, for instance, has always been defined as transcendental and therefore beyond the bounds of empirical investigation. Far more philosophically interesting and informative, they claimed, is an analysis of key religious concepts within their various contexts of real-life uses. The meaning of duty, for instance, varies according to context: the duty to turn up to work on time differs from the duty to honour the sacraments. The love of God is different from an individual's love of select Châteauneuf-du-Pape wines. The concept of religious sacrifice is different from sacrificing one's comfort to go to the gym. The idea of having been made in the image of God is different from the idea of the image of a selfie, etc. In each of these cases, understanding the meaning of these terms requires understanding their specific *uses* within their respective real-life contexts.

Another noteworthy area to which the Wittgensteinian method was put to novel positive use was literature. Rather than being viewed as mere entertainment, the cultural, psychological, and social insights afforded by the literary classics were viewed as distinctive modes of understanding and potential sources of moral or phenomenological illumination in their own right, which could then be used as correctives to philosophical confusion.[5] Suffice it to say that with its scope spanning religious and moral epistemology, the grammatical analysis of key religious concepts, literature and aesthetics, and the relation between language, culture and nationality, the Swansea School was anything but a narrow enterprise of 'merely linguistic' conceptual analysis. As Walford Gealy put it, analysing concepts within their proper socio-cultural contexts is a challenging but creative activity, necessary to avoiding essentialism.[6] Indeed, by elucidating the differences rather than forcing generalisations, one comes to see the richness of our manifold forms of life while simultaneously avoiding conceptual confusion.

Consistent with the Wittgensteinian ethos of the Swansea School, it is important to focus on an area of relevance to Wales: the relation between language and national identity. Perhaps it is unsurprising that, given their aversion to philosophy as an impersonal and socially disengaged analysis of merely intellectual problems, D. Z. Phillips and J. R. Jones have already addressed this topic to some extent. In his 'Pam Achub Iaith?', for instance, Phillips argues that if language were simply an instrumental device used solely for communicating information (à la Locke), it would be impossible to explain what is wrong with language extinction[7]. For on a purely instrumental view of language, the replacement of one language by another would result in no corresponding cultural loss: one could communicate the exact same information in any other language and no cultural shift would ensue. However, a consideration of Wittgenstein's account of language reveals that to lose a language is to lose a form of life, i.e. the speakers' collective cultural distinctiveness and *Weltanschauung*.

Similarly, J. R. Jones argued in his articles and pamphlets throughout the 1960s that the anglicisation of Wales is eroding the country's 'linguistic microcosm', resulting in epic-scale pathological psychological symptoms and cultural degeneration. Although Jones did not explicitly make use of Wittgenstein's philosophy, it is arguably no accident that his arguments were developed within the Swansea School since the cultural-linguistic link which formed the basis of his work is implicit in Wittgenstein's philosophy of language and was a live issue for many of his colleagues.

Wittgenstein's account of linguistic meaning and language acquisition implies linguistic relativity, which is the empirically substantiated mechanism whereby language embeds culture and influences the speakers' *Weltanschauung*. What then are the implications of this for Welsh cultural-linguistic identity as articulated by the twentieth century nationalist intellectuals, epitomised by the idea of the interpenetration of land and language? Although it may be problematic to draw any direct explanatory conclusions about the relation between Welsh nationalism as a social movement and the intellectual content of its ideology, any Wittgenstein-related exploration should nonetheless shed light on their mutual relevance and should provide scope for further investigation, both socio-culturally and philosophically.

The idea of language as a vehicle of culture has formed the basis of much nationalist and anticolonial political thought, beginning with J. G. Herder (1744–1803) who was the first to systematically formulate it and articulate its implications for linguistic nationalism, i.e. the promotion of indigenous languages a fundamental condition of political legitimacy within nation-states. According to Herder, every nation has its own unique cultural identity (*Volksgeist*) embodied in its indigenous language(s).[8] This cultural-linguistic link is characterised in terms of (1) the essential dependence of thought on language,[9] and (2) that linguistic meaning derives from use: how words are conventionally used within a given socio-cultural context determines their meanings. This notion of *Volksgeist*, in turn, was adapted by J. G. Fichte whose *Reden an die deutsche Nation* (1808) influenced the regeneration of German national consciousness which was central to Germany's eventual unification in 1871, as well as the political evolution of numerous nation-states in nineteenth century Europe.[10] Indeed, most nationalist and anticolonial movements of the nineteenth and twentieth centuries were strongly associated with language *qua* a vehicle of culture, and the projects of language standardisation which were central to both Renaissance humanism and Modernity were equally informed by this principle.[11]

In modern parlance, the idea of *Volksgeist*/language as a vehicle of culture is known in cognitive linguistics as linguistic relativity, which has been substantiated by a proliferation of experimental evidence over the past two decades. Linguistic relativity is defined as the view that language mirrors its speakers' cultural particularities and influences their cognition accordingly. It is characterised by the two necessary conditions that (1) there are differences in conceptual repertoires across languages, and (2) that the concepts embedded in language influence or determine thought. If these two premises are true, it follows that the speakers' thought processes differ according to which language they speak, in line with the cultural heritage embodied therein. As Herder puts it:

> Has a nation anything more precious than the language of its fathers? In it dwells its entire world of tradition, history, religion, principles of existence; its whole heart and soul.[12]

Linguistic relativity's first premise of cross-linguistic conceptual variation is uncontroversial, since it is common knowledge that different languages vary considerably in their conceptual repertoires. Lexical, grammatical, and syntactical differences are part of its definition. The common expression *lost in translation* represents the well-documented problem of failing to achieve exact conceptual equivalence between the source and target languages. Take the German word *kitsch* which refers to worn-out clichés such as Christmas decorations and pop songs, Santa Claus smiling lovingly, the music of Einaudi, or sentimental pictures of cats and dogs: in other words, fake art which elicits fake emotions on the cheap. Since there is no direct synonym in English, the direct loan *kitsch* is used instead. In terms of grammar: different languages grammatically classify different objects into different genders, e.g., *grasshopper* is feminine in French and masculine in Russian. Regarding time orientation: languages such as Malagasy have a back-to-front system whereby future events are designated by terms which refer to the past (*aoriana, any aoriana* (after, behind)) while past events are conceived of as being in front (*taloha, teo aloha*).[13] It has even been argued that this grammatical idiosyncrasy is what explains their tradition of *Famadihana* ('turning of the bones') whereby people dig out their deceased ancestors' bodies and dance with them.[14]

The rifest form of cross-linguistic variation, however, concerns metaphorical and figurative language: different languages are laden with different metaphors, many of which are culture-specific. Take the German idiom *unter aller Sau*, which would not make sense if directly translated part-for-part into English. Likewise, the English idiom *Bob's your uncle* which means *done and dusted* would be equally unintelligible if directly translated into any other language. To this end, cognitive linguistics has, since the publication of Lakoff and Johnson's *Metaphors We Live By*,[15] come to view metaphors and figurative meanings as all-pervasive building blocks in language and cognition.[16]

Linguistic relativity's second premise of the inextricability of language and thought is also substantiated by the evidence to date. First, framing effects are well-established in decision and behavioural science: using apparent synonyms with differing connotations affect the way that people conceptualise a given topic by highlighting specific associated semantic domains at the expense of others.[17] Second, research on the influence of gender on object categorisation suggests that gendered language can at least prime or induce gender-specific thought.[18] Third, the work of linguist Daniel Everett on the Amazonian hunter-gatherer tribe, the Pirahã, evidences radical cultural-linguistic constraints on cognition. The Pirahã language lacks numerals, quantification, perfect tense, recursion, colour terms, and any capacity to conceive of events in the distant past.[19] Consequently, the Pirahã are unable to think in such terms. This is due to an 'immediacy of experience' cultural norm whereby surviving and avoiding predators requires an in the moment mindset which cannot afford to entertain distant historical events. The Pirahã language therefore evidence both cross-linguistic variation, and the strong influence of language on cognition.

Turning from the empirical evidence base to Wittgenstein's analytic arguments: how do these imply linguistic relativity? Wittgenstein's succession of arguments presented in the *Philosophical Investigations*, collectively known as the 'private language argument', conclusively established the logically incoherent and self-defeating nature of psychologised views of linguistic meaning. These psychologised views of linguistic meaning originate in the British Empiricists' accounts of the relation between perception and language, whereby words simply function as labels for concepts acquired via sense perception. According to Locke, all mental states are comprised of ideas (mental images) derived from sense perception, and words function as labels which designate these ideas.[20] On this account, language has no necessary (only contingent) connection to culture or cognition, since cognition is both epistemically and temporally prior to language. It is therefore incompatible with linguistic relativity in both its denial of the inextricability of language and thought, and its assumption that linguistic meaning is private, individualistic, and detachable from culture.

Although this view is no longer held in its original introspection-based 'armchair psychology' guise, its legacy persists in contemporary linguistics, cognitive science, and philosophy of mind; not least Chomsky's theory of Universal Grammar (UG),[21] and its spin-off descendant theories such as 'Mentalese' or 'language of thought' (LOT).[22] These contemporary psychologised theories of the relation between language and thought are equally incompatible with linguistic relativity in virtue of their claim that linguistic meaning is fundamentally internal and psychological: it is UG or LOT which determine our linguistic abilities, rather than natural, communally-embedded languages.

What Wittgenstein's 'private language argument' underlines, however, is that if internal psychological states were *sufficient* for conceptual understanding (as psychologised views of linguistic meaning entail), then a counterfactual situation in which an individual spoke a private language should at the very least be conceivable without turning out to be self-defeating. As the following summary of the argument demonstrates, however, such a scenario turns out to be logically incoherent once its consequences are followed through to their extremes.

Suppose that a person living in solitude spoke a private language which he himself had invented, and which was necessarily incomprehensible to others. 'The words of this language are to refer to what can be known only to the speaker; to his immediate, private, sensations. So, another cannot understand the language'.[23] This private linguist keeps a diary solely for the purpose of recording his own private sensations.

With each occurrence of a given sensation which he terms S, he writes S in the diary: this is supposed to ensure that the right connection between the word and the specific sensation is both established and maintained for future use.[24]

The problem that emerges, however, is: how can the private linguist know whether he is continuing to use the word correctly in future cases? As far as he is aware, he might have unwittingly started connecting S with a different sensation from the original one; and there would be no way of checking its accuracy. This is because there would be no external, public criteria of correctness for the private linguist to consult. It might seem to him that he is using the word correctly, but this could easily be an illusion. (Indeed, there is ample evidence that memory distortion is rife (e.g., Tompary 2021, Fukuda 2022).[25] Checking one's own memory alone for the right meaning would be 'As if someone were to buy several copies of the morning paper to assure himself that what it said was true'.[26] Indeed, even the meaning of the word 'right' might not be stable or consistent, for the private linguist might have unwittingly started to connect the word with a different concept from the original one. 'Whatever seems right will be right', and 'that only means that here we can't talk about "right".'[27]

What this illustrates is that the private, psychologised account of linguistic meaning is self-defeating. If linguistic meaning was determined by inner, psychological words (or language-like representations) or ideas, which themselves are subject to change, then, necessarily, the language would be unintelligible to its user. For without external criteria of correctness, one could be inadvertently mistaken about the correct meaning of an indeterminate number of one's own words, including the word correct, with no reliable criterion for checking its accuracy. Moreover, it is an inextricable feature of language that we presuppose that linguistic meaning remains reasonably stable and consistent. But one cannot rationally state that one's use of words might be inconsistent while simultaneously presupposing that they are in fact consistent. For to do so is itself inconsistent. Herein lies the self-defeating status of the psychologised, internal conception of the relation between thought and language.

The bottom line, then, is that since linguistic meaning cannot possibly be internal and private, it must therefore be external and public. Objective, socially derived criteria of correctness are necessary to the existence and feasible functioning of languages. It is on this basis that Wittgenstein advanced the replacement account according to which 'the meaning of a word is its use in the language'.[28] Thought, in turn, is derivative of this: 'When I think in language, there aren't "meanings" going through my mind in addition to the verbal expressions: language itself is the vehicle of thought'.[29] Language is interwoven with forms of life (i.e. behavioural and social conventions), and it is these which give rise to meaning: 'the speaking of language is part of an activity, or of a form of life'.[30] Language acquisition consists in learning how to use words competently in line with the social practices which delineate their various purposes: it is these which determine linguistic meaning and standards for use.

The fact that language is inescapably grounded in culture-specific forms of life, as well as being the vehicle of thought, implies both linguistic relativity and communitarianism. The linguistic relativity implications should be obvious: first, since different cultural-linguistic communities have different cultural norms and therefore different uses for words (and linguistic meaning is determined by these), the first condition of cross-linguistic variation is automatically implied on *a priori* grounds. Second: since, on the Wittgensteinian view, 'language is the vehicle of thought', linguistic relativity's second condition of the inextricability of language and thought is also directly entailed.

In terms of the communitarian implications: synoptically, communitarianism is typically understood in both descriptive and prescriptive terms. Descriptively, it states that people's identities are socially embedded in the sense of being fundamentally shaped by their community. That is to say: people are inescapably moulded by intersubjective communication with others, as well as the civil society associations in which they participate. Prescriptively, communitarians tend to advance arguments for the value of the community, the rejection of self-centred individualism, and the importance of civic virtue. Political principles, therefore, should be designed and implemented in a manner that is congruent with the (national) community's underlying culture and values.

How does Wittgenstein's view of language support communitarianism? Descriptively: it is a socially embedded account of language and linguistic meaning. Language carries the sum total of concepts derived from a given community's forms of life, and those concepts have been accumulated through the course of history. Therefore, language is the repository into which its speakers historically amassed cultural norms, outlooks, and values have been compressed. This yields a de-individualised conception of personal identity and human nature: since the concepts through which people think are interwoven with their linguistic community's cultural particularities, so too are their thoughts (i.e., the main feature of personal identity). This drastically consolidates the link between an individual's identity and their cultural embeddedness, thereby directly justifying communitarianism's descriptive claim.

Prescriptively: although Wittgenstein never advanced any normative political arguments, a few prescriptive communitarian political implications can nonetheless be indirectly drawn from his philosophy. For instance, Wittgenstein's admonition against taking language on holiday[31] i.e. detaching language from its ordinary contexts of applicability, thereby misusing words to cause confusion via equivocation or unwarranted conceptual inflation, implies a type of status quo bias, for lack of a better term. Consider, for instance, a national conversation about anti-discrimination legislation, cultural or academic decolonisation measures, safe spaces, or gender identity recognition reforms. On the Wittgensteinian view, key buzzwords such as *safety* (emotional and psychological), *trauma*, *violence*, *equity*, *oppression*, *power*, *fascism*, *domination*, *colonialism*, *capitalism*, or *privilege* should not be uncritically adopted in a manner which involves serious conceptual inflation and departure from their ordinary default uses. Rather, they must be brought back to their original home, i.e., their everyday real-life uses from which they derive their central, default meanings.[32] The 'normative' prescription which can be inferred from this view, therefore, is that the public discussion should be conducted consistently with the pre-existing, historically accumulated concepts embedded in the language, which places common sense-based constraints on the debate's parameters.

This prioritisation of ordinary language as the court from which there is no appeal underlines the value of the community (emphasised by 'prescriptive' communitarianism) since it implies that it is by default the ultimate authority, and any public discussion should be partly biased in favour of, and thereby help perpetuate, the historically rooted national culture with which the language is associated. For, as illustrated by linguistic relativity and Wittgenstein's philosophy of language, the socially embedded nature of language entails that linguistic meaning is bottom-up: it tracks the cultural norms and sensibilities of the majority population. This yields the democratically inclusive conclusion that national conversations about, e.g., political reforms or cultural policy should not be uncritically framed in buzzwords which take language on holiday. Rather, the parameters of the debate should be mainly constrained by ordinary language which *ipso facto* frames the debate in terms of the (national) community's underlying culture and values.

The linguistic dimension to Welsh nationalism gained currency with the establishment of the Welsh nationalist party Plaid Cymru in 1925. The party's founding aims were Home Rule and the promotion of Welsh to official language status in Wales; though the latter aim received by far the greatest priority due to the overwhelming influence of its chief founder, ideologue, and first president Saunders Lewis. Language was also a prime focus among the party's other founders who were mainly right-of-centre intellectuals influenced by the likes of Hilaire Belloc and G. K. Chesterton, and to a lesser (and certainly more selective) extent, the non-fascist elements of the ideology of Charles Maurras, Maurice Barrès and the Action Française, as well as its Italian counterpart, as articulated in Pietro Gorgolini.[33] Among these co-founders were historian Ambrose Bebb, Iorwerth Peate (who, influenced by the rural folk movements of Scandinavia, founded the St Fagans National Folk History Museum) and theologian and classicist J. E. Daniel, the first Welshman to gain a triple first from Oxford. The party's membership was originally comprised of farmers, academics and professionals, and their prime goal was to reverse the decline of Wales's rural and literary civilisation, to which the language was central.

Perhaps unsurprisingly, Plaid Cymru's near-exclusive focus on language was a consequence of an underlying commitment to linguistic relativity (though clearly, the hypothesis was never referred to by its name). Lewis, who was also a literature Nobel Prize nominee, medievalist, translator, historian, and literary critic, became convinced during the First World War, under the influence of Maurice Barrès, that writing in one's original language is necessary to achieving one's literary authenticity.[34] Relatedly, the project of Welsh linguistic nationalism was partly driven by the need to establish continuity with the existing body of indigenous literature (and the cultural heritage it represents), which

Lewis argued had not properly fed into the Anglo-Welsh genre.[35] This, in turn, was based on the premise that language is a vehicle of culture.[36] Moreover, that culture A cannot be properly represented in language B was a recurring theme in his writings. Upon disowning his own drama, *The Eve of St John* (1921), which he had attempted to write in an Anglo-Welsh idiom by replicating the rhythms and grammatical patterns of Welsh in English diction, he concluded that Anglo-Welsh is in fact 'the horrible jargon of men who have lost one tongue without acquiring another ... no feebler stuff is spoken in these islands'.[37]

Ultimately, the revitalisation of the Welsh language is presented as the *conditio sine qua non* of reviving a Welsh national consciousness and securing Welsh cultural continuity and longevity. In addition to masterminding the party's earlier political programme and communications, inciting radical political activism, and committing a symbolic arson attack on the RAF bombing school of Penyberth, Lewis's greatest influence can retrospectively be ascribed to his 1962 public address *Tynged yr Iaith* (The Fate of the Language). In it, he predicts the imminent extinction of the Welsh language within an historical and political analysis of the status of the Welsh language and urges radical political action. The impact of this lecture was profound. In addition to sparking various acts of civil disobedience, arson, demonstrations, and small-scale insurgencies, it also kick-started the formation of Cymdeithas yr Iaith Gymraeg (The Welsh Language Society), the pressure group whose campaigning led to the creation of the Welsh language radio station (1977), television channel S4C (1982), the Welsh Language Acts of 1967 and 1993, and indeed the entire linguistic dimension to Wales's contemporary nation-building project.

The main intellectual influence on Cymdeithas yr Iaith Gymraeg was J. R. Jones, who was a professor at the Swansea School. In line with Plaid Cymru's fundamental emphasis on promoting language *qua* a vehicle of culture, Jones took this theme several steps further in his books, pamphlets and addresses while presenting them in a more overtly philosophical guise. Jones's view of language amounted to linguistic relativity, since his works include frequent approving references to Herder's and Fichte's remarks on the culture-laden nature of language and its significance. Further, his main book on the necessity of language for safeguarding cultural longevity, *Prydeindod* (Britishness),[38] begins with a definition of a nation which emphasises language, which is defined as:

the source of their [a People's] spirit, which is their language: not as a medium or technique for communication as much as a tradition, an inheritance enriched by the succession of the centuries – 'language' in the sense ascribed to the word when it is claimed that the whole of a People's cultural past has been compressed into their native language.[39]

Jones applied the language-centric nationalism of Herderian Romanticism to various related areas, addressed in a distinctively charged and polemical fashion. Among these were the need for cultural roots in one's own nation; the inferiority complex instilled by the legacy of historical conquest, colonisation, and cultural-linguistic domination; and the need for everyday symbols which mediate and tacitly reinforce people's sense of national/ cultural identity (what Billig calls 'banal nationalism').[40] Perhaps most interestingly, Jones also propagated the two related ideas that (1) the erosion of the Welsh language and corresponding anglicisation of Wales are causing moral and spiritual degeneration; and (2) that nationality requires the interpenetration of land and language, in the sense that they continually permeate each other.[41]

The paradigmatic example of interpenetration is place names: 'the names they gave in their own native language to their mountains and vales, their rivers, and villages',[42] since these represent the native peoples' sense of local rootedness and pride, given the extent to which language reflects their culture and environment. In this regard, the land was understood in non-urban terms since, as we shall shortly see, the idealisation of the rural community as the heartland of Welsh identity was a common theme in the assertion of Welsh national identity throughout the twentieth century. Indeed, the urbanisation, industrialisation, and concomitant anglicisation of Welsh communities (resulting in and perpetuated by language erosion) were viewed as major sources of moral, spiritual, and cultural degeneration.

Jones elaborates on this cultural erosion in 'Cristnogaeth a Chenedlaetholdeb' (Christianity and Nationalism, 1963)[43] and *Prydeindod* (1966), where he predicts that the uprooted Welsh are in danger of declining back to barbarism and lurking in the shades of primitive life.[44] Here, he merges the spiritual and national decline of the Welsh, insisting that they are inextricable: 'We now face the emergency of the erosion of the nationality of the Welsh people. And it is clear enough that this is a spiritual emergency.'[45] An example of this spiritual degeneration is found in *Prydeindod*:

> Imagine a countryside girl coming into the town of Carmarthen to work. She was raised in an expressive Welsh which gave her some mental breadth. But in the town she 'tries to conceal the fact that she is Welsh' and turns to speaking an impoverished English slang (*bratiaith*), meagre in resources, which stifles her spirit, debases her sensibilities, and shrinks her mind until she melts in the end into the unvaried and vacuous swarm of pop songs and betting papers.[46]

Such spiritual degeneration is also intertwined with the unravelling of mental health.[47] The above depiction is presented by Jones as representative of ever-increasing sections of Wales's population, given their cultural uprootedness. Central to this diagnosis is an account of human nature according to which we all need a 'microcosm' which 'introduces to us the psychic heritage of the ages',[48] since civilised life depends on people being rooted in a cultural setting which makes evident their cultural heritage and the importance of its transgenerational continuity. Simplifying somewhat, this idea of a linguistic microcosm refers to an aggregate of unique, unprecedented, and non-exchangeable interpretations and experiences of the world, embodied in the language. That is: the language cumulatively embeds the surviving concepts of bygone generations; thus an imprint of the deceased's microcosms / world outlooks is transmitted across generations via the language's sustained use.[49]

It can be seen, then, that both linguistic relativity and communitarianism were constant undercurrents to the main intellectual and ideological influences driving twentieth century Welsh nationalism. Granted, this is nothing new as such. After all, most nationalist and anticolonial movements of the nineteenth and twentieth centuries were strongly associated with language *qua* a vehicle of culture (e.g., Norway, Ireland, Iceland, India, Italy, Greece, Romania, Sweden, Hungary, Poland, Bulgaria, Albania, Finland, Estonia, Latvia, Bangladesh, Lithuania, Turkey, Philippines, Israel, to name a few). However, the idea of 'interpenetration' of land and language warrants further examination as an original and philosophically interesting way of conceiving of the relation between urbanisation and cultural erosion vis-à-vis communitarianism and the cultural-linguistic link.

As mentioned, the idealisation of the agricultural heartland as the power point of national identity was a recurring theme in twentieth century Welsh nationalism, gaining renewed momentum during the inter-war years.[50] This type of theme had originated in nineteenth century Romanticism but was systematically developed by early twentieth century human geographers, anthropologists, agricultural scientists and geneticists within a neo-Lamarckist framework which emphasised the modification of organisms via changes in the natural environment and the heritability of those organisms.[51] While American neo-Lamarckism had focused predominantly on the biological sciences, its British counterpart drew equally on the human and social sciences, placing particular emphasis on human consciousness in relation to 'the continuous interaction and interpenetration of man and environment'.[52] This involved analysing regionally concentrated human 'types' in terms of their physical, mental, spiritual, social, and environmental characteristics across Britain and Europe, where regional distinctions were viewed as embodying 'cumulative expressions of the human spirit'.[53]

This emphasis on regional environmental distinctions as being closely interconnected with people's mental, spiritual and social characteristics, pioneered by the likes of H. J. Fleure (1877–1969), Patrick Geddes (1854–1932) and George Stapledon (1882–1960), echoed a broader European ideological trend of 'habitat, economy and society'.[54] Here, the countryside was seen as the living reservoir of cultural inheritances: Germany's rural peasantry, for instance, were viewed as 'an arsenal of pre-modern characteristics',[55] while rural sociology and ethnology proliferated in post-First World War France for similar reasons.[56] Ideologically, the countryside was viewed as the embodiment of tradition, which politically translated into drives for rural revitalisation policies.

This approach of emphasising the importance of countryside and its rural peasantry as the backbone of cultural diversity, vitality and civilisation was given a distinctively salient and densely concentrated expression among Wales's nationalist intellectuals during the inter-war years. Plaid Cymru's founders where strongly influenced by the human geography of British neo-Lamarckism, mainly via Iorwerth

Peate whose doctoral research was supervised by H. J. Fleure, its chief pioneer. This theme, in turn, was converted by Plaid Cymru into a systematic political programme of back to the land policies for rural revitalisation,[57] articulated most extensively by its president Saunders Lewis's political articles, pamphlets, and literary works.

In this regard, Lewis's political programme was also strongly influenced by contemporaneous European and English political and economic thought, such as the distributism of G. K. Chesterton and Hilaire Belloc, the economic autarky of J. M. Keynes, the neo-Thomism of Étienne Gilson and Jacques Maritain (particularly the subsidiarity principle), European federalism, guild socialism, organic society, and cooperativism.[58] All of these were designed to be capable of bringing about a more culturally rooted, sustainable, self-sufficient, decentralised and more evenly distributed (in terms of industry and property) society which was less exploitative, culturally alienating, and socially deprived than the status quo. This, in turn, would *ipso facto* result in cultural-linguistic revitalisation.

Take the two ideals of distributism and guild socialism,[59] which informed Plaid Cymru's economic programme of a relatively decentralised system of co-operative associations. These, it was argued, would help restore workers' control in agriculture, industry, and commerce, thereby acting as non-governmental curbs on corporate monopolies, as well as correctives to what was perceived as the increasingly centralising, homogenising and dehumanising state control of society. These ideals were coupled with a doctrine of economic autarky whereby independent farming and cooperative industries would form a self-sufficient national economy based mainly on the agricultural sector.[60] Since this programme would inevitably result in rural reconstruction, it would automatically function as a vehicle of cultural-linguistic national renewal. This is because the agricultural communities of the north and west of Wales had remained Welsh language strongholds while the heavy industrialisation of southern Wales had, as early as 1911, began to cause its rapid anglicisation. Unsurprisingly, therefore, given the extent to which language was viewed as a vehicle of culture, rural revitalisation was viewed as a two-way system whereby its rollout would strengthen the Welsh language, while correspondingly, the Welsh language would strengthen its associated culture.

At risk of oversimplifying, however, it should also be noted that this agenda was neither anti-urban, anti-capitalist, nor anti-English (indeed, Lewis was a self-confessed anglophile). Rather, the anglicisation of Wales which was the target of their critique referred to the conditions caused by Wales's rapid heavy industrialisation, to which their solution was not outright de-industrialisation, but rather a more even redistribution of heavy industry which would combine technological advancement with the rural *Gemeinschaft*. In terms of their portrayal of the anglicised industrial south as culturally uprooted and morally degenerate, this referred specifically to the spread of individualistic, materialistic, and consumerist side-effects of international capitalism; a theme partly developed via the influence of F. R. Leavis. It is this aspect of English culture, rather than Englishness in its own right, which was equated with English political and economic encroachment, exacerbated by the proliferation of the English mainstream media, rapid in-migration, trade unionism and Labourism which were collectively displacing chapel attendance and accelerating cultural and linguistic homogenisation. Nonetheless, the role of language as an intrinsic carrier of culture cannot be overstated: it remained a constant undercurrent spanning the entire intellectual content of their political programme, and therefore cannot be read in isolation from it.

As the above summary of twentieth century Welsh nationalism's main intellectual content illustrates, the idea of language *qua* a vehicle of culture was given a distinctively varied, though systematic, expression within the context of the back to the land policies for rural revitalisation. This was driven by the principle of interpenetration of land and language which itself recruited from a vast array of geographical, anthropological, philosophical, and economic and political thought materials. The interpenetration of land and language, in turn, hinges on the truth of linguistic relativity: the vehicle for embodying the regionally differentiated cultural inheritances in question is the language, and the continuation of the language's use viewed as the means of safeguarding cultural continuity and civilisation.

Wittgenstein's philosophy of language both implies and justifies linguistic relativity on analytical grounds; and moreover, its meaning-as-use principle provides a straightforward lens with which to elucidate the cultural significance of the interpenetration of land and language. That is: the socially embedded nature of language entails that cross-regional differences in forms of life, determined to varying degrees by environmental differences, become cumulatively embedded in the language, which is the repository into which its speakers' historically amassed cultural norms, outlooks, and values have been compressed. Given that language is the vehicle of thought, this has a feedback effect on the speakers *Weltanschauung* such that linguistic continuity sustains its associated historically rooted culture.

Further, the communitarianism implicit in the ideological programme of twentieth century Welsh nationalism is evident in both the descriptive and prescriptive senses. Descriptively: the emphasis on rural vitality and characterisation of the interpenetration of land and language as the cumulative expression of the human spirit and vehicle of a collective consciousness and civilisation is nothing if not communitarian. Prescriptively: the *raison d'être* of the language revitalisation and back to the land policies were reversing the atomising effects of mass industrialisation and its individualistic, materialistic, and consumerist side-effects, which in turn would promote civic virtue.

Hence, it could be contended that the idea of interpenetration has not received the scholarly attention it deserves. This is presumably because it may be too easily associated in hindsight with the *Blut und Boden* ideology of the Third Reich, where the previously innocuous study of the perceived spiritual importance of remote rural areas and their peasantry was corrupted into the racial supremacist Nordic Myth. However, while no ideology is immune from being appropriated into perverse extremism, the exception cannot be the rule. Indeed, the human geographer H. J. Fleure who pioneered the subject in Britain and directly influenced Wales's nationalist intellectuals, consistently attacked notions of 'racial purity' and was active in anti-racist campaigns.[61] The fact remains that the study of national attachments and diversity – taking a Wittgensteinian approach – is no less relevant today than it was in the early-mid twentieth century, and notions of interpenetration continue to resurface through the back door. Whether reframed in terms of 'belonging', or anticolonial raciolinguistics, such as in Gegentuul Baioud's 2022 study of linguistic purism in Inner Mongolia which equates 'pure' (free from Mandarin loanwords) Mongolian with an untarnished agrarian, poetic, ancestral Mongolian worldview and tradition, its legacy undoubtedly persists.[62]

As such, overlooking its relevance risks, as it were, throwing out the Châteauneuf-du-Pape with the cork.

Notes

1 Ludwig Wittgenstein, *Philosophical Investigations* (Oxford; Wiley-Blackwell. 1953), §464.
2 Wittgenstein, *Philosophical Investigations*, §127.
3 Wittgenstein, *Philosophical Investigations*, §§122, 415.
4 Ludwig Wittgenstein, *Blue and Brown Books* (Oxford: Wiley-Blackwell, 2nd edn, 1969), p. 18.
5 Mario von der Ruhr, 'Rhees, Wittgenstein, and the Swansea School School', in John Edelman (ed.), *Sense and Reality: Essays Out of Swansea*, Publications of the Austrian Ludwig Wittgenstein Society (Hessen: Ontos Verlag, 2009), pp. 219–35.
6 Walford Gealy, 'Athroniaeth Crefydd yn yr Ugeinfed Ganrif a Chyfraniad D. Z. Phillips Iddi', in Gwynn Matthews (ed.), *Cred, Llên a Diwylliant: Cyfrol Deyrnged Dewi Z. Phillips* (Talybont: Y Lolfa, 2012).
7 D. Z. Phillips, 'Pam Achub Iaith?', *Efrydiau Athronyddol*, 1–12 (1993).
8 J. G. Herder, *On the Spirit of Hebrew Poetry* (Illinois: Aleph Press, 1971), 1782–3.
9 J. G. Herder, *A Metacritique on the Critique of Pure Reason* (Paris: PUF, 2022).
10 See G. H. Turnbull, 'Introduction', in *Addresses to the German Nation*, trans. R. F. Jones and G. H. Turnbull (Totnes: Franklin Classics, 2018), pp. 19–21.
11 See Lodi Nauta, 'Linguistic Relativity and the Humanist Imitation of Classical Latin', in *Language and Cultural Change: Aspects of the Study and Use of Language in the Later Middle Ages and the Renaissance* (Leuven: Peeters, 2006), pp. 173–86; Alan Patten, 'The Humanist Roots of Linguistic Nationalism', *History of Political Thought* (2006), 223–62; and Kevin Absillis and Jürgen Jaspers, 'Reconsidering purism: The case of Flanders', in G. Rutten and K. Horner (eds), *Metalinguistic Perspectives on Germanic languages: European case studies from past to present* (Lausanne: Peter Lang, 2016).
12 J. G. Herder, *Vico and Herder: Two Studies of the History of Ideas*, trans. Isaiah Berlin (New York: The Viking Press, 1976 [1881]).
13 See Øyvind Dahl, 'When the future comes from behind: Malagasy and other time concepts and some consequences for communication', *International Journal of Intercultural Relations* (1995), 197–209.
14 See https://www.youtube.com/watch?v=oFaItWmAoBQ for a representative video of this ritual.
15 G. Lakoff and M. Johnson, *Metaphors We Live By* (Chicago: University of Chicago Press, 1980).

16 M. Danesi, *Linguistic relativity today: Language, mind, society, and the foundations of linguistic anthropology* (London: Routledge, 2021).
17 See Daniel Kahneman, *Thinking, fast and slow* (New York, NY: Farrar, Straus and Giroux, 2011); Eran Amsalem and Alon Zoizner, 'Real, but Limited: A Meta-Analytic Assessment of Framing Effects in the Political Domain', *British Journal of Political Science* (2022), 221–37.
18 See W. Phillips and L. Boroditsky, 'Can Quirks of Grammar Affect the Way You Think? Grammatical Gender and Object', *Proceedings of the Annual Meeting of the Cognitive Science Society* (2003); R. P. Cubelli, 'The effect of grammatical gender on object categorization', *Journal of Experimental Psychology: Learning, Memory, and Cognition* (2011), 449–60; Steven Samuel, Geoff Cole and Madeline J. Eacott, 'Grammatical gender and linguistic relativity: A systematic review', *Psychonomic Bulletin & Review* (2019); Nan Elpers, Greg Jensen and Kevin J. Holmes, 'Does grammatical gender affect object concepts? Registered replication of Phillips and Boroditsky (2003)', *Journal of Memory and Language* (2022).
19 D. Everett, 'Cultural Constraints on Grammar and Cognition in Pirahã', *Current Anthropology* (2005), 621–46.
20 John Locke, *An Essay Concerning Human Understanding*, III. 2.2, ed. Peter H. Nidditch (Oxford: Clarendon Press, 1975 [1689]).
21 Noam Chomsky, *Things No Amount of Learning Can Teach*, 1983 interview by John Gliedman; and Noam Chomsky, *Aspects of the Theory of Syntax* (Cambridge, MA: MIT Press, 1965).
22 J. Fodor, *The Modularity of Mind* (Cambridge, MA: MIT Press, 1983); S. Pinker, *The Language Instinct: How the Mind Creates Language* (New York: Perennial, 1994).
23 Wittgenstein, *Philosophical Investigations*, §243.
24 Wittgenstein, *Philosophical Investigations*, §258.
25 See A. Tompary and S. Thompson-Schill, 'Semantic influences on episodic memory distortions', *Journal of Experimental Psychology* (2021), 1800–24; K. Fukuda, A. Pereira, J. Saito, T. Tang, H. Tsubomi and G. Bae, 'Working Memory Content Is Distorted by Its Use in Perceptual Comparisons', *Psychological Science* (2022), 816–29.
26 Wittgenstein, *Philosophical Investigations*, §265.
27 Wittgenstein, *Philosophical Investigations*, §258.
28 Wittgenstein, *Philosophical Investigations*, §43.
29 Wittgenstein, *Philosophical Investigations*, §329.
30 Wittgenstein, *Philosophical Investigations*, §23.
31 Wittgenstein, *Philosophical Investigations*, §38.
32 Wittgenstein, *Philosophical Investigations*, §116.
33 For more on this line of thinking, see Pietro Gorgolini, *The Fascist Movement in Italian Life* (London: Creative Media Paertners 2021).
34 See Saunders Lewis, 'Dylanwadau' (Influences), *Taliesin*, 2 (1961).
35 See A. R. Jones and G. Thomas, *Presenting Saunders Lewis* (Cardiff: University of Wales Press, 1973).

36 See Saunders Lewis, 'Cenedlaetholdeb a chyfalaf' (Nationalism and capitalism), *Y Ddraig Goch* (1926).
37 Bruce Griffiths, *Saunders Lewis* (Cardiff: University of Wales Press, 1989).
38 J. R. Jones, *Prydeindod* (Llandybie: Llyfrau'r Dryw, 1966).
39 Jones, *Prydeindod*, p. 10 (author's translation).
40 Michael Billig, *Banal Nationalism* (London: Sage Publications Ltd, 1995). Banal nationalism is an often-cited theory of everyday casual nationalism and national sentiment.
41 Jones, *Prydeindod*, p. 13.
42 Jones, *Prydeindod*, p. 14.
43 J. R. Jones, 'Cristnogaeth a Chenedlaetholdeb' (Christianity and Nationalism), 1963; E-print: Coleg Cymraeg Cenedlaethol, available at *https://llyfrgell.porth.ac.uk/View.aspx?id=1985~4x~8wS88MtU*.
44 Jones, 'Cristnogaeth a Chenedlaetholdeb', 1–2.
45 Jones, 'Cristnogaeth a Chenedlaetholdeb', 1–2.
46 Jones, *Prydeindod*, p. 42 (author's translation).
47 Jones, *Prydeindod*.
48 Jones, 'Cristnogaeth a Chenedlaetholdeb', 3.
49 See J. R. Jones, 'Cenedligrwydd a Chrefydd' (Nationhood and Religion), 1970; E-print: Coleg Cymraeg Cenedlaethol, available at *https://llyfrgell.porth.ac.uk/View.aspx?id=1986~4y~AkgxJXFh*.
50 See Wil Griffith, 'Saving the Soul of the Nation: Essentialist Nationalism and Interwar Rural Wales', *Rural History* (2010), 177–94.
51 See J. A. Campbell and D. N. Livingstone, 'Neo-Lamarckism and the development of geography in the United States and Great Britain', *Transactions of the Institute of British Geographers* (1983), 267–94.
52 H. J. Fleure, 'Human regions', *Scottish Geographical Magazine* (1919), 94.
53 H. J. Fleure, *Human geography in western Europe: a study in appreciation* (London: Williams & Norgate, 1918).
54 J. Langton, 'Habitat, economy and society revisited: peasant ecotypes and economic development in Sweden', *Cambria* (1986), 5–24; Pyrs Gruffudd, 'Back to the Land: Historiography, Rurality and the Nation in Interwar Wales', *Transactions of the Institute of British Geographers* (1994), 61–77.
55 I. Farr, '"Tradition" and the peasantry: on the modern historiography of rural Germany', in R. J. Evans and W. R. Lee (eds), *The German peasantry: conflict and community in rural society from the eighteenth to the twentieth centuries* (London: Croom Helm, 1986), pp. 1–36.
56 See L. Lévi-Strauss and H. Mendras, 'Rural studies in France', *Journal of Peasant Studies* (1974), 363–78; and Gruffudd, 'Back to the Land'.
57 See Gruffudd, 'Back to the Land'.
58 See Emyr Williams, 'The Social and Political Thought of Saunders Lewis', PhD thesis, 2005; available at *https://orca.cardiff.ac.uk/id/eprint/54521/1/U584622.pdf*; and Griffith, 'Saving the Soul of the Nation'.
59 Respectively, these are: the principle that the ownership of property and industry should be distributed more widely, not via state redistribution

but rather cooperative societies and policies which favour the interests of small and medium-sized enterprises over corporate monopolies; and the principle which specifically advocates a system of national guilds whereby workers collectively and democratically manage their respective industries' means of production and output.

60 It is important to note that economic autarky was by no means some quaint, inward-looking isolationist ideal during the interwar years. The abject poverty and unemployment caused by the Depression (which, in Wales alone, had forced an exodus of hundreds of thousands), coupled with the realisation since the First World War of the extents to which supply chains could be disrupted, meant that, for many, it was seen to be the most feasible means of minimising the risk of total economic ruin.

61 Gruffudd, 'Back to the Land', 63–4.

62 G. Baioud and C. Khuanuud, 'Linguistic purism as resistance to colonization', *Journal of Sociolinguistics* (2022), 315–34.

8

'Change and decay in all around I see':
The Wittgenstein School of English
at Swansea

M. Wynn Thomas

I entered University College Swansea in October 1962 to read for a degree in English. But at the time the enlightened regulations of the University of Wales (of which Swansea was a constituent college) required every undergraduate to study not one but three subjects during their first year – a requirement modelled on the regulations of the University of London. My A-level subjects had been English, Welsh and History. But as I approached eighteen, I felt ready to spread my wings intellectually and so opted to replace Welsh with Philosophy. I was emboldened so to do because I had been trained in the Sunday School of a Welsh Congregational chapel to reflect on the great questions of life and supposed that this would provide me with a good grounding in the basics of Philosophy. I was very soon to be disabused of that hopeful, naïve supposition.

Although I was unaware of it at the time, my three Philosophy lecturers during that interesting and challenging year were luminaries. One was Peter Winch, who was in the early stages of establishing an international reputation for his work on the philosophy of social science. In 1968, he was to publish a ground-breaking book, *The Idea of a Social Science and its Relation to Philosophy*, a work influenced by the ideas of R. G. Collingwood and Ludwig Wittgenstein. In later years, he became Professor at King's College London. But his duties at Swansea involved introducing freshers to the Philosophy of Perception, using Bishop Berkeley's *An Essay Towards a New Theory of Vision* (1709) as his set text. Winch's emphasis, as I remember it, was on the distinction between understanding the mechanics of eyesight and reflecting on its philosophic implications, central to which was a meditation on the exact status of the world that was perceptible to human beings.

Winch was a dry lecturer. J. R. Jones was his opposite. Impassioned in his every word and gesture, he had the drawn, gaunt features of an Old Testament prophet and the dramatic 'pulpit' manner of the lay preacher he actually was. One would therefore have thought that he would have been the last person to take us through the rudiments of logic (courtesy of Susan Stebbing's handbook). But, undaunted by the challenge, he paced mesmerically like a caged tiger from one side of the podium to the other, eyes feverishly aglitter like the Ancient Mariner, as he incanted such false syllogisms as 'This car is a Saab. This car is blue. Therefore, all Saabs are blue.' To attend his lectures was an experience at once thrilling and exhausting. He would shortly publish a number of Welsh-language books on the philosophy of linguistic nationality that were to prove very influential among the young people who by the later 1960s embarked on a series of peaceful law-breaking campaigns to gain legal parity for Welsh – a legally proscribed language since 1536 – with English.[1] His emphasis on an anciently inherited language as the indispensable product, producer and carrier of cultural values, and thus the sustainer of a people, obviously owed a great deal to his readings in Wittgenstein.

And then there was the strangest of the three lecturers: Rush Rhees. He made no attempt to lecture. He simply stood compellingly still before us, lost in refined processes of thought to which we the listeners were made privy. For him, philosophical discourse was not to be heard but to be overheard. I later learned it was his habit to devote a whole hour ahead of a lecture to immersing himself in the knotty train of thought that would then simply be continued when he appeared before us. He despised rhetorical performance of any kind. Ascetically lean, softly spoken, and quietly intense, he sported a crew-cut that I later came to realise was a kind of relic of his American origins.

Rhees scorned the very idea of 'teaching philosophy'. For him that was a complete travesty of what it really meant to live a life devoted to philosophical thought, which he regarded as a kind of holy and intellectually heroic undertaking. His responsibility as teacher was to convey the nature of such a life by practising philosophy before us, thereby demonstrating before our eyes what it was like to ponder some of life's deepest and most insoluble questions. As Coleridge once put it, his was an effort to put us into a way of thinking. The books he set for us to read were all by Plato: the Gorgias, the Symposium, and the Republic. These he regarded not as historic texts – not once did he ever attempt to set them in their cultural and intellectual context – but as texts that were completely contemporary in their challenge to thought. He put his finger on my own (alas ineradicable) inadequacies as a budding philosopher in a comment he added to one of my essays. 'An excellent summary,' he wrote, 'but what do *you* think?'

As his choice of texts implicitly indicated, Rhees was an admirer and practitioner of the 'Socratic method'. But instead of mercilessly interrogating a companion to expose the fallacies and contradictions underlying his position, Rhees preferred to interrogate himself, painstakingly winnowing every word of every sentence. To read him can be a frustrating experience, as every statement seems to lead to further complication. The experience is rather like trying to make your way through a nest of serpents, each of which has its tail in its mouth. During this time, I don't remember him ever referring to Ludwig Wittgenstein (although he may have done so – at that time I had never heard of him and so would in any case have paid little attention). A figure to whom he did repeatedly refer (and indeed defer) was Simone Weil, whose writings in the little collection translated from the French under the title *Waiting on God* were also revered by J. R. Jones.[2]

Compared with the Department of Philosophy, the Department of English at Swansea unfortunately carried a great deal of dead wood at this time, although there were several stars of the future amongst the younger staff, and these were the saving of me. Howard Erskine-Hill eventually (and somewhat reluctantly) moved from Swansea to Cambridge, where he ended up Professor of English and a Fellow of the British Academy. He became the author of a classic study *The Augustan Idea in English Literature*.[3] George Dekker was a young American, a pioneering scholar of Pound's *Cantos*, who moved on from Swansea to join his friend Donald Davie at Essex, before returning to the States where he became a Professor at Stanford. And then there was the brilliant young scholar Brian Way, who had been one of F. R. Leavis's star pupils at Cambridge, and who passed away at a cruelly early age. For me, these proved to be the saving grace of a rather moribund (and, frankly lazy) department – the colourful Kingsley Amis had departed the scene just a year before I arrived.⁴

There were, however, two other lecturers of singular intellect worthy of special note, David Sims and Ian Robinson. Their trenchant original work was in due course to provide a bridge between the Department of English at Swansea and the Wittgenstein school in the Department of Philosophy, a school much augmented by the arrival, shortly after my brief sortie into Philosophy, of an electrifying young talent. He was Dewi Zephaniah Phillips, a dazzlingly quick-witted and charismatic talker and lecturer, a natural debater, and an inexhaustible and indefatigable source of jokes. He would become a devoted friend and disciple of Rush Rhees's (a surname deriving from the Welsh surname 'Rhys'),⁵ and his many works on the Philosophy of Religion were to light up the field worldwide. Dewi was a former student in the Swansea English Department, and he retained a deep interest in literature for the remainder of his life.

In due course, a richly symbiotic relationship was to develop between the writings of the literary critics Sims and Robinson and those of the linguistic philosopher Dewi Z (as he was universally known). He himself published several significant works of literary criticism, the most notable probably being *R. S. Thomas: Poet of the Hidden God*.⁶ In it, he displayed his deep interest in a poet whom Wittgenstein would have probably recognised as a particularly brilliant 'tight-rope walker' of the kind he had described in one of his notebooks:

> An honest religious thinker is like a tight-rope walker. He almost looks as though he were walking on nothing but air. His support is the slenderest imaginable. And yet it really is possible to walk on it.⁷

Direct references to Wittgenstein are very rare in Phillips's book (much more common are his appreciative acknowledgements of the work of Simone Weil), but his thinking throughout is infused with the German's key concepts about the nature of language. As Phillips trenchantly points out, in R. S. Thomas's 'fascination with the notion of a *Deus Absconditus*, the poet sees God's will as not being contingently mysterious to us, but as born of a sense of mystery. On this view, we are not hidden from God by an inherently inadequate language. On the contrary, the idea of God in the language is of a hidden God.' (xviii)

At the end of that introductory year of study, it seemed to me that my dabblings in Philosophy had come to a full stop. It was perfectly obvious that I had been tried and found sorely wanting. I gratefully retreated to grapple with English. But if I had finished with Philosophy, Philosophy had not finished with me, because due to an unexpected turn of events – a turn I have found rather embarrassing to recall ever since – I found myself engaged in philosophical discussions once more, and this time at a very exalted level. Having completed my degree in English and embarked unenthusiastically on a course of distinctly desultory doctoral study, I found myself prematurely appointed to the department's staff at the absurdly young age of twenty. My performance at undergraduate level had attracted the attention of Robinson and Sims, and they it was who seem to have proposed to Dewi Z. Phillips that I read a paper to a highly select forum, the research seminar of the Philosophy Department.

Thoroughly intimidated by the prospect, I came up with the idea of offering reflections on the (suggestively contrasting) treatment of evil in English and American novels – a subject on which I had originally proposed to write my PhD, until wisely discouraged from doing so by my kind, patient supervisor, the scholarly Professor Cecil Price, who pointed out it was very unlikely that I'd come up with anything that was remotely original. Anyway, the treatment of evil was what I proposed as topic for my talk. Having delivered it, I was thoroughly discomfited when reports came back that Rush Rhees had been very impressed, and that I had inadvertently gained a reputation among his many disciples and acolytes of being a penetrating thinker!

Rhees had apparently been much taken by my pointing out that no exact equivalent for 'evil' existed in the Welsh language. The Welsh word for it is 'drwg', but that can also mean simply 'naughty' or mildly 'bad'. Accordingly, I mulled over the possible philosophical implications of such a word as this. It was this (wholly spurious) reputation for profundity that shortly led to my being invited to join the select company who gathered to reflect on Wittgenstein's theories of language under the leadership of Rush Rhees. It had become his custom to host a discussion meeting attended not only by members and postgrads from the Philosophy Department, but also a few invited representatives from other departments as well.

In attending, of course, I immediately found I was totally out of my depth. I was further disorientated by the practice of all those attending of referring to each other solely by their surnames – an Oxbridge practice that seemed, and still seems, to me to be unbearably pretentious. These occasions purported to be scrupulously egalitarian in character, another pretence I found annoying because it was perfectly obvious that Rhees was a cut above all others present, and that, whether consciously or not, they invariably deferred to his privileged interpretations. And that, in turn, alerted me to what might be called the infinitely subtle game of power politics that was being conducted between them, but always under the elaborately courteous pretence of complete equality. Then there was the intriguing contrast in manner between Dewi Z and Rush Rhees; the former invariably fluent (yet exact) and inclined to 'talk for victory', the latter parsimonious of speech.

That said, the intellectual calibre of the group was undoubtedly of the very highest, and everyone respected the tone set by Rhees – a tone of reverent concentration on linguistic issues that were of the very knottiest. There were one or two in attendance who stood out, for very different reasons. Dewi Z was a man whose brilliance of mind was evident throughout, and he was naturally given to adversarial philosophical encounters, in which he always prevailed. John Rees was a straight-speaking former union official. He had established a reputation as a scholar of the work of John Stuart Mill, had been promoted to professor, but had then demoted himself, disgusted by what becoming a 'Chair' entailed even in those far more enlightened university days. He was fearless in his forthright bearding of Rhees, and it was obvious that each highly respected the other. And then there was Gabriel Jacobs, a talented and talkative lecturer in French, who was never shy of asking questions even when they sounded brash and naïve. And of course, David Sims and Ian Robinson were also in attendance, although they mostly chose to observe a dignified silence.

Rhees prepared for these sessions with all the devotion with which he had prepared for his undergraduate 'lectures'. As text for study, he had chosen the edition of the Blue Book and the Brown Book that had been published a couple of decades earlier, to which he had provided an informative Preface.[8] He then circulated 'appendices' to these texts, in the form of stencilled sheets. I recently discovered that I had retained two of these. One of them, dated 6.5.70 , consisted of notes on Wittgenstein's statements that had been prepared by 'MM' (one of the students to whom he dictated the Blue Book) on 3.12.34. The other was a brief collection of Rhees's own reflections – at once lucid and impenetrable – on one or two of Wittgenstein's typically lapidary, gnomic observations.

Rhees was particularly interested in the early evolution of Wittgenstein's seminal concept of 'language games' – an explanation of how language could have meaning that was totally at variance with Bertrand Russell's insistence that words could have meaning only when firmly pinned to external 'realities'. Such a model necessarily led to the conclusion that the language of literature lacked any substantive meaning – whereas for Wittgenstein, the arts were one of the richest repositories of human meaning available to humankind.

But understanding that involved first understanding the *kind* of meaning that was instanced in artistic expression – understanding, that is, the *kind* of language game being played on such occasions. Here is a sample of Rhees's discussion of such points in his stencilled notes:

> Wittgenstein would remark that we do not always use 'language' to mean 'the language of communication' – or language in which we convey information to someone. So we may speak of music as a language, and at the same time hold that the music does not say anything except itself. (It says something, but it says only itself.) Of course, this does not mean that in music there are no rules of no composition or rules of harmony; or that there is a difference between a funeral march and a song of joy at the coming of spring. Not just any conjunction or sequence of notes would *say* anything. There are certain sequences that would be 'meaningless'; and so on. A piece of music is not independent of the musical tradition in which the composer has learned to write music at all. This is especially clear when we speak of 'innovations'.

Such a train of thought would be certain to appeal to literary critics such as David Sims and Ian Robinson. As would the distinctly conservative, if not reactionary, character of the sceptical observation by Rhees that follows: 'What is electronic music – why is it called music. It seems like "painting" by flicking the brush.'

* * *

As adopted by Sims and Robinson, Wittgenstein's language theory would take on a distinctly conservative cast. Not for nothing, after all, had Ian Robinson been one of F. R. Leavis's most brilliant and cherished students. Like Leavis, the maintenance of traditional 'Englishness' was very close to Robinson's heart, and in due course he was to prove hostile to any attempts at linguistic innovation, because they seemed to him to threaten the precious integrity of England's great literary heritage. This obsession it was that made him completely blind to Wales, the country which had become his home, and supremely indifferent to the contemporary campaigns to protect the imperilled Welsh language with whose parlous state both J. R. Jones and Dewi Z. Phillips were very actively concerned. As he once confessed to me, that was no business of his. It was up to the Welsh to do something about it.

Both David Sims and Ian Robinson were 'state of England' men, in the tradition of the likes of the magisterial Matthew Arnold, D. H. Lawrence (who had recently been canonised of course by F. R. Leavis)[9] and George Orwell. And when they adopted aspects of Wittgenstein's philosophy of language, it was to reinforce and advance their work in these national (and even nationalistic) contexts. By the same token, both were High Anglicans of a markedly conservative theology and temperament who hated the reforms in language and liturgy the Church was at that very time in the process of implementing.

Ian was very much of Edmund Burke's turn of mind, one to whom all things traditional, not least the 'received' version of the English language as most richly mediated through literature, were sacrosanct. All of his work on language and literature may be described as a grand work of mourning for the steep decline in values consequent, he believed, upon a progressive erosion of the signifying power of the English language at its peak. It is no coincidence that the quotation he chose as epigraph for perhaps his most important book, *The Survival of English*,[10] was the following: 'O gentile Engleterre, a toi j'escrits/ Pour remembrer ta joie qu'est novelle' (Gentle/noble England, I write to you to recall your joy, which is new'). These are the words of the fourteenth-century poet John Gower, dedicating his work to the cause of the English nation.

One of the first books that Ian Robinson published advertised its intention in its title. Called *Chaucer and the English Tradition*,[11] it was a deliberate riposte to Charles Muscatine's landmark study *Chaucer and the French Tradition*.[12] In it, Robinson set out to reclaim Chaucer for England by demonstrating his indebtedness to the English language and its literary tradition. A like animus against 'foreign' influence was apparent in his dismissive attitude towards American literature, about which I suspect he knew very little, like his mentor F. R. Leavis. I well remember the occasion when I read a paper on Walt Whitman's Civil War collection *Drum-Taps* to a staff-student seminar. Ian was unwilling to admit Whitman's originality, or to acknowledge the origins of his poetry in a literary culture already very different from that of England. He triumphantly demonstrated that if you carefully scanned some of the poems they turned out to have been written in that good old English staple, blank verse.

In that way, Ian was a typical product of the period – as Britain lost it worldwide political power so intellectuals sought to compensate by advancing their own version of a linguistic and cultural imperialism. It was hardly a surprise when later he turned out to be a great supporter of Mrs Thatcher and her government. What was a surprise – and indeed a disappointment – to me was that David Sims should also become a Thatcher fan. After all, he was himself a product of the industrial society that Thatcher's policies cruelly savaged – a native of one of the eastern valleys of the great south Wales coalfield. He must have grown up there during the terrible Depression years, and I could never understand how he ended up on Thatcher's side. His seemed to me to be a dreadful act of cultural betrayal. But David was a formidable personality of impressive and singular intellectual powers. He had been one of Kingsley Amis's boon drinking companions during the latter's years in the Department, but by the time I came to know him he was a thoroughly reformed character.

Ian's attendance at Rush Rhees's seminars fed directly into work he had in progress at that time. It was in 1973 that he published his typically polemical and controversial study *The Survival of English*, a work that announced his arrival as an important right-wing thinker of the day about language and literature. It was a work heavily influenced from beginning to end by his understanding of the implications of Wittgenstein's philosophy of language, as inflected by Ian's conservative cultural philosophy. Its central theme was the steady corruption and degeneration of the English language and the consequent erosion of hallowed values that were wholly sustained and transmitted by it. In short, his book was a cultural Jeremiad.

The subtitle of *The Survival of English* is 'essays in criticism of language' (a formulation distantly reminiscent of the writings of Matthew Arnold, one of Robinson's most important forerunners in this field),[13] and the epigraphs identify the thinkers on the subject of language to whom Ian Robinson admits being most indebted: Wittgenstein (on the link between a style of language and a style of living) and F. R. Leavis. The main concepts underpinning the book's whole project are clearly explained in the Introductory Essay. 'If things exist as meaning, the context where they do so can only be our lives. We are the people to whom things signify ... Sometimes we can change the meaning of a thing by seeing it in a different aspect (cf. L. Wittgenstein, *Philosophical Investigations*)' (2). 'Our view of the world, the way the individual sees things, is also the way we put things together ... It wouldn't be stretching the word far to call this composing itself language' (5). There was therefore a connection between the work of shaping and verbal language, and so, Robinson added, his book was all about 'different examples of the interplay between language and life' (6).

The production and use of language, Robinson argued – with a glance at Wittgenstein's famous assertion that there can be no such thing as a private language – was a group activity not a lone enterprise, even though it was an activity differently modified by different individuals. Together, human societies carefully maintained a common stock of words that were used in several different collectively agreed ways for different purposes, and in the case of speakers of English, it was the correct use of language at the correct time and in the way appropriate to one or other of this variety of forms that constituted 'standard English'. It was the ability to recognise when one or other of these forms of language was being used correctly and when not that constituted 'common judgement'.

Behind Robinson's thinking here there lay not only F. R. Leavis with his idea of the 'common pursuit of true judgement',[14] but also T. S. Eliot, most particularly his discussion of the relationship between tradition and innovation in his great essay 'Tradition and the Individual Talent'.[15] So Robinson proceeded to emphasise that while these different forms of language were fundamentally inherited by speakers of a language, and were therefore 'given', they were far from being static. They were constantly being modified through changes that nevertheless had to remain basically consistent with the whole tenor of accepted usage or become meaningless. And any meaningful change would invariably result in alterations of sense that were also alterations in one's perception of the world and indeed of one's relation to it. In short, it resulted in a different way of living.

It was at this point that Robinson began to pay attention to his real subject, the disturbing changes in the way the English language was used that were becoming ever more evident in contemporary society. His first (prescient) example was a change in the terms used to describe the function of university study, changes that clearly indicated that such study was beginning to be viewed, and assessed, in terms imported from the world of business and finance. British universities, he added, were busily changing their very nature. He then proceeded to show how the term 'friendship' had begun to be used in a slack, promiscuous fashion that threatened to make the very experience of friendship so all-embracing as to become meaningless. By now, it had become very evident that Ian Robinson was deeply disturbed by the dramatic change he saw on all sides and in every sphere of life, a change that was not only reflected in changes of language use but was also actively enabled and promoted by them.

For him, nowhere was this more evident than in recent attempts to 'modernise' the language of the King James Bible as well as of the Anglican liturgy and related forms of worship that were couched in the same 'outmoded' terms. Robinson followed Wittgenstein in arguing that to change the traditional language was to change the experience. With the modernisation of religious language there must inescapably come the dilution of faith, to a point where it threatened to become meaningless. Worship of any spiritual depth or integrity became next to impossible. His was a movingly profound analysis, based on an exceptionally sensitive awareness of the inherent poetry of any authentic religious belief. And it carried unmistakeable echoes of Leavis's famous diatribe against a 'technological-Benthamite or scientifico-industrial civilization'.[16]

Leavis had been very wary of Wittgenstein when both had been colleagues at Cambridge, not least because he strongly believed that philosophers 'should be kept the hell away from literary criticism'. But as the work of Ian Robinson intriguingly demonstrated there was nevertheless a fruitful convergence between critic and philosopher when it came to understanding the nature and function of language. Setting aside Leavis's particular animus against Science – which Wittgenstein did not share – the Englishman would have assented to Ray Monk's succinct account of the Austrian's key conclusions about:

> the wretched effects that the worship of science and the scientific method has had upon our whole culture. Aesthetics and religious belief are two examples – for Wittgenstein, of course, crucially important examples – of areas of thoughts and life in which the scientific method is not appropriate, and in which efforts to make it so lead to distortion, superficiality and confusion. (*DG*, Chapter 20)

In successive chapters of *The Survival of English*, Ian Robinson passionately advanced linguistic evidence of baleful change for the worse across a number of key fields of human activity, including politics and journalism, and he devoted two lengthy discussions to concerned demonstrations of how human relationships of love and sexuality were being disturbingly cheapened as a result of the new ways in which they were being discussed and thereby experienced.[17] His blanket term for these developments was 'pornography', a phenomenon he believed to stem from a failure to 'take sex seriously' by equating it with mere sensual pleasure. (This was one of the points in his book where his interest in the work of D. H. Lawrence became very evident.) Pornography, he emphasised, should not be judged according to how coarsening were its effects; rather, pornography should be understood as being in itself inherently coarse.

Of particular interest in this connection was Robinson's subtle demonstration of the contribution traditionally made by the language of love poetry to the mature experience of love. He clearly believed it was this language, particularly as used by the likes of Shakespeare and John Donne, that provided the gold standard for human experience in this seminal field. Their aliveness to what Robinson called the 'demonic' dimension to sexual passion seemed to him particularly important, and deeply instructive because along with the coarsening of relationships consequent upon 'pornography' (in the broad sense in which Robinson used it) there went a correspondingly decadent current tendency to sentimentalise love, to treat it as if were always and inherently sweet and good. Never, in Robinson's opinion, did any of the great love poet lose sight of the dangerous, volatile, destructive character of the experience with which they were dealing. This was implicitly recognised in the rich and subtle language in which they treated it.

So impoverished had the English language become since the war, in Ian Robinson's angry opinion – following the decline of the British ruling classes of the Victorian era (241) – that it was impossible for any major creative work to be fashioned out of it. 'The pop world, the growth-worshippers, and the manipulators become the meek inheritors of English – which we have to go on speaking and living in' (234). What was, however, not only possible but an imperative necessity was a major critical effort that would review the 'minor' products of the present in the light of the very best and highest that the past had to offer – and here Robinson acknowledged the relevance of Matthew Arnold's magisterial phrase 'the best that is known and thought in the world'. For him, one person stood out as the perfect exemplar of a critic of the highest order, and that was his own teacher F. R. Leavis, who, he wrote, 'is a *great* writer because of the passion of his devotion to criticism and to the creative part it must play at the present time in our literature and our life' (234). He had, added Robinson, again deliberately echoing Arnold, widened 'literary criticism into a criticism of life' (235).

A man of formidable intellectual gifts, and a brilliant controversialist, Ian Robinson had an unfortunate weakness for what Pope memorably styled 'the Parnassian sneer'. Nowhere was this more apparent that in the inflammatory attack he launched on Noam Chomsky's linguistics in his book *The New Grammarians' Funeral*. And it was there that he nailed his philosophical colours most firmly to the mast when he provocatively declared that he had 'learned far more about language both from the philosophy of Collingwood, and of Wittgenstein and Rhees, and from the literary criticism of Leavis, than from the whole corpus of established linguistics'.[18]

As a Coda for his book, Ian Robinson published the 1970 prospectus for *The Human World*, a new quarterly review, modelled on the great compendious periodicals of the Victorian era, which had included not only literary features but also meaty essays on the whole spectrum of public intellectual life and political affairs. Published by the Brynmill Press that Robinson had recently established, it was co-edited by him and his close friend and collaborator David Sims, and all the contributions were to be grounded in the kind of understanding of Wittgenstein's linguistic philosophy that Robinson was to demonstrate in *The Survival of English*. Over the brief four-year-period of its existence, the review came to be recognised as a powerhouse of right-wing cultural thought, attracting contributors as distinguished as Elizabeth Anscombe.[19]

The two seminal figures for *The Human World* were F. R. Leavis (several of whose major essays appeared in its pages for the first time)[20] and Wittgenstein – the very first issue flagged up an intention shortly to review both a new, definitive edition of Wittgenstein's *On Certainty* and Rush Rhees's *Without Answers* (HW 1, 68–9). It was therefore appropriate that the February 1973 number should include Leavis's 'Memories of Wittgenstein', a source of information about his life that has been thoroughly mined since. In it, Leavis spoke of the 'basic lack of intellectual sympathy' between them while also stressing Wittgenstein's 'unmistakeable genius'. He pointedly declared that for him 'the fullest use of language is to be found in creative literature', adding acidly that 'philosophers are always weak on language' (*HW* 10, 66–79).

For Robinson, of course, Rush Rhees proved to be an invaluable conduit of Wittgenstein's thought, and so the May 1971 issue featured Rhees's translation (along with A. C. Miles) of the Austrian's 'Remarks on Frazer's *Golden Bough*' (HW 3, 18–42). The thrust of the discussion, Rhees explained, was that we needed to 'understand ritual or magical practices', not by translating them, as Frazer had done, into the terms of science and historical enquiry, but as though we were 'understanding a language'. It was, moreover, a language with which we were already unconsciously familiar, as it continued to be used by us today, albeit not in the same cultural contexts as those of earlier societies.

The February 1974 number of *The Human World* featured a highly critical, not to say scathing, review by Rhees of William Bartley III's *Wittgenstein*, a biographical study that gave prominence to the claim that Wittgenstein had lived the life of a tormented homosexual (*HW*, 14, 66–85). Rhees was disgusted by that claim not, as he emphasised, because he had any moral objection to gayness, but first because Bartley had completely failed to produce any detailed, convincing corroborative evidence so support his thesis, and secondly because while the Wittgenstein whom Rhees had known so well was certainly troubled by sexual desires, these had never been a dominant feature of his life and he had never felt any anguish about their character. Love, Rhees stressed, had occupied and 'perplexed him much more than "sex" did'.

Rhees's concern over such matters had already become evident in a discussion he had contributed to an earlier number of the periodical under the title 'The Tree of Nebuchadnezzar' (*HW*, 4, 23–7). There, he had been preoccupied with the developing contemporary tendency to discuss sexual issues, even at school level. What disturbed Rhees was that however well-intentioned such attempts might be, they demonstrated a complete failure to understand that 'the ... *talk* about sex brings no understanding, no more than doing it in public does' – this latter remark pertaining primarily to the increasing tendency for plays and films to include graphic representations of intimate sexual activity.

As for the issue, raised by Bartley, about Wittgenstein's concern with sex, Rhees's attempt to set the record straight in this regard continued to rumble on right into the final number of *The Human World* (*HW* 15–16, 152–62), in which he tried to explain what he had understood by the term 'philosophy'. The same number had opened with the 'Valedictory' statement of the two editors in which they announced that after this *The Human World* would be ceasing publication. Its closure, they admitted, did indeed amount to a failure on their part, but they remained defiantly confident that it had performed an invaluable service. They remained 'unrepentant and hopeful – confirmed, indeed, in a sense of necessity and also of possibility' (*HW* 15–16), 5–7. They still believed, they added, that 'criticism is the light we need' in a period they regarded as one of alarming decline in 'human' standards. They proudly reprinted Peter Simple's statement in the *Daily Telegraph* that 'we were in the proper sense, a light in darkness'. For both Sims and Robinson, the Biblical source of that remark seemed perfectly apt. Theirs had after all been a kind of sacred enterprise. And in bringing it to an end they made wry reference to a light that had come into the world and the world had comprehended it not.

The story of the fruitful relationship between the English Department and the Wittgenstein School in the Philosophy Department doesn't end there, however. One of the very earliest of Rush Rhees's pupils, after his arrival at Swansea, was a young man from the nearby village of Dunvant who was named John Ormond Thomas. As John Ormond, he went on to become one of the most important of Wales's post-war poets and a BBC documentary filmmaker who won international prizes and achieved considerable renown.

On entering upon his undergraduate career, John Ormond had studied Philosophy with Rush Rhees while reading for his degree in English. And throughout his life, what he had then learnt about language was to influence all his creative output. He was particularly fascinated by Wittgenstein's distinction between what it was possible to say and what not. As I have written elsewhere, 'Ormond became a devotee of Wittgenstein's language philosophy and, mediated through the bravura language games of Wallace Stevens's poems, this proved to be a significant influence on his mature work.'[21] Indeed, it was through Rush Rhees's own collection of modern American poetry that Ormond first encountered the work both of Stevens and of many other of the poets whose work remained important to him.

And then there was the intriguing connection with Wittgenstein supplied by my late friend Neil Reeve, a first-class critic and scholar, whose own brilliant and innovative work on J. H. Prynne (by whom he had been taught and with whom he kept closely in touch) demonstrated his intense interest in the implications of contemporary language use. Neil was the nephew of Basil Reeve, who had been a close friend and associate of Wittgenstein's during the war years when the latter had left his post at Cambridge to work as orderly and porter at a hospital. They first met when Reeve was a young doctor at Guy's Hospital researching traumatic shock – a condition then vaguely labelled 'wound shock' and inadequately understood.

As Monk explains (*DG*, Ch. 20), Reeve was then concluding it would be best to avoid such a diagnosis 'and to replace it by an accurate and complete record of a patient's state and progress together with the treatment given'. Wittgenstein was impressed by such a radical approach. He realised the problem lay in language, in the traditional medical reliance upon an unusable concept. So engrossed in the research did he become that he accompanied Reeve when he moved to work in Newcastle. Neil Reeve's indirect association with Wittgenstein through his distinguished uncle therefore provides us with a fitting conclusion to this brief discussion of a fascinating phenomenon that has so unfortunately been hitherto overlooked by specialists in Wittgenstein.

Notes

1. See in particular J. R. Jones, *Yr Argyfwng Gwacter Ystyr* (Llandybie: Llyfrau'r Dryw, 1974); *Prydeindod* (Llandybie: Christopher Davies, 1966); *Gwaedd yng Nghymru* (Liverpool/Pontypridd: Cyhoeddiadau Modern Cymreig, 1970). For a useful overview, see Dewi Z. Phillips, *J. R. Jones* (Cardiff: University of Wales Press, 1995).
2. Simone Weil, *Waiting on God*, trans. Emma Craufurd (London: Routledge and Kegan Paul, 1951).
3. Howard Erskine-Hill, *The Augustan Idea in English Literature* (London: E. Allen, 1983).
4. I should add that the next generation of academics attached to the Department, and therefore contemporary with myself, included a number of outstanding talents. These included Margaret Doody (currently Distinguished Professor at the University of Notre Dame), and a trio of scholars who together formed a cohort of impressive scholars and critics of D. H. Lawrence: John Worthen (later eminent biographer of Lawrence and holder of the Chair of Lawrence Studies at Nottingham University), John Turner (who combined his work on Lawrence with important work on Wordsworth) and Graham Holderness, a passionate young Marxist iconoclast who later became Professor at the University of Hertfordshire. Add to these the gifts of an emerging young scholar Glyn Pursglove, and it becomes evident what an exceptional collection of younger, highly varied, talents there was in the Department by the time that Robinson and Sims began to involve themselves in publication.
5. He was named for Morgan John Rhys (1760–1804), a Nonconformist minister radicalised by the French Revolution who railed against the iniquity of slavery and emigrated to the US to establish what he hoped would become a Welsh settlement in western Pennsylvania that would live and worship according to his progressive principles. In the states he was befriended and assisted by Benjamin Rush, one of the Founding Fathers of the US, and a signatory of the Declaration of Independence. For a vivid historical account of Rhys's achievements, see Gwyn A. Williams, *The Search for Beulah Land: the Welsh and the Atlantic Revolution* (New York: Holmes and Meier, 1980). For a fascinating account in fiction of Rhys's community, see Emyr Humphreys, *The Anchor Tree* (London: Hodder and Stoughton, 1980).
6. D. Z. Phillips, *R. S. Thomas: Poet of the Hidden God* (Pennsylvania: Pickwick Publications, 1986).
7. Quoted in Ray Monk, *Wittgenstein: The Duty of Genius* (London: Vintage, 1991), Chapter 22 (hereafter *DG*).
8. Ludwig Wittgenstein, *The Blue and Brown Books: Preliminary Studies for the 'Philosophical Investigations'* (Oxford: Blackwell, 1958; 2nd edn 1969).
9. F. R. Leavis, *D. H. Lawrence: Novelist* (London: Chatto and Windus, 1955).

10 Ian Robinson, *The Survival of English: Essays in Criticism of Language* (Cambridge: Cambridge University Press, 1973).
11 Ian Robinson, *Chaucer and the English Tradition* (Cambridge: Cambridge University Press, 1972).
12 Charles Muscatine, *Chaucer and the French Tradition: A Study in Style and Meaning* (Berkeley: University of California Press, 1957).
13 See, for example, *Essays by Matthew Arnold* (London: Oxford University Press, 1914).
14 F. R. Leavis, *The Common Pursuit* (London; Chatto and Windus, 1952).
15 T. S. Eliot, *Selected Essays, 1917–1932* (London: Faber and Faber, 1932).
16 The phrase was coined by Leavis in the two Richmond lectures he delivered at Downing College Cambridge in 1962, as part of his notorious riposte to C. P. Snow's 'The two Cultures and the Scientific Revolution', the two Rede lectures delivered at Cambridge in May 1959. Snow's core argument was that humankind should look to the application of science and technology to supply it with its future needs. Leavis was scathing on the crass simple-mindedness of any such vague concept of the human good.
17 I drew upon the thinking in these discussions some fifty years later, when I wrote an essay on Whitman's treatment of gay love in his pioneering *Calamus* sequence of poems; M. Wynn Thomas, '"Till I hit upon a name": *Calamus* and the language of love', *Huntingdon Library Quarterly*, 73/4, 641–58.
18 Ian Robinson, *The New Grammarians' Funeral* (Cambridge: Cambridge University Press, 1975), 184.
19 G. E. M. Anscombe, 'Contraception and Chastity', *The Human World*, 1, 9–31 (hereafter *HW*); Elizabeth Anscombe, 'Mr Truman's degree', *The Human World*, 10, 32–41 (hereafter *HW*). She is objecting to the award to the former US President of an Honorary Degree by Oxford University; 'I vehemently object to *our* action in offering Mr Truman honours because one can share in the guilt of a bad action [i.e. the bombing of Hiroshima and Nagasaki] by praise and flattery, as also by defending it.'
20 See the following: 'Elites, Oligarchies and an Educated Public' (*HW* 4, 21–2); 'Justifying one's valuation of Blake' (*HW* 6, 42–64); '"Believing in" the University' (*HW* 15–16, 98–110).
21 M. Wynn Thomas, *John Ormond* (Cardiff: University of Wales Press, 1997), p. 10.

9

Strange Country:
The Cosmopolitan Particularism
of Ludwig Wittgenstein and Ralph Ellison

Daniel G. Williams

1. Introduction: Swansea, January 1944

> When the Stranger says, "What is the meaning of this city?
> Do you huddle together because you love each other?"
> What will you answer? "We all dwell together
> To make money from each other"? or "This is a community"?[1]

In this passage from T. S. Eliot's 'Choruses from "The Rock"', urban civilisation is looked at from the point of view of a stranger. The question as to the 'meaning of this city' suggests that the stranger's otherness is mirrored in the unnerving inscrutability of the landscape being viewed and the ambiguous motivations of those living within it. The year 1944 saw two notable strangers visiting the city of Swansea, which was itself the site of visible, unnerving devastation at that time. Of all Welsh towns and cities, it was Swansea that suffered most severely during the war years, with forty-four air raids being mounted on the town between 1940 and 1943. A total of 369 people were killed, including 230 who died in the three-night blitz of February 1941 that destroyed the entire town centre. 'Where is your husband?' a Swansea woman was asked during the height of the bombing. 'In the army, the coward' was her answer.[2]

Wittgenstein in Swansea

Swansea's blitzed landscape is the subject of a striking scene in an unpublished short story by the first of my strangers: African American novelist Ralph Ellison. Ellison, whose seminal novel *Invisible Man* would be published in 1952, served in the merchant marine as second cook and baker from 1943 to 1945, seeing this as a means of contributing to the war effort without serving in the segregated American army. The boat on which he travelled was the *Sun Yat Sen*, part of convoy HX 273 that arrived in Swansea on 16 January 1944. It departed on the 5 February, heading towards Belfast to join convoy ON 203 sailing back to New York.[3] Born in Oklahoma in 1913 and attempting to establish himself as a writer in the early 1940s, Ellison was in Swansea for twenty-one days. This would have been his first experience of another country and in an unpublished autobiographical short story entitled 'The Red Cross in Morriston, Swansea, SW' he narrates his arrival as follows:

> At the gates a constable examined my pass and told me how to get the bus for the city. The bus, like those which run on Fifth Avenue but traveling much faster, was filled with people going into town from nearby villages. I settled back, listening to the strange English and to a language which I learned later was Welsh. In five minutes I got off at the bottom of what I was told was Wind Street, paid the conductor four pence as I left and started heading for the Red Cross Club.
> Moving along the street by flashlight I sensed rather than saw the wrecked buildings, as when you approach Colorado Springs in the early morning you *feel* the mountains before you see them. Then when a bus flashed by I saw demolished masonry fenced off along the side walk. Those barrage balloons I'd seen from the ship were not for show. In the early days of the war Swansea had been badly blitzed; and unlike London, where the debris is quickly cleared away, Swansea had neither the money nor the facilities to do so. I was told that several bodies were sealed beneath one of the wrecked buildings. Looking up the hill to the intersecting street at the top was like looking at the will-o-wisp glowing of cigarettes around a dark cinema balcony and up ahead, a lot of people were singing. It was Saturday and by the time I reached the

top of the hill I felt I had stumbled into a *Mardi Gras* procession. Hundreds of flashlights and cigarettes flickered on and off revealing soldiers' trousers and women's legs as they moved leisurely along.[4]

In blackout conditions the narrator 'listens' and 'senses' before he 'sees' the reality of wartime destruction as a bus flashes by. The jarring juxtaposition of buried bodies and 'a *Mardi Gras* procession' captures the contingency of national and cultural encounters during the war years. We are told later in the story that it is 'bad blackout etiquette to flash one's light in another's eyes', a fact that is already indicated here in the foregrounding of 'trousers' and 'legs'.

It is possible that among those trousers illuminated by Ellison's flashlight would have been those worn by the second stranger with whom I'm concerned: the Austrian philosopher Ludwig Wittgenstein. As Alfred Schmidt's research in this volume indicates, Wittgenstein spent the Christmas of 1943 and following New Year with his Welsh-American friend, acolyte and philosopher at Swansea University, Rush Rhees. It is not clear when Wittgenstein left Swansea to return to his work at a Clinical Research Unit in Newcastle, but it is 30 January by the time Rhees writes to thank him for his visit. (That Rhees, the host, writes to thank Wittgenstein for the visit reveals something of the teacher-disciple nature of their relationship.)[5] Be that as it may, the fact that both Wittgenstein and Ellison were in Swansea in the same month is the suggestive coincidence that gives rise to what follows. While Ellison would continue to refer back to his time in Swansea in letters throughout his life and even described himself as a 'Welsh nationalist' in 1968, he never returned to Wales.[6] Wittgenstein, on the other hand, would continue to visit Swansea between 1942 and 1947, with the longest sojourn being from March to September 1944.

2. Affinities and Estrangements

There is no evidence that Wittgenstein was ever aware of Ellison, or *vice versa*. Yet there are some similarities between them, both superficial coincidences and areas where a comparative reading sheds an illuminating light on their thinking and writing. Wittgenstein died in

1951, with his *Tractatus Logico-Philosophicus* (1922) being the only volume published during his lifetime. Ellison's novel *Invisible Man* was published a year later in 1952 and would prove to be his only completed novel. Ray Monk subtitles his biography of Wittgenstein 'The Duty of Genius', while Lawrence Jackson's subtitle for his account of Ellison's first fifty years is 'Emergence of Genius'.[7] If it would seem that publishing one text and struggling for the rest of one's life to complete an unpublished second is a sign of genius, the use of the term may also be linked to the ways in which both are seen to have avoided clubability, cultivating reputations for being dedicated to their writings and development of their thought. Their shared tacit Communist sympathies in the 1930s (famously retracted in the case of Ellison) did not entail a desire for communality.[8] Lawrence Jackson, among others, comments on Ellison's haughtiness, noting that 'social isolation contributed to Ellison's impatience with others incapable or uninterested in dwelling in a theoretical and almost esoteric plane'.[9] Terry Eagleton evokes Wittgenstein's 'extreme personal asceticism'. In tracing Wittgenstein's development from life as an engineer to a philosophical career 'via flights into seminary gardening and village school-teaching' Eagleton emphasises periods of 'solitary self-communings in Norway and the west of Ireland'.[10] Wittgenstein's periods in Swansea are often occluded as his engagements with those with whom he stayed and conversed do not wholly fit this model of willed isolation. (The biography by Ray Monk is a notable exception, where a chapter is dedicated to Swansea).[11] Similarly, Ellison's emphasis on social interactions and cultural engagements while in Wales are somewhat at odds with his reputation for self-reflexive contemplation.

On a visit to County Wicklow, Ireland, in 1947, Wittgenstein noted that 'there is nothing like the Welsh coast here', indicating a fondness for the Welsh landscape that mirrored a fondness for the people.[12] 'It's good to be away from Cambridge and to be here, and among friendly people', he noted of Swansea in 1946, reinforcing his earlier observation that

> I know quite a number of people here whom I like. I seem to find it more easy to get along with them here than in England. I feel much more often like smiling e.g. when I walk in the street, or when I see children etc.[13]

Strange Country: Cosmopolitan Particularism

In a letter to editor Senora Babb, with whom he'd had a brief relationship, Ellison noted effusively of the Welsh 'that I love them like my own people', and expressed his pleasure 'that hundreds of Negro boys are acquiring their first notions of real democracy among these people who, strangely, are culturally so similar'.[14] The narrator of 'The Red Cross' notes that these alleged cultural similarities meant that 'it was not as difficult as ... expected' for 'Negro troops'.

> For although American Negro and Welsh historical backgrounds were different, there were also certain cultural and temperamental similarities. Both Welshmen and Negroes loved to sing, to dance, to talk long over drinks, to laugh, to enjoy a good argument.[15]

It would seem, in returning to the lines by T. S. Eliot with which I began, that the answer offered by Swansea as to the 'meaning of this city' was that 'this is a community'; a community which these strangers could engage with and embrace. That answer is significant given the wartime context which foregrounded questions of nationality and citizenship in the lives of Wittgenstein and Ellison.

Despite being brought up Catholic in one of the wealthiest families in Vienna, 'by the annexation of Austria by Germany' as he was to write to John Maynard Keynes, Wittgenstein had 'become a German citizen, and by the German law, a German Jew' (as three of his grandparents had been baptised only as adults).[16] After 12 March 1938, to return to Austria would be to risk his life. While being unable to return to Vienna, Wittgenstein was also worried about his status as an 'alien' in Britain. In the year 1939, while visiting his Irish friend and former student Maurice O'Connor Drury (1907–76), then employed as a doctor in Pontypridd, south Wales, Wittgenstein had a sense of his precarious situation. The owner of the hotel in which he was staying called for an unnecessary blackout and upon hearing a man with a foreign accent joking about the ensuing drama, the manageress called the police who took Wittgenstein in for questioning.[17] Eventually, with the assistance of Keynes and others, Wittgenstein took the oath of allegiance to the British Crown on 12 April 1939. Receipt of his British passport on 2 June allowed him to return to Vienna to try and secure the safety of his sisters. This would involve 'proving' that one of the

Jewish grandparents was actually Aryan, and depositing 'a staggering 1.7 tonnes of gold – equivalent to two per cent of the Austrian gold reserves taken over by Berlin in 1939' into the coffers of the Third Reich.[18]

American racism differed from German anti-Semitism in that American racist practices entailed the segregation rather than the complete expulsion or extermination of African Americans. This extended to the army where at the outset of war, African Americans were barred entirely from the marines and air force, and only allowed to enlist in the navy as messmen. It is perhaps no surprise, then, that the protagonist of the story 'In a Strange Country' (the only story based in Wales to be published in Ellison's lifetime) feels ambivalent about his American identity. Having been beaten by white America troops, he is saved by a group of Welshmen who take him to a choir rehearsal. 'Are there many like me in Wales?' he asks.

'Oh yes! Yanks all over the place. Black Yanks and white.'
'Black *Yanks?*' He wanted to smile.[19]

Unlike all other Allied forces in Britain, the US had been accorded exclusive jurisdiction over its own troops and followed its own laws in areas such as segregation and the death penalty. Even the American Red Cross, according to *The Crisis* in 1943, was unofficially 'running a segregated Jim-Crow setup for soldiers abroad'.[20] Indeed, Ellison's narrator in 'The Red Cross' arrives at the Swansea American Red Cross club only to realise that 'this club was attended principally by white soldiers'. He is then driven out to the club in Morriston, which Ellison recalled in 1977 was 'located a few miles north of Swansea' and was 'frequented mostly by Afro-American GIs'.[21] The Swansea that Ralph Ellison witnessed in 1944 was the site of unofficial segregationist practices.

Here lies the profoundest connection between Ellison and Wittgenstein; a sense of strangeness and otherness, exacerbated by the fact that their identities – at least as they related to national citizenship – lay in the hands of others. It is this that perhaps explains the fact that the interlocutory voice in Wittgenstein's posthumously published *Philosophical Investigations* seems, often, to be that of a stranger. The volume's influential meditations on language seem to develop from a re-iterated scenario: 'Suppose you came as an explorer to an unknown country with a language quite unknown to you.'²² One 'human being can be a complete enigma to another', notes Wittgenstein:

> One learns this when one comes into a strange country with entirely strange traditions; and, what is more, even though one has mastered the country's language. One does not *understand* the people.²³

Furthermore, Wittgenstein argues that 'a philosophical problem has the form: "I don't know my way about"'.²⁴ He notes in the preface that the book is like 'a number of sketches of landscapes which were made in the course of ... long and meandering journeys', and offers 'sketches' drawn 'from different directions ... in order to give the viewer an idea of the landscape. So this book is really just an album'.²⁵ Alfred Schmidt suggests that 'a substantial part of the *Philosophical Investigations*, as they were published posthumously by his executors in 1953, was written at Swansea, expanding the work to about twice its original size'.²⁶ In Swansea, notes Schmidt,

> Wittgenstein wrote most of the central passages on rule-following and – logically connected to this – the private language arguments and inner experience (§198-421).²⁷

If some of the most significant passages in *Philosophical Investigations* were written in Swansea, Ralph Ellison suggests that his brief sojourn in Wales played a significant role in the evolution of some of the central themes of *Invisible Man*. Ellison described *Invisible Man* as having 'erupted out of what had been conceived as a war novel', and in his introduction to the thirtieth anniversary edition he recalled the gestation of his most famous work as follows:²⁸

> I had published yet another story in which a young Afro-American seaman, ashore in Swansea, South Wales, was forced to grapple with the troublesome 'American' aspects of his identity after white Americans had blacked his eye during a wartime blackout on the Swansea street called Straight (no, his name was *not* Saul, nor did he become a Paul!). But

here the pressure toward self-scrutiny came from a group of Welshmen who rescued him and surprised him by greeting him as a 'Black Yank' and inviting him to a private club, and then sang the American National Anthem in his honor. [The story was] published in 1944, but now in 1945 on a Vermont farm, the theme of a young Negro's quest for identity was reasserting itself in a far more bewildering form.[29]

That 'pressure toward self-scrutiny' seems to have been stimulated through encountering Wales, and if Wittgenstein asks his readers to imagine themselves to be explorers in an 'unknown country', the narrator of Ellison's 'In a Strange Country' comes 'ashore from the ship' and feels 'the excited expectancy of entering a strange land'. The encounter with Welsh national identity leads Parker, the central protagonist and narrator, to wish that 'we only had some of what they have':

> they are a much smaller nation than ours would be, yet I can remember no song of ours that's of love of the soil or of country. Nor any song of battle other than those of biblical times.[30]

What Wales 'had' was under threat in the 1940s as wartime propaganda sought to 'disseminate the notion that Britain was totally united'. Widespread strikes in the coalfields suggested otherwise.[31] The depression of the 1930s had given rise to radical working class politics, ultimately propelling the Welsh socialist Aneurin Bevan – expelled from the Labour Party in 1939 for 'persisting with public agitation for Popular Front alliances' – to the role of Minister of Health in the new Labour Government following Clement Attlee's landslide victory of 1945.[32] The depression years also formed the context for a less widespread but widely observed growth in Welsh national consciousness, particularly following the burning of an RAF bombing school in Penyberth, in the Welsh-speaking heartland of the Llŷn Peninsula in 1936 by three leading Welsh nationalists. Saunders Lewis, one of the founders of Plaid Cymru, was dismissed from his lecturing post in Welsh at Swansea University as a result of his part in this act. A guilty verdict, condemning the three men to nine months in Wormwood Scrubs prison, was only achieved after the case had been transferred from Caernarfon (where the jury failed to reach a verdict) to the Old Bailey in London. An emergent cultural and political sense of Welshness in the 1930s was served a severe blow with the onset of the Second World War. Many distinctive Welsh journals ceased publication and programmes for the BBC's 'Welsh region', created after considerable protest in 1937, came to an end from the first day of the war as broadcasts became limited to a unified 'Home Service'.[33] If war transformed the British economy, pulling Wales out of depression, even a staunch supporter of Britain's stand such as W. J. Gruffydd could see the potential cultural devastation: 'England could win the war and Wales could lose it. [...] The impact of [this war] on the future of Wales and the Welsh language will be inexpressibly greater than [the impact of the last war]'.[34]

It is difficult to gauge to what extent either Wittgenstein or Ellison would have been aware of this wider context as Britain sought unity in the face of class and national fractures. In an uncompleted draft of 'A Storm of Blizzard Proportions' Ellison suggestively scribbled in pencil on the margin, 'love of soil if not of government'.[35] This deceptively simple statement speaks of a people who retain a distinctive identity without the protective buttressing of their own political structures, and who preserve a sense of cultural difference while contributing to the war effort of a larger nation state. He could be speaking of African America or Wales. Ellison's stories demonstrate a striking awareness of Welsh cultural particularities, from hearing the Welsh language and accent – 'incidentally, they do speak the way you heard in *The Corn Is Green*' – to commenting on the fact:

> that Welsh drama had developed out of the nonconformist religious movement, which instituted amature [sic] dramatics; thus the stage; thus, at longer range, such contemporary Welsh dramatists as Emlyn Williams and Richard Llewellyn.[36]

Wittgenstein was also aware of Welsh distinctiveness. He signed off a letter to his lover Ben Richards of 31 December 1946 with the correctly mutated 'pob llwyddiant yn y flwyddyn newydd as I always say when I'm speaking Welsh'.[37] Rush Rhees, Wittgenstein's friend and disciple recalled that:

> At a meal in a Welsh-speaking home, those present turned to speaking English with each other in deference to Wittgenstein's

presence. He insisted that they should not stop speaking Welsh to each other.³⁸

These responses to Wales are a minor example of the myriad contingent encounters between peoples and nationalities that occurred during the war and immediate post-war years. Ellison's belief that his story 'In a Strange Country' depicted 'a group of Welshmen' exerting a 'pressure toward self-scrutiny' on the central character indicates that the wartime context in which his thinking and writing developed should not be dismissed. In what follows I hope to suggest that Swansea was the site of an emergent strain of thought that was to prove profoundly influential in the post war years. As I hope to demonstrate, Wittgenstein and Ellison – in their different ways and in their different fields of activity – rejected the coerced sameness of assimilationism. In its place they embraced a 'cosmopolitan particularism'; a form of cosmopolitanism in which our common humanity is rooted in the appreciation of difference, particularity and diversity.

3. Forms of Life

From the late 1920s onwards, Ludwig Wittgenstein argued that 'forms of life' were the legitimate bedrock of social thought. A private language is inconceivable, he argues in the passages of the *Philosophical Investigations* that were probably written in Swansea, because language is a rule-governed activity. The rules of any language game can only exist, and can only be recognised as normative, in a public setting. Public consent is required for any rule's efficacy. Thus 'forms of life' – the social contexts of all utterances – are the basis from which an understanding of linguistic practice must begin. In making this case Wittgenstein was rejecting referential theories in which words denote objects or ideas (as in empiricism, and as in his own early writings), and departing from formal systems in which meaning derives from internal relations between signs (as in Saussurean structuralism). He used the term 'language game' to indicate that the 'speaking of language is part of an activity, or a form of life'.³⁹ Issues of value and rationality therefore arise from within a form of life and within the practices of a certain community. It is only against such a shared background that questions such as 'is this so' or 'is that reasonable' can be asked.

Strange Country: Cosmopolitan Particularism

We cannot imagine ourselves as independent from our loyalties and convictions because 'living by them is inseparable from understanding ourselves as the particular persons we are'.[40]

Rush Rhees described Wittgenstein's later method as 'anthropological'.[41] It is a suggestive description for, although Wittgenstein was not an anthropologist, his insistence that words and their meanings should be understood within the rituals, practices and gestures of a broader 'form of life' can be read as a manifestation in philosophy of the embrace of cultural pluralism in anthropology. Franz Boas (1858–1942) is usually seen as the person who initiated a tendency to think in terms of plural cultures across time and space, as opposed to espousing a notion of ever evolving development towards a superior universal civilisation. He illustrated his beliefs by arranging museum exhibitions according to 'culture area' as opposed to an evolutionary plotting of human civilisation towards greater technical mastery and social complexity. Boas believed that a fishhook, for example, should be properly displayed alongside other products of the culture to which it belonged – baskets, weapons, jewellery etc. – rather than next to earlier 'primitive' and later 'advanced' fishhooks. He insisted that artefacts be analysed and discussed in relation to their cultural context and in their own terms. Utterances for Wittgenstein, and objects for Boas, can only be interpreted within their broader 'form of life'. There is, then, some merit in the notion of an 'anthropological turn' in Wittgenstein's thought.[42]

The 'anthropological' aspect of Wittgenstein's thought, and its broader implications, are indicated in a review that he wrote of James George Frazer's (1854–1941) *The Golden Bough* (1890).[43] The review was largely written in 1931–2, but only published posthumously.[44] Wittgenstein's rejection of Frazer's evolutionist premises is particularly forceful here. He notes that 'all that Frazer' and Victorian anthropologists like him did was to make primitive practices 'plausible to people who think as he does'.[45] As Greg Chase notes, this incorporation of unfamiliar practices of the past into familiar rubrics amounts to a form of 'intellectual imperialism', which becomes a defence of imperialism itself at several moments in Frazer's text such as when 'intellectual and industrial' progress are associated with 'the great conquering races' of the West.[46] Wittgenstein resisted teleological accounts of history and thought, believing that the notion of progress 'dazzles and misleads our culture more than any other'.[47] Those attending a lecture by the Irish Marxist historian of science Benjamin Farrington (1891–1974) at Swansea in 1943 would have witnessed Wittgenstein humorously undermining the self-validating narratives of civilisationist progress that informed much social and scientific thought. Farrington referred to the coal and iron industries of the surrounding landscape in the Swansea Valley and acknowledged the environmental and aesthetic devastation wrought by slag heaps and disused mines. His conclusion, however, was that despite 'the ugly side of our civilisation, I am sure I would rather live as we do now than have to live as the caveman did'. Wittgenstein responded: 'Yes of course you would. But would the caveman'?[48] This is an example of the way in which Wittgenstein appealed to the primitive in order, as Luke Gibbons notes, 'to question whether language and knowledge, including mathematics and the higher sciences, could obviate the "forms of life" and social contexts that made them intelligible'.[49] Evoking the allegedly 'primitive' offers a means for Wittgenstein to question common sense assumptions.[50] It also allowed him to turn the anthropological gaze on to modern societies, noting the persistence of ritualistic practices such as 'kissing the picture of one's beloved' or 'walking quickly past a cemetery' in contemporary industrialised society.[51] The primitive, for Wittgenstein, was therefore as much a feature of the present as it was of the past. Writing to Maurice O'Connor Drury in the mid-1930s he feared, presciently, that the 'dark ages are coming again. I wouldn't be surprised, Drury, if you and I were to see such horrors as people being burned alive as witches'.[52]

The prescience of Wittgenstein's words need no elaboration. Though he never aligned himself with his Jewishness nor homosexuality, Wittgenstein would have been aware that the ritualistic scapegoating he feared became based on ethnicity and sexuality in the gruesome mass murders of the Third Reich. For Ralph Ellison, the dark ages had always been present. Though the practice of lynching was on the wane in the 1930s, the year 1933 had seen brutal acts of burning, dragging and dismembering in Maryland and Texas, and the late 1930s saw the use of blowtorches in the lynchings of Tom McGehee in Mississippi, Willie Reed and John Dukes, both in Georgia.[53] Furthermore, he noted that 'racial violence was no stranger' to his native Oklahoma.[54] Ellison sought to understand how ritualistic violence of the mob functioned as a symbolic compensation for poor Southern whites who 'lynched as one of the leading symbolic and ritualistic means of asserting their dominance'.[55] A purely economistic Marxism seemed unable to explain the psychological benefits that 'economically deprived Southern whites seemed to acquire when they organised into lynch mobs'.[56] Ellison sought alternative models of explanation and in addition to Kenneth Burke on symbolic action and (Welsh anthropologist) Lord Raglan's account of heroic sacrifice, Ellison was reading Frazer's Golden Bough alongside Freud's *Totem and Taboo* (which also drew on Frazer).[57] Faced with the history of racism and lynching Ellison, like Wittgenstein, rejected the evolutionist, teleological implications of Frazer's armchair anthropology with its clear sense of development from magic through religion to science. The narrator of *Invisible Man* warns us that the world moves '[n]ot like an arrow, but a boomerang', and that we should therefore '[k]eep a steel helmet handy'.[58] For Ellison and Wittgenstein alike, the primitive does not designate an early stage of society left behind by history. 'Primitive' forms of scapegoating were all too present.

This was a truth of which African American troops stationed in Britain during the war years were fully aware. African American journalist Roi Ottley noted that Americans from the South in particular feared 'that on his return the Negro will be mighty difficult to remold into the Jim Crow pattern'.[59] Returning African American soldiers described the ways in which 'in England a few of the narrow minded possibly Southern white American soldiers have already poisoned the mind of a few of the British people toward us', and a Mississippi Black Veteran remembered that the first obstacle he faced overseas was an idea implanted in the British mind by white GIs that blacks were so low on the evolutionary scale that they had tails that appeared at night.[60] Ralph Ellison has one of his characters recount a similar story in the conclusion to his story 'The Red Cross'. The narrative shifts from the main narrator to Doc at this point, and this technique of creating a story within the story creates a sense of dialogue and emphasises the collective nature of the African American GI's experience. Doc describes the way in which a group of Welshmen gathered around him in rural pub:

> I noticed that every time I'd have a round the folks would stand back and watch me a while, like they was waiting for something to happen. Finally I asked the man what the hell is

going on. First he acted embarrassed like, then he told me to wait a second. And man, next thing I know he's rapping for everybody to be quiet and making a speech. He gave them hell for even believing it.

Believing what? Well, what had happened was that before we were sent to that camp somebody had been around telling them folks not to have anything to do with us. They said that we was bad fellows and not fit to associate with. That was all. They hadn't ever seen any of us and they believed it."

"Oh no, that's not all", somebody else said. "You know that's not all. Tell him the rest."

"Why don't you be quiet?" he said. "Nobody believes the last part noway".

I asked him what it was people expected him to do.

"That's just it" he said reluctantly. "They was waiting for me to show my tail".

"Your tail?"

"See there", he said, "you don't believe it. But it's the truth. Whoever got there ahead of us told these people that whenever we got a little high we had a long black tail that would stick out behind."

"Why didn't you show it to the people, Doc?"

"Doc didn't say they brought him *that* much liquor".[61]

The humorous conclusion reflects the GIs' high spirits on a night out, but Ellison does not end the story on a comical note. One of the African Americans responds to Doc's story by stating 'seriously' that 'the people must have been mighty ignorant'. 'They wasn't no more ignorant than some of us when the army took us out of Alabama' is Doc's response.

4. The World and the Jug

The conclusion to 'The Red Cross at Morriston' suggests that cultural encounters need not result in conflict, that one culture has the ability to instruct another, correcting its prejudices and fostering understanding. Doc's consideration of the Welshman's ignorant and limited perspective is a characteristic of the shifting perspectives and attempted bridging of divides in Ellison's writing. This process of influence across 'forms of life' or 'language games' in the story relates to an area of disagreement in accounts of Wittgenstein's thought. Influential accounts of our contemporary 'postmodern condition' argue that the teleological grand narratives of modernity have collapsed, whether they be a belief in an evolutionary progress towards the common standards of consent (Friedrich Hayek, Karl Popper), or the view that the persistence of ethno-nationalisms and primitivist rituals indicate that modernity remains an 'unfinished project', yet to fulfil its whole potential (Jürgen Habermas).[62] In place of participation in the 'grand narratives' of the past, we are trapped, argues Jean-François Lyotard, in a plethora of Wittgensteinian 'language games'.[63] This analysis of the 1980s seems prophetic today as social media intensifies the sense that people are screaming at each other from predetermined subject positions within their isolated silos, as opposed to working towards consensus through dialogue. The Wittgenstein who underpins Lyotard's analysis believes, in Rod Mengham's lucid summary, that:

> everything we say belongs to one or another category of utterance, but never to more than one category. Every speaker or listener is a player in a game whose rules do not apply in any other games.[64]

Wittgenstein in this reading is the philosopher of limits and of impermeable boundaries. The result is that his philosophy leaves 'everything as it is', or 'simply ... underwrite[s] the commonplaces of ordinary parlance'.[65] Yet, given this analysis, it is striking how often Wittgenstein stresses transformation in language. Wittgenstein accepts that concepts can have 'blurred edges', for example.[66] Furthermore, 'diversity' in language, he notes, 'is not something fixed, given once for all; but new types of language, new language-games, as we may say, come into existence, and others become obsolete and get forgotten'.[67] Alice Crary and Doris Sommer argue that Wittgenstein is no 'quietist'; he is not one who interprets established practices as being unchangeable. Rather, he is 'a philosopher of human agency who enjoins us to leave prejudice behind and investigate how meanings are made'.[68]

This tension between a view of language games or forms of life as sealed entities, and the alternative that they are in some ways porous and have the ability to influence one another, offers an interesting context for discussing a well-known – if often misunderstood – debate between Ralph Ellison and critic Irving Howe regarding African American literature. In his essay 'Black Boys and Native Sons' (1963) Howe – a leading critic, author of several volumes on American and European literature and founder editor of the New Left's journal *Dissent* – used the exposure of racism and social ills that characterised the work of Richard Wright to chastise Ralph Ellison and James Baldwin for their alleged refusal to embrace 'protest' as an inevitable consequence of the 'Negro writer's' lived reality in America. Howe reads 'Black literature' as a distinctive canon, a 'category of utterance' or 'language game' with its own rules. Even the aesthete Ellison, argued Howe, could not escape from 'being caught up with the idea of the Negro'.[69] Howe speaks in the voice of a critical meta-language; a position of objective knowledge from which to comment on all other uses of language. The following passage reflects Howe's ability to identify the various voices present in Ellison's Invisible Man, and from there to generalise about the African American condition.

> There is a great deal of superbly rendered speech: a West Indian woman inciting men to resist an eviction, a Southern sharecropper calmly describing how he seduced his daughter, a Harlem streetvendor spinning jive. The rhythm of Ellison's prose is harsh and nervous, like a beat of harried alertness. The observation is expert: he knows exactly how zootsuiters walk, making stylization their principle of life, and exactly how the antagonism between American and West Indian Negroes works itself out in speech and humor. He can accept his people as they are, in their blindness and hope: – here, finally, the Negro world does exist, seemingly apart from plight or protest. And in the final scene Ellison has created an unforgettable image: 'Ras the Destroyer', a Negro nationalist, appears on a horse dressed in the costume of an Abyssinian chieftain, carrying spear and shield, and charging wildly into the police – a black Quixote, mad, absurd, pathetic.
> But even Ellison cannot help being caught up with the idea of the Negro. To write simply about "Negro experience" with the esthetic distance urged by the critics of the fifties, is

a moral and psychological impossibility, for plight and protest are inseparable from that experience, and even if less political than Wright and less prophetic than Baldwin, Ellison knows this quite as well as they do.[70]

Ellison did indeed 'know this' but, in a response entitled 'The World and the Jug', felt it curious that Howe should deny 'esthetic distance' to the Black writer, while adopting an 'Olympian' distance of his own in mounting his critique.[71] Howe, argued Ellison, was presumptively denying African Americans the capacity to adapt and adopt modes of expression from beyond the parameters of Black culture. If one of Wittgenstein's essential observations is that there is no metalanguage – that analysing language by means of language is an impossibility akin to a 'tin opener slic[ing] itself open' – then Ellison draws attention to the hidden particularity of Howe's seemingly disinterested critical voice.[72] If Howe could be prescriptive about the obligations of the 'Negro writer', he made no such claims about Jewish American writers. Howe had, and would, write extensively about the Jewish-American experience elsewhere, but had rendered that identity invisible when writing about African American literature in 'Black Boys and Native Sons'. Ellison thus seeks to unmask the particular background hidden by Howe's adoption of a universalist position:

> If I would know who I am and preserve who I am, then I must see others distinctly whether they see me so or no. Thus I feel uncomfortable whenever I discover Jewish intellectuals writing as though they were guilty of enslaving my grandparents, or as though the Jews were responsible for the system of segregation [...] Speaking personally, both as a writer and as Negro American, I would like to see the more positive distinctions between whites and Jewish Americans maintained. Not only does it make for a necessary bit of historical and social clarity, at least where Negroes are concerned, but I consider the United States freer politically and richer culturally because there are Jewish Americans to bring it the benefit of their special forms of dissent, their humour and their gift for ideas which are based upon the uniqueness of their experience.[73]

If the richness of America derives from the diversity of its people and their unique histories, Ellison also emphasises 'the basic unity of human experience that assures us of some possibility of empathetic and symbolic identification with those of other backgrounds'.[74] He draws attention to the 'performance of the slaves in re-creating themselves, in good, part, out of images and myths of Old Testament Jews'.[75] Wright 'was no father of mine' notes Ellison for culture does not conform to geographical or racial divisions. In 'Macon County, Alabama', he notes, 'I read Marx, Freud, T. S. Eliot, Pound, Gertrude Stein and Hemingway. Books which seldom, if ever, mentioned Negroes were to release me from whatever "segregated" idea I might have had of my human possibilities'.[76]

It is in relation to this argument that Ellison introduces his notorious distinction between 'relatives' (those who are 'given', of whom one has no choice) and 'ancestors' (who the writer can choose). Richard Wright and Langston Hughes are his 'relatives', notes Ellison, while Hemingway, Eliot, Dostoyevsky and Faulkner are 'ancestors'. 'Consult the text!' was Ellison's instruction to Howe, for then he would see that 'I sought out Wright because I had read Eliot, Pound, Gertrude Stein and Hemingway'.[77] If Ellison challenged Howe's generalising by suggesting that the text be consulted, Wittgenstein seldom insisted on anything so vehemently as when, in the face of homogenising generalisations, he instructed his readers 'don't think, but look!'

> Don't say: 'There must be something common, or they would not be called games' – but *look and see* whether there is anything common at all.[78]

If Ellison spoke in terms of 'ancestors' and 'relatives', Wittgenstein spoke in terms of 'family resemblances'.[79] What we see if we look closely is that games do not in fact have something in common, notes Wittgenstein, nothing that unites the sheer plethora of activities designated by the word 'game'; a word that designated activities from solitary card games to mass competitive games. The concept 'game' relies on a range of 'family resemblances', a criss-crossing without an essential core. The word 'game' thus resembles a thread, where 'the strength of the thread resides not in the fact that some one fibre runs through its whole length, but in the overlapping of many fibres'.[80]

Strange Country: Cosmopolitan Particularism

Wittgenstein's meditation on the multiple uses of terms sheds light on Ellison's thought on the literary canon. Ellison questions Howe's tendency to read *Invisible Man* in relation to works by other Black writers. Indeed, in the years of the Civil Rights Movement, he sees Howe perpetrating in the realm of culture the segregation that is being challenged in society.[81] Howe's attempt at identifying that which is distinctive about African American is similar to the claims of distinctiveness made by Black nationalists and later formulators of an African American literary canon. From this perspective, the critique of Howe could be read as evidence of Ellison's assimilationism. Writing from a militant class perspective, Ernest Kaiser described Ellison as 'an Establishment writer, an Uncle Tom, an attacker of the sociological formulations of the Black freedom movement', and 'a denigrator of the great tradition of Black protest writing'.[82] Speaking of a 'New York Literary Establishment' that was 'afraid of the competition from a wave of young 1960s African American writers', Ishmael Reed viewed Ellison an establishment figure whose 'job was to keep the natives down, a designated role that he played for forty years'.[83] For Black Nationalist Addison Gayle Jr., Ellison 'bought the propaganda of the academic critics, accepted the image of the faceless, universal man, trapped in the narrow world of his own ego' along with 'the modern idea of a raceless world'. Gayle despaired over *Invisible Man*'s 'assimilationist denouement'.[84] But Ellison's foregrounding of Howe's Jewish-American identity, and desire that it be preserved, indicates that he was no assimilationist. In rejecting Howe's insistence on reading his work in relation to other African American writers, and in emphasising the personal choice of ancestral influence, Ellison may be seen to jettison the idea of a consistent 'core' and, as with Wittgenstein's metaphor of the thread, to be emphasising the criss-crossing multiplicity of influences and resemblances within the literary canon. Having said that, just as this multiplicity does not render the term 'game' redundant, or the thread unwound, neither does Ellison wish to do away with the cultural distinctiveness of African Americans.

Indeed, Ellison believed that the African American community was culturally distinct. In his letters to the African American critic and novelist Albert Murray in particular, Ellison speaks in a distinctive Black voice that he would refer to as 'the idiom'.[85] Drawing on African American usage of the Exodus story, Ellison spoke of 'bringing the mose view' to bear on America, and his letters are often humorously chauvinistic (and occasionally, unfortunately, homophobic) such as when he tells Murray to ignore the establishment critics and 'Stick to mose, Man. He's got more life in his toenails than these zombies have in their whole bodies.'[86] He explained the lack of appreciation received by Melville's *Moby-Dick* by the fact that 'the thing's full of riffs; no wonder the book weren't understood in its own time, not enough moses were able to read it!' Ellison turned down an opportunity to teach at Brandeis University on the basis that he wouldn't enjoy 'living in an environment in which there are no Moses'. While living in rural New York with Saul Bellow, he regretted that 'there are no Moses to keep me tuned in', and while in Rome he required the company of his Duke Ellington and Count Basie records to recreate 'my only true atmosphere'. After an evening of entertaining others he would retire to his records in order to feel a 'little less lonely. I'd heard the idiom and relived a bit of the past – which is really the same thing.'[87]

Timothy Parrish suggests that 'Ellison could not resolve the conflict between his public positions on art and aesthetic integration and what seem to have been his private attitudes toward community and identity'.[88] It may perhaps be more accurate to suggest that the dominant binaries informing social thought – assimilationism vs particularism, purity vs hybridity, isolation vs interaction – are inadequate if we are to accurately describe Ellison's position. Deploying his titular metaphor, Ellison argues that Howe

> seems to see segregation as a steel jug with the Negroes waiting for some black messiah to come along and blow the cork. [...] But if we are in a jug it is transparent, not opaque, and one is allowed not only to see outside, but to read what is going on out there; to make identifications as to values and human quality.[89]

Those who interpret Ellison's position as that of an assimilationist or integrationist ignore the fact that he is not doing away with the jug. The jug, the container of cultural particularity, remains and can itself sustain its own internal diversity. Ralph Ellison wondered with some exasperation 'why is it that so many of those who would tell us the meaning of Negro life never bother to learn how varied it really is?'[90]

While sustaining its own inner diversity, the jug is also transparent. Inhabitants within the jug can see and respond to what is happening outside its transparent walls, with the result that, in Wittgenstein's words, 'new types of language, new language-games, as we may say, come into existence, and others become obsolete and get forgotten'.[91] Ellison's jug may be usefully related to Wittgenstein's 'form of life'; both offer a frame for pluralism and a basis for a respecting other particularities within the broader context of the interactions and influences that constitute the human family.

5. Acknowledging Otherness

Given my attempt above to trace similarities in their thought, it is striking that critiques of Wittgenstein and Ellison often seem to be mirror images of one another. In the case of Wittgenstein, his acknowledgment of transformation and change is ignored as he becomes viewed as a defender of boundaries, within the confines of which 'any internal elimination or addition of one game by another' is precluded. The duty of the philosopher for Wittgenstein, according to this misleading reading, is 'the stability of the set'.[92] In the case of Ellison, it is his commitment to the jug, to the bounded particularity of the African American form of life, that is occluded, with even sympathetic critics – let alone his nationalist detractors – viewing him a 'militant integrationist'.[93] Commentators and critics seem unwilling to allow for a position that argues for the integrity of particularistic language games *and* for the possible impact and influence of one form of life on another. The case for a particularism that co-exists with a cosmopolitan universalism fails, it seems, to convince.

The problem, perhaps, lies in the question of influence; by what mechanism can one culture or 'form of life' impact another without that entailing some form of assimilation? 'To bring the foundation of a certain linguistic game to the surface' notes Paolo Virno, 'is the only way to move gradually onto a different game, one governed by a different set of rules'.[94] Comparison is presumably one way of bringing one language game into dialogue with another, of exposing the foundational rules of one game, and in extreme cases of potentially replacing them with a different set altogether. Yet, cultural comparison is only possible if there is mutual accessibility between cultures at the cognitive level. There is a danger here that we fall into the trap that Wittgenstein identified in the work of James Frazer; that we make the practices of others plausible to people who think as we do.[95] On the other hand, there's the potential inability to recognise another culture at all. To express acknowledgment and sympathy, or to criticise, entails a mutuality between cultures or selves. Stefan Collini notes that even the most hostile critics require a 'bridgehead' or 'some commonality of values' with the objects of their scorn if their views are 'to gain any purchase at all'.[96] A. C. Grayling makes the same point in a more philosophical vein when he notes that 'if we are to talk of "other forms of life" at all we must be able to recognize them as such; we must be able to recognise the existence of practices which go to make up a form of life'.[97] Moreover, 'if we are to see that another form of life is different from our own we have to be able to recognize the differences; this is only possible if we can interpret enough of the other form of life to make those differences apparent'.[98] Is there a way of expressing sympathy or dissatisfaction with what Wittgenstein described as the 'rough ground' of particularistic forms of life, without drawing on transcendent and universal standards that pose a challenge to all particularisms?[99]

Wittgenstein raises this issue in relation to our understanding of 'pain'. Firstly, he distinguishes between my pain and that of others in relation to everyday language. Can I 'know' that I am in pain? In ordinary usage, this question is not asked as my pain, for me, is beyond doubt. Yet I can not be so sure about the pain of others. Here some doubt does exist, yet the phrase 'I know that you are in pain' can be sensibly uttered. The basis for such knowledge is unclear.[100] Are we reliant on the 'performance' of pain – grimaces, screams and so forth – on what Wittgenstein describes as 'pain-behaviour'.[101] This can only be said of 'a living human being' and it is only of 'what resembles (behaves like) a living human being can one say: it has sensations; it sees; [...] is conscious or unconscious'.[102] The suggestion seems to be that there is a universal humanity for whom external actions are expressive of internal consciousness. Yet,

> [c]ould someone who had *never* felt pain understand the word 'pain'? – Is experience to teach me whether this is so or not? – And if we say 'A man could not imagine pain without having

sometime felt it', how do we know? How can it be decided whether it's true?[103]

When he talks about 'pain', it is clear here that Wittgenstein is not primarily interested in matters of epistemological fact. Stanley Cavell suggests that Wittgenstein 'does not negate the concluding thesis of scepticism, that we do not know with certainty the existence [...] of other minds'.[104] Indeed, Cavell argues that Wittgenstein affirms this thesis, but turns attention to the fact that the 'fundamental importance of someone's having pain is that he has it; and that he is suffering, that he requires attention'.[105] Doris Sommer notes that the acknowledgement of other language games can fail 'because of our underdeveloped skills for hearing differential meanings', and it seems that Wittgenstein encourages us to notice those differentials that signify and matter.[106] To say 'I know you are in pain' is then not an expression of certainty, but of acknowledgement and sympathy. Yet in learning to hear those differentials are we, inevitably, becoming more alike? Does the acknowledgement of the Other become, over time, a denial of difference and a threat to pluralism?

These questions are raised with dramatic and complex form in Ellison's writings. The protagonist of 'A Storm of Blizzard Proportions', speaking of Wales and the United States respectively, finds that 'to love this land was to more deeply love the land which gave one pain'.[107] 'In a Strange Country' dramatises this process where encountering Wales leads to a greater identification with America. The story's opening traces the ebb and flow of identification and alienation, indifference and acknowledgement. Bumping into someone in blackout conditions, Parker registers their expression of shock – 'Jesus H. Christ' – and recognises the accent. He realises that he's knocked 'someone from home', so grins and apologises 'into the light they flashed in his eyes'. Their response is to yell 'It's a goddamn nigger' before beating him up.[108] A not wholly dissimilar scene occurs, more famously, in the opening pages of *Invisible Man*. The 'invisibility to which I refer' states the narrator of the novel's 'Prologue':

> occurs because of a peculiar disposition of the eyes of those with whom I come in contact. A matter of the construction of their *inner* eyes, those eyes with which they look through their physical eyes upon reality. I am not complaining, nor am

I protesting either. It is sometimes advantageous to be unseen, although it is most often rather wearing on the nerves. Then too, you're constantly being bumped against those of poor vision. Or again, you often doubt if you really exist.[109]

As Anne Anlin Cheng notes, Ellison locates identity 'not in uncompromising individualism, but in painful interpersonal negotiations'.[110] Here, the narrator does not attempt to acknowledge or define the other. He does not question the other's experience but asks why his own experience is rendered invisible. The shift in perspective is striking in a scenario that dramatises a question asked by Wittgenstein:

> Could there be human beings lacking the ability to see something *as something* – and what would that be like? What sort of consequences would it have? – Would the defect be comparable to colour-blindness [...] ?[111]

The emphasis on sight resonates with Ellison's description, and recalls an earlier observation of Wittgenstein's that if 'someone has a pain in his hand [...] one does not comfort the hand, but the sufferer: one looks into his eyes'.[112] The result of this empathetic look is 'pity' which 'one might say, is one form of being convinced that someone else is in pain'.[113] Yet the eyes of the dominant society are blind to the African American experience in Ellison's encounter. The acknowledgment that Cavell believes central to Wittgenstein's meditations on pain and human sympathy, is denied. On the other hand, and paradoxically, African American distinctiveness is maintained as a result of its invisibility in the eyes of the dominant society.[114]

This Emersonian play between 'eye' and 'I' in *Invisible Man* is also present in Ellison's Wales-based short stories.[115] Parker initially incudes the Welsh 'in his blind range' in 'In a Strange Country' before acknowledging that 'they're a different breed; even from the English'.[116] The story anticipates *Invisible Man* in that it is saturated by symbols of sight and blindness. Upon entering a club with his Welsh hosts the light strikes Parker's injured eye 'as though it were being peeled by an invisible hand'. The story's exploration of the layers of identity that constitute the African American self – the black 'I' – reaches a conclusion with the performance of a series of anthems.[117]

When the opening bars were struck, he saw the others pushing back their chairs and standing, and he stood, understanding even as Mr. Catti whispered, "Our national anthem".

There was something in the music and in the way they held their heads that was strangely moving. He hummed beneath his breath. When it was over he would ask for the words.

But even while he heard the final triumphal chord still sounding, the piano struck up "God Save the King." It was not nearly so stirring. Then swiftly modulating they swept into the "Internationale", to words about an international army. He was carried back to when he was a small boy marching in the streets behind the bands that came to his southern town ...

Mr Catti had nudged him. He looked up, seeing the conductor looking straight at him, smiling. They were all looking at him. Why, was it his eye? Were they playing a joke? And suddenly he recognized the melody and felt that his knees would give way. It was as though he had been pushed into the horrible foreboding country of dreams and they were enticing him into some unwilled and degrading act, from which only his failure to remember the words would save him. Only now the melody seemed charged with some vast new meaning which that part of him that wanted to sing could not fit with the old familiar words. And beyond the music he kept hearing the soldiers' voices, yelling as they had when the light struck his eye. He saw the singers still staring, and as though to betray him he heard his own voice singing out like a suddenly amplified radio:

> "... Gave proof through the night
> That our flag was still there ..."

It was like the voice of another over whom he had no control. His eye throbbed. A wave of guilt shook him, followed by a burst of relief. For the first time in your whole life, he thought with dreamlike wonder, the words are not ironic. He stood in confusion as the song ended, staring into the men's Welsh faces, not knowing whether to curse them or to return their good-natured smiles.[118]

Ellison's comparativist impulse results in his awareness of the range of identities being embraced simultaneously by a national minority within the British state. The plurality of identities expressed by the Welsh choir – from Welsh distinctiveness to Britishness to Socialist Internationalism – creates a space where Parker can ultimately, with 'The Star-Spangled Banner' as a background, identify himself as an American. Yet this affirmative reading is not wholly convincing as a sense of guilt and ambivalence is also communicated. If the gesture of the 'look' is inseparable from the documentary strategy of Ellison's semi-autobiographical short stories, this passage revolves around forms of blindness (thus offering an ironic gloss on the opening words of the US anthem, 'O say can you see'). In failing to recognise that their Black guest may not wish to identify with the 'Star Spangled Banner', the Welsh are in a sense blind to American racism. Yet in that blindness, they give voice to the unfulfilled promise of American democracy. The story's resolution remains far from clear. Parker joins the singing in the 'voice of another', and a 'wave of guilt' shakes him, followed by the relief of feeling that for the first time 'the words are not ironic'. There's clearly a change in consciousness here as 'his eye throbbed'. If we follow Wittgenstein's meditations on the meaning of words, such a shift would also indicate a transformation in the 'form of life' or 'language game'. The scene may exemplify the way on which comparison engenders change. The juxtaposition of Welsh and African American perspectives results in the 'foundation of a certain linguistic game' (that of American racism and segregation) being exposed, and therefore opens the possibility of a 'move gradually onto a different game, one governed by a different set of rules' (that of a more capacious, colour-blind democracy).[119]

If there can be acknowledgment and mutual influence between language games, then Wittgenstein is not the quietist who 'devotes much acumen and space to the analysis of "My broom is in the corner"'.[120] African American philosopher Cornel West recalls reacting negatively to such dismissals, for he 'was impressed by the contextualism' that he 'detected in the *Philosophical Investigations*. It opens itself on to a broader historical reading, even though Wittgenstein himself didn't do it'.[121] In wartime Wales, Ralph Ellison may be seen to offer that historical contextualism in short stories that engage in fictional form with a number of concerns that he shares with Wittgenstein. The connecting anthem, between those of Wales, Britain and America is the Internationale which takes Parker back to boyhood memories of 'marching in the streets behind the bands that came to his southern town'.[122] The anthem of international Communism thus connects the anthems of Wales and Britain with the anthem of the United States. Barbara Foley suggests that 'In a Strange Country' is 'embedded in the discourse of CPUSA [the Communist Party of the United States] politics', which had adopted the policy of 'a Black Belt nation' along the lines of the Soviet Union's support for folk languages and cultures on its non-Russian republics.[123] Similarly, the British Communist Party recognised the right for Welsh self-determination in 1939.[124] The use of the 'Internationale' as a means of connecting the Welsh and British anthems with the American anthem reinforces a connection made earlier in the story between Wales and Russia:

> And as the men sang in hushed tones [Parker] felt a growing poverty of spirit. He should have known more of the Welsh, of their history and art. [...] [I]n his mind's eye he saw a Russian peasant kneeling to kiss the earth and rising wet-eyed to enter into battle with cries of fierce exultation.[125]

Writing to Senora Babb, Ellison noted that the Welsh were 'like the Russians' in being 'a mature people while we Americans are in painful adolescence'.[126] The connections between the Welsh, Russians and African Americans in his native 'southern town' creates a transnational web of connections between folk cultures. Such connections were being fostered at the time by America's leading Communist-affiliated performer, the bass baritone Paul Robeson who supplemented his performances of spirituals with an array of folk songs from the mid-1930s onwards.[127] Indeed, this final scene of 'In a Strange Country' could have been lifted from the film of 1940, *Proud Valley*, in which Robeson plays an African American miner who settles in south Wales. That Welsh folk songs remind Parker of Russia, and that the 'Internationale' functions as a link between the Welsh and American anthems, suggest that 'In a Strange Country' is embedded in the 'form of life' of a Popular Front internationalism that emerged in the 1930s and continued to inform Ellison's thought in the early 1940s.[128]

Ellison would later offer a searing critique of the Communist Party in the shape of the 'Brotherhood' in *Invisible Man*, and was deeply critical of Paul Robeson's views on African Americans and Africa which he viewed as 'neo-Garveyism from a wealthy singer'.[129] But as we saw in his debate with Howe, the simultaneous commitment to the cultural particularism of the jug within a wider universalism continued to inform his work. Michael Denning has suggested that Cold War liberalism was 'the Popular Front without Communists'.[130] While Ellison had expunged the Communist and Socialist content of his thought by the 1950s, its structure in relation to the legitimacy of minoritarian identities within a broader international web of connections remained intact. 'The role of the writer', he argued at West Point in 1969, 'is to structure fiction which will allow a universal identification, while at the same time not violating the specificity of the particular experience and the particular character'.[131]

6. Conclusion

In his simultaneous commitment to 'universal identification' and 'particular experience', Ralph Ellison offers a succinct expression of the cosmopolitan particularism that this chapter has sought to both explore and substantiate. Though there is no evidence that Ellison read Wittgenstein, there is (as I hope to argue in the future) a Wittgensteinian thread that informs this structure of thought in the post war years. The earlier Wittgenstein of the *Tractatus Logico-Philosophicus* comprehended the world as a 'whole', a bounded realm of 'facts': 'The World is all that is the case'.[132] Slavoj Žižek, among others, notes that every 'whole' presupposes 'an exception'. In the case of the early Wittgenstein this exception was the 'mystical ineffable'; those ethical and theological questions that lie beyond language and which function as its limit. In the *Philosophical Investigations* the universe is no longer comprehended as 'a whole regulated by the universal conditions of language'. It is, rather, made of 'lateral connections between partial domains'.[133] This shift in perspective also entails a shift in tone. Several critics have noted that whereas Wittgenstein adopted a voice in the *Tractatus* that spoke in direct assertions and logical propositions with no space for dissent, *Philosophical Investigations* contains voices in dialogue and is therefore less assertive and more exploratory in approach. The notion of language as a system defined by a set of universal features is thus replaced by the notion of language as a plurality of dispersed practices with their meaning deriving from their use within the rituals, gestures and extra-linguistic practices of broader 'forms of life'.

It is in relation to this pluralisation that the figure of the stranger appears as a teasing interlocutor in the *Philosophical Investigations*. Like T. S. Eliot's stranger in 'Choruses from "The Rock"', this figure asks questions and seeks answers. We can assume that Eliot's stranger did not have Swansea in mind when he asked about 'the meaning of this city?' Indeed, Swansea appears in Eliot's 'The Function of Criticism' (1923) as a place where 'those who ride ten in a compartment to a football match at Swansea' contribute to a mass culture characterised by 'the eternal message of vanity, fear and lust'.[134] If the city functions metonymically for unthinking provincial homogeneity in Eliot's essay, both Wittgenstein and Ellison encountered a Swansea characterised by internal difference and diversity. It is, perhaps, appropriate that Abertawe/Swansea proved a significant context for the development of a strain of thought that allowed 'for universal identification' while respecting 'the specificity of the particular experience'. For according to Dylan Thomas, the city's most famous son (absent from his home town in January 1944), the ocean that carried Ralph Ellison to the shores of Wales and that Ludwig Wittgenstein appreciated on his coastal walks, was a 'two-tongued sea'.[135]

Notes

1 T. S Eliot, 'Choruses from "The Rock"', *Collected Poems 1909–1962* (London: Faber and Faber, 1963), pp. 170–1.
2 Quoted in John Davies, *A History of Wales* (London Penguin, 2007 [1990]), p. 580. See also Deirdre Beddoe, *Out of the Shadows: A History of Women in Twentieth-Century Wales* (Cardiff: University of Wales Press, 2000), p. 126.
3 I offer a detailed account and analysis of Ralph Ellison in Wales in 'The Invisible Man's Welsh Routes: Ralph Ellison in Wartime Wales', *Black Skin, Blue Books: African Americans and Wales 1845–1945* (Cardiff: University of Wales Press, 2012), pp. 208–52. Phil Treseder of Swansea Museum, has done further work on the *Sun Yat Sen*. See his blog entry here: http://www.swanseamuseum.co.uk/blog/black-history-month-ralph-waldo-ellison (Accessed 1 July 2023).
4 Ralph Ellison, 'The Red Cross in Morriston, Swansea, S.W.' Several Drafts. The Ralph Ellison Papers. Library of Congress, Washington DC. Box 165. Files 3 and 7. This introductory material is omitted from later drafts of the story but offer a fascinating account of Ellison's first encounters

with Wales. I am grateful to Professor John F. Callahan, executor of the Estate of Ralph Ellison, for allowing me to quote from the unpublished short stories.

5 Alfred Schmidt, '"It is good to be away from Cambridge and to be here and among friendly people": Wittgenstein's letters to Ben Richards and his philosophical work in Swansea'. Presentation at the *Ludwig Wittgenstein: An Austrian in Swansea* conference, Swansea University, 16 June 2022.

6 Ralph Ellison, *The Selected Letters of Ralph Ellison*, ed. John F. Callahan (New York: Random House, 2019), pp. 194–5, 734–5, 994. Ralph Ellison, William Styron, Robert Penn Warren and C. Vann Woodward, 'The Uses of History in Fiction' (A panel discussion at the thirty-fourth meeting of the Southern Historical Association in New Orleans, 6 November 1968), *The Southern Literary Journal*, 1/2 (Spring, 1969), 73. I am grateful to Martin Davies for drawing my attention to this. See Schmitt for the dates of Wittgenstein's visits.

7 Ray Monk, *Ludwig Wittgenstein: The Duty of Genius* (London, Vintage, 1991 [1990]). Lawrence Jackson, *Ralph Ellison: The Emergence of Genius* (New York: John Wiley and Sons, 2002).

8 John Moran 'Wittgenstein and Russia', *New Left Review*, 1/73 (May/June 1972), 85–96. Barbara Foley, *Wrestling with the Left: The Making of Ralph Ellison's* Invisible Man (Durham: Duke University Press, 2010).

9 Jackson, *Ralph Ellison*, p. 155.

10 Terry Eagleton, 'Wittgenstein's Friends', *New Left Review*, 1/135 (September/October 1982), 86. See also David Edmonds and John Eidinow, *Wittgenstein's Poker: the story of a ten-minute argument between two great philosophers* (London: Faber, 2001), p. 155.

11 Monk, *Ludwig Wittgenstein*, pp. 458–70.

12 Wittgenstein, 'Letter to Rush Rhees: 5 June 1948' in *Wittgenstein in Cambridge: Letters and Documents, 1911–1951*, ed. Brian McGuinness (Oxford: Wiley Blackwell, 2011), p. 421.

13 Ludwig Wittgenstein, 'Letter to Ben Richards', 28 July 1946 (Austrian National Library. 1840/5-1 HAN). 'Letter to Norman Malcolm', 15 December 1945. Quoted in Monk, *Ludwig Wittgenstein*, p. 459.

14 Ralph Ellison, 'Letter to Senora Babb', 18 August 1944. Ralph Ellison Papers, Library of Congress. Quoted in Arnold Rampersad, *Ralph Ellison: A Biography* (New York: Vintage, 2008 [2007]), pp. 170–1.

15 Ellison, 'The Red Cross'.

16 Quoted in Edmonds and Eidinow, *Wittgenstein's Poker*, p. 105. See Monk, *Ludwig Wittgenstein*, pp. 394–400. Most deprivations of citizenship for German Jews took place under the 25 November 1941 'Eleventh Decree to the Law on the Citizenship of the Reich', which automatically stripped all Jewish Germans of their German citizenship if they had taken up residence abroad.

17 See Edmonds and Eidinow, *Wittgenstein's Poker*, p. 105.

18 See Edmonds and Eidinow, *Wittgenstein's Poker*, p. 108. Monk, *Ludwig Wittgenstein*, p. 400.
19 Ralph Ellison, 'In a Strange Country' in *Flying Home and Other Stories* (London: Penguin, 1998 [1996]), p. 139.
20 'This American Red Cross Centre is Strictly Jim Crow', *The Crisis*, 50/3 (March 1943), 76–7.
21 Ellison, 'Letter to Mr. G. A. Smith: March 20, 1977', *Selected Letters*, p. 734.
22 Wittgenstein, *Philosophical Investigations*, trans. G. E. M. Anscombe, P. M. S. Hacker and Joachim Schulte (Oxford: Wiley-Blackwell, 2009 [1953]), 206 (henceforth PI followed by section number).
23 Wittgenstein, 'Philosophy of Psychology' (Previously known as *Philosophical Investigations Part II*) in *Philosophical Investigations*, 325.
24 PI §123.
25 PI, pp. 3–4.
26 Alfred Schmidt, *Ludwig Wittgenstein: An Austrian in Swansea* conference, Swansea University, 16 June 2022.
27 Alfred Schmidt, *Ludwig Wittgenstein: An Austrian in Swansea* conference, Swansea University, 16 June 2022.
28 Callahan, 'Introduction' to *Flying Home and Other Stories* (1996. London: Penguin, 1998), p. xxxvi.
29 Ralph Ellison, 'Introduction' to *Invisible* Man (New York: Vintage, 1995 [1981]), p. xiv.
30 Ellison, 'In a Strange Country', p. 142.
31 Davies, *A History of Wales*, pp. 588–9.
32 On the war context and the rise of Labour, see Kenneth Morgan, 'Power and Glory: War and Reconstruction, 1939–1951', in Deian Hopkin, Duncan Tanner and Chris Williams (eds), *The Labour Party in Wales 1900–2000* (Cardiff: University of Wales Press, 2000), pp. 166–88.
33 Davies, *A History of Wales*, pp. 575, 585–6. The 'Welsh Region' was re-established in 1945.
34 Quoted in Davies, *A History of Wales*, p. 585. Gruffydd was primarily concerned about the effects of evacuees from English cities.
35 The comment appears on an unpaginated page of typescript beginning, 'He sat now in the Red Cross Club and gazed into the glowing coals ...'. Ralph Ellison, 'A Storm of Blizzard Proportions'. Several Drafts. The Ralph Ellison Papers. Library of Congress, Washington DC. Box 165. File 7.
36 Ellison, 'The Red Cross'.
37 Quoted by Alfred Schmitt in a paper at the *Ludwig Wittgenstein: An Austrian in Swansea* conference, 16 June 2022. The Welsh means 'I wish you every success in the New Year'.
38 Quoted by Dewi Z. Phillips in 'Rush Rhees: A Biographical Sketch', in Rush Rhees, *Wittgenstein and the Possibility of Discourse*, ed. D. Z. Phillips (Oxford, Blackwell, 2006), p. 273.

39 PI §23.
40 Michael Sandel, *Liberalism and the Limits of Justice* (Cambridge: Cambridge University Press, 1982) p. 179. Sandel is quoted by Kwame Anthony Appiah, *The Ethics of Identity* (New Jersey: Princeton University Press, 2005), p. 46.
41 Rush Rhees, *Discussions of Wittgenstein* (London: Routledge and Kegan Paul, 1970), p. 51. See Ludwig Wittgenstein, *Culture and Value*, ed. G. H. von Wright, trans. Peter Winch (Oxford: Basil Blackwell, 1980), p. 37e. Michael North offers an illuminating analysis in *Reading 1922: A Return to the Scene of the Modern* (Oxford: Oxford University Press, 1999), pp. 39–64.
42 Michael North suggests that there is an 'intimate connection' between the anthropological emphasis and 'that other modern preoccupation, the feeling of social rootlessnes'. Michael North, *Reading 1922*, p. 64. See also Greg Chase, *Wittgenstein and Modernist Fiction: The Language of Acknowledgment* (London: Anthem Press, 2022), p. 67.
43 Wittgenstein, 'Remarks on Frazer's *Golden Bough*', in *Philosophical Occasions, 1912–1951*, ed. James C. Klagge and Alfred Nordmann (Indianaoplis: Hackett, 1993), pp. 115–55.
44 See the discussion in Chase, *Wittgenstein and Modernist Fiction*, pp. 61–5.
45 Wittgenstein, 'Remarks on Frazer', p. 119.
46 Chase, *Wittgenstein and Modernist Fiction*, p. 64.
47 Wolfram Eilenberger, *Time of the Magicians: Wittgenstein, Benjamin, Cassirer, Heidegger and the Decade that Reinvented Philosophy* (New York: Penguin, 2020), p. 359.
48 Quoted in Rush Rhees, 'Postscript', in *Recollections of Wittgenstein*, ed. Rush Rhees (Oxford: Oxford University Press, 1984), p. 201.
49 Luke Gibbons, 'Coast-Modernism: Wittgenstein, Primitivism, and the West of Ireland', in Clara Fischer and Áine Mahon (eds), *Philosophical Perspectives on Contemporary Ireland* (New York: Routledge, 2020), p. 186.
50 Gibbons, 'Coast-Modernism, p. 180.
51 Wittgenstein, 'Remarks on Frazer', p. 131.
52 M. O'Connor Drury, 'Conversations with Wittgenstein', in *The Selected Writings of Maurice O'Connor Drury: On Wittgenstein, Philosophy, Religion and Psychiatry* (London: Bloomsbury, 2017), p. 121.
53 Ashraf H. A. Rushdy, *The End of American Lynching* (New Brunswick: Rutgers University Press, 2012), p. 93.
54 Ellison, 'Letter to Stewart Lillard' (28 August 1973), *Selected Letters*, p. 711.
55 Lawrence Jackson, *Ralph Ellison: Emergence of Genius* (New York: John Wiley and Sons, 2002), p. 196.
56 Donald E. Pease, 'Ralph Ellison and Kenneth Burke: The Nonsymbolizable (Trans)Action', *boundary 2*, 30/2, (2003), 67.

57 Jackson, Emergence of Genius, p. 182. Arnold Rampersad, *Ralph Ellison: A Biography* (New York: Vintage, 2008 [2007]), p. 164. On Raglan, see Daniel G. Williams, *Black Skin, Blue Books*, pp. 236–8.
58 Ellison, *Invisible Man* (London: Penguin, 1965 [1952]), p. 9.
59 Roi Ottley, 'Ottley Reports on Negro-White Troop Relations', *PM*, Thursday, 21 September 1944, p. 10. Copy in Ralph Ellison Papers, Library of Congress. Box 203. File 12.
60 Quoted in Phillip McGuire, *Taps for a Jim Crow Army: Letters from Black Soldiers in World War II* (Oxford: ABC-Clio, 1983), p. 229. Neil R. McMillen, 'Fighting for What We Didn't Have: How Mississippi's Black Veterans Remember World War II', in Neil R. McMillen (ed.), *Remaking Dixie: The Impact of World War II on the American South* (Jackson: University Press of Mississippi, 1997), p. 97.
61 Ralph Ellison, 'The Red Cross in Morriston, Swansea, S.W.' This version is to be found in the Ralph Ellison Papers, Box 165. File 7.
62 Friedrich A. Hayek, *The Road to Serfdom* (London: Routledge, 1944). Karl Popper, *The Open Society and its Enemies* (London: Routledge, 1945). Jürgen Habermas, *Strukturwandel der Öffentlichkeit* (Darmstadt: Mermann Luchterhand, 1962). Translated as *The Structural Transformation of the Public Sphere: An Inquiry Into a Category of Bourgeois Society* (Cambridge: Polity Press, 1989).
63 Jean-François Lyotard, *The Postmodern Condition*, trans. Geoff Bennington (Manchester: Manchester University Press, 1984), p. 4.
64 Rod Mengham, *The Descent of Language* (London: Bloomsbury, 1993), p. 175.
65 'It [philosophy] leaves everything as it is' is Wittgenstein's own phrase. PI §124. Perry Anderson, *English Questions* (London: Verso, 1992), p. 66.
66 PI §71
67 PI §23
68 Alice Crary, 'Wittgenstein's Philosophy in Relation to Political Thought', *The New Wittgenstein*, ed. Alice Marguerite Crary and Rupert J. Read (New York: Routledge, 2000), pp. 118–45. The quotation is from Doris Sommer, *Bilingual Aesthetics: A New Sentimental Education* (Durham NC: Duke University Press, 2004), p. 162.
69 Irving Howe, 'Black Boys and Native Sons', *Dissent* (Autumn 1963), 353–368. Collected in Howe, *A World More Attractive: A View of Modern Literature and Politics* (New York: Horizon Press, 1963).
70 Howe, 'Black Boys and Native Sons', p. 363.
71 Originally published in two parts in *New Leader*. The first piece entitled 'The World and the Jug' appeared on 9 December 1963. Howe responded and received 'A Rejoinder' from Ellison in the edition of 3 February 1964. Collected in Ellison, *Shadow and Act* (New York: Quality Paperback Book Club, 1994 [1964]), pp. 107–143.
72 PI §120–4. See Marjorie Perloff, *Wittgenstein's Ladder: Poetic Language and the Strangeness of the Ordinary* (Chicago: University of Chicago

Press, 1996), pp. 71–2. The 'tin-opener' analogy is from Terry Eagleton, 'My Wittgenstein', in Eagleton, *The Eagleton Reader*, ed. Stephen Regan (Oxford: Blackwell, 1998), p. 336.
73 Ellison, 'World and the Jug', pp. 126–7.
74 Ellison, 'World and the Jug', p. 123.
75 Ellison, 'World and the Jug', p. 117.
76 Ellison, 'World and the Jug', p. 116.
77 Ellison, 'World and the Jug', p. 140.
78 PI §66 (italics in original). See also PI §340.
79 PI §67
80 PI §67
81 Ellison, 'World and the Jug', p. 115.
82 Ernest Kaiser, 'Negro Images in Negro Writing', *Freedomways*, 7/2 (Spring 1967), 152–63. The comments on Ellison are on p. 157. These comments are usually traced to Kaiser's 'A Critical Look at Ellison's Fiction and Social and Literary Criticism about the Author', *Black World*, 20/2 (December 1970), 95–7. But Kaiser was here repeating his analysis of three years earlier.
83 Ishmael Reed, *The Ishmael Reed Reader* (New York: Basic Books, 2000) p. xix.
84 Addison Gayle Jr., *The Way of the New World: The Black Novel in America* (Garden City, NY: Anchor Press, 1975), pp. 212–13.
85 Ellison, 'Letter to Albert Murray' (22 October 1955), *Selected Letters*, p. 390.
86 Ellison, 'Letter to Albert Murray' (1 February 1954), *Selected Letters*, p. 348.
87 Ellison, Letters to Albert Murray (12 April 1956, 28 July 1957), *Selected Letters*, pp. 431, 493–6.
88 Tim Parrish, 'Invisible Ellison: the fight to be a Negro leader', in Ross Posnock (ed.), *The Cambridge Companion to Ralph Ellison* (Cambridge: Cambridge University Press, 2005), p. 153.
89 Ellison, 'World and the Jug', p. 116.
90 Ellison, 'World and the Jug', p. 108.
91 PI §23
92 Anderson, *English Questions*, p. 67.
93 Henry Louis Gates Jr., *Thirteen Ways of Looking at a Black Man* (New York, Vintage, 1998 [1997]), p. 22.
94 Paolo Virno, *Multitude: Between Innovation and Negation*, trans. Isabella Bertoletti, James Cascaito and Andrea Casson (Los Angeles: Semiotexte, 2008), p. 129. Quoted by Gibbons, 'Coast-Modernism', p. 183.
95 Wittgenstein, 'Remarks on Frazer', p. 119.
96 Stefan Collini, *Speaking of Universities* (London: Verso, 2017), p. 223.
97 A. C. Grayling, *Wittgenstein: A Very Short Introduction* (Oxford: Oxford University Press, 2001 [1998]), p. 121.
98 Grayling, *Wittgenstein*, p. 121.

99 PI §107
100 PI §244–53.
101 PI §281
102 PI §281
103 PI §315.
104 Stanley Cavell, *The Claim of Reason: Wittgenstein, Skepticism, Morality and Tragedy* (Oxford: Oxford University Press, 1999 [1979]), p. 45.
105 Stanley Cavell, *Must We Mean What We Say?* (Cambridge: Cambridge University Press, 2002 [1969]), p. 245. See Greg Chase's lucid discussion in *Wittgenstein and Modernist Fiction*, pp. 12–13.
106 Doris Sommer, *Proceed with Caution when engaged by minority writing in the Americas* (Cambridge MA: Harvard University Press, 1999), p. 7.
107 Ralph Ellison, 'A Storm of Blizzard Proportions'. Several Drafts. The Ralph Ellison Papers. Library of Congress, Washington DC. Box 165. File 7. The 2016 edition of *Flying Home and Other Stories* includes the story.
108 Ellison, 'In a Strange Country, p. 138.
109 Ralph Ellison, *Invisible Man* (New York: Vintage, 1995 [1952]), pp. 3–4.
110 Anne Anlin Cheng, 'Ralph Ellison and the Politics of Melancholia', in *The Cambridge Companion to Ralph Ellison*, p. 135.
111 Wittgenstein, 'Philosophy of Psychology' (previously known as Philosophical Investigations Part II) in PI, 257.
112 PI 286.
113 PI 286.
114 One is reminded of the word 'neb' in Welsh, which can signify absence and presence simultaneously.
115 Ralph Waldo Emerson, 'Nature' (1836), in *Nature and Selected Essays* (New York: Penguin, 2003) p. 39.
116 Ellison, 'In a Strange Country', pp. 138–9.
117 Ellison, 'In a Strange Country', p. 140.
118 Ellison, 'In a Strange Country', pp. 145–6.
119 Paolo Virno, *Multitude: Between Innovation and Negation*, trans. Isabella Bertoletti, James Cascaito and Andrea Casson (Los Angeles: Semiotexte, 2008), p. 129. Quoted by Gibbons, 'Coast-Modernism', p. 183.
120 Herbert Marcuse's phrase in *One Dimensional Man* (London: Routledge, 1991 [1964]), p. 173.
121 Cornel West, 'American Radicalism', in Peter Osborne (ed.), *A Critical Sense: Interviews with Intellectuals* (London: Routledge, 1996), p. 129.
122 Ellison, 'In a Strange Country', p. 145.
123 Barbara Foley, 'Reading Redness: Politics and Audience in Ralph Ellison's Early Short Fiction', *Journal of Narrative Theory*, 29/3 (Fall 1999), 332.
124 Gwyn A. Williams, *When Was Wales? A History of the Welsh* (London: Black Raven Press, 1985), p. 274.
125 Ellison, 'In a Strange Country', p. 142
126 Ralph Ellison, 'Letter to Senora Babb', quoted in Rampersad, *Ralph Ellison*, p. 171.

127 See my discussion in *Black Skin, Blue Books*, pp. 165–8.
128 See Barbara Foley, *Wrestling with the Left*, pp. 31–53.
129 Jackson, *Ralph Ellison*, p. 318.
130 Michael Denning, *The Cultural Front: The Laboring of American Culture in the Twentieth Century* (London: Verso, 1997), pp. xiii–xx.
131 Ellison, 'On Initiation Rites', p. 56.
132 Wittgenstein, *Tractatus Logico-Philosophicus* (New York: Routledge, 2001 [1922]), p. 5.
133 Slavoj Žižek, *Less than Nothing: Hegel and the Shadow of Dialectical Materialism* (London: Verso, 2012), p. 756.
134 T. S. Eliot, *Selected Essays* (London: Faber, 1932), p. 27.
135 Dylan Thomas, 'A Child's Christmas in Wales', in *Collected Stories*, ed. Walford Davies (London: Weidenfeld & Nicolson, 2014 [1983]), p. 304.

10

The Psychogeography of Swansea as a Stimulus for Wittgenstein's Cerebration

Alan Sandry

W. H. Auden's poem *Night Mail* was a tour de force reflecting a postal rail journey through the English countryside and into Scotland's Central Belt.[1] Ludwig Wittgenstein never wrote, or commissioned, an equivalent Welsh Night Mail, but imagining that initial foray onto Welsh soil, and the different landscapes that Wittgenstein would have viewed as he made his first journey to Swansea in 1942, could easily have induced an equally memorable verse. Wittgenstein may not have witnessed too much of the 'cotton grass and moorland boulder' that Auden encountered in England but the imagery on arrival in Scotland, where Auden observes 'the fields of apparatus, the furnaces set on the dark plain like giant chessmen', would have been akin to Wittgenstein emerging into the Copperopolis of the heavily industrialised lower Swansea valley and spilling into Swansea itself.

How very apt that Wittgenstein entered Swansea by locomotive. Trains have played a key part in the identity and personality of Swansea since 1807, when it was graced by the world's first passenger railway, one which Wittgenstein would have hopped on and hopped off on numerable occasions. The Mumbles Railway was seen as Swansea's internal rail, acting as its great cardiac vein. It was a rickety train and track that tempted, on a twice-daily basis, the Swansea tides to wash it away. That washing away never came until the Council decided, in its ineluctable wisdom, that the car would be king and the jewel in Swansea's crown was confined to the breakers' yard.

Wittgenstein's first impression of Swansea's holistic topography would have been the view from his room at 96 Bryn Road, Brynmill. This was Rush Rhees's home and, being a mere hundred metres from the beach, it allows panoramic views of the Neapolitan-like Swansea Bay. It was here, also, that Wittgenstein would have first observed Brynmill Station, servicing the Mumbles Railway, where five years later in 1947 the famous *esprit de corps* Ben Richards photograph would be taken.[2] This was the occasion when Richards snapped Wittgenstein, and he kindly returned the favour. Wittgenstein's image inhabits our lives to this day, whilst the photograph of Richards has dissipated over time. A simple photographic moment, metres away from the golden sand of Swansea Bay, but a visual image that could have been part of an intricate *mis-en-scène*, such is its arresting effect on the eye of the observer. From first glance in 1942 to legacy moment in 1947, this was a circular journey, of sorts, and all visible from the moored home of Rush Rhees.

Water is inescapable in Swansea, as a bird's eye view highlights the prominence of the Bay, with its massive tidal range.[3] Sealed against the sea is the *terra firma* of Swansea, with its array of tightly packed terrace housing, which either boast panoramic or partial sea views or, at minimum, allow the inhabitants refreshment through their perpetual salt air intakes. So, the eyes and chests of Swansea's residents cannot escape the effects of its soggy surroundings. Throughout his life Wittgenstein sought comparable calming, near water, zones. Not exactly isomorphic examples but the similarities between some of these venues is conspicuous. Thales, the ancient Greek who is generally acknowledged as the first philosopher, was attracted to water, which influenced his peripatetic lifestyle and line of thought.[4] For Thales, the arche, or first principle, is water. One could comfortably transpose that onto Wittgenstein's shoulders. Swansea's voluminous bay, with its clear day views of the green and black Somerset and Devon coastlines, would have allowed for much conjecture from a philosopher at the height of his creative and intellectual powers. Water brings hope, and it stimulates production.

For a philosopher of language Swansea offered boundless possibilities. Bilingualism is conspicuous in sound and sight. Brynmill, home of Rhees, is a portmanteau – half Welsh, half English. A 4/4 split. 'Bryn' means hill, but Bryn is also a first name. There isn't any common use of hill in English as a first name. 'The words are part of the experience', Searle and Magee once ruminated.[5] Thus, the word 'Swansea' is part of the experience of Swansea. Split it and you have Swan, followed by sea. All very straightforward, one would think. There are swans in Swansea and there is a sea, or at least a bay, in Swansea. We know what a swan looks like, and we have all seen a sea, or at the very least water. Hence, we have those concepts in our picture of Swansea. But the name Swansea is supposedly derived from Sweyn's Ey,[6] and has nothing to do with swans or sea. In many respects Swansea's Welsh name, Abertawe, acknowledges this reclaimed islet because 'aber' is the river's mouth. Therefore, mouth of the river Tawe signifies the zone where Sweyn may, or may not, have camped. So, there are similarities and differences, perfect for Wittgensteinian analysis.

In the early part of 1944, Wittgenstein lodged with reputable Mrs Mann at 10 Langland Road. This house had been a private school in Victorian times, and it contained an atmosphere of learning within its crafted walls. So, two decades plus after his vacillating adventures as a schoolteacher in Austria, we can site the spectre of children and education – the pedagogical act – in the middle of the Wittgenstein story; a leitmotif that synergises with his philosophical musings. From his bedroom window at number 10, he would have overlooked Underhill Park, where he would have observed people at play and recreation. A rightward glance from the same spot would have granted him a unblemished view of Oystermouth Castle, whose history of colonial (mis)management would have chimed with his knowledge and understanding of the Austrian Empire. The name of the road and district would have unquestionably captured his imagination. Langland in Welsh would be 'llan', meaning shore, with 'glan' translating as bank. An early modern name for the area was Llan y Llan, which translates as houses (glebe) by the shore.[7] The descriptive precision of Welsh place names chimes with Wittgenstein's early philosophy.

During his time in the west of Swansea, Wittgenstein would have also pondered upon a place name such as Mumbles, an onomatopoeia – to mumble – for not talking clearly.[8] Indeed, Mumbles has a vernacular distinct from the rest of Swansea. It is a Devon-infused mode of speech emanating from its maritime history, which saw a predominance of sea crossings and interactions between the fishing and quarrying folk of Mumbles, and indeed the south flank of Gower, and those of the

Devon seaside communities. In contrast, the north of Gower, where Wittgenstein sometimes ventured, has a more traditional accent which blends Swansea and Llanelli tones and mannerisms. Pronunciation and accentuation may differ, but labelling sometimes spans both areas. For example, the horses that run wild across Gower's common land, which Wittgenstein witnessed and wrote about,[9] are known as Gower ponies in the parlance of the people right around the Gower peninsula.

Though, using academic applications, he could have torn it apart at any given moment, Wittgenstein would have greatly appreciated the Swansea demotic; the entertaining admixes of English, Welsh and Jack.[10] This was a version of English that was very different to that exercised in Cambridge. Added to that, Welsh would have been hitherto inaudible to Wittgenstein's ears, whilst Jack was the *lingua franca* that would have been saltily fused with the sea air with which Wittgenstein, like the inhabitants of Swansea, would have filled his lungs on a daily basis. All in all, therefore, for a philosopher of language this would have been an aural delight.

Along with the captivating Gower ponies, as Wittgenstein strolled around he would have encountered and absorbed the industrial milieu of the area. On Gower, that would have comprised fishermen in the south and women cockle pickers at Penclawdd in the north. Urban Swansea would have offered him copperworkers, steelworkers, labourers galore, and miners from the hinterland. All forms of heavy industry intermingled, as these were people who earned their living off the sea and transportation – such as the Swansea dockers – or in the production of materials and the mining of resources. It was a cornucopia of strength and guile. There would have been welders aplenty, including Rush Rhees, whose experience in that field in the late 1930s may not have been entirely fulfilling.[11] In terms of trade identification, Swansea presented a third estate sweep which enriched Wittgenstein's overall experiences during his visits and undoubtedly satiated his empathy for the working classes.

One thing that Wittgenstein would have taken on board was the fact that the Swansea he saw, and got to love, was then a mosaic – and is even more so in contemporary times – of various sectors, cultures, geographies and related factors. Territorial demarcations were visible as you walked west or east from the Uplands,[12] his home for the latter visits.

The Psychogeography of Swansea

Wittgenstein's movement around Singleton (the site of Swansea University), Brynmill (the home of Rhees), and the Uplands allowed him to be part of Swansea's unique area of creativity. Globally, areas of creativity are not uncommon. Greenwich Village, New York, and Laurel Canyon, California, are two well-known American examples. The Left Bank and Montmartre are Parisian versions; again, famous, and often cited. Into this category must come the Uplands in Swansea, or more specifically the perimeter of Cwmdonkin Park, the majestic green space of the Uplands, which is as inextricable as Central Park is to Manhattan. Swansea did not have Brahms and Mahler performing in Wittgensteinian palaces, but the symphonies of Daniel Jones may have drifted across from Jones's home at 16 Cwmdonkin Terrace.[13] Wittgenstein savoured the artistic coterie of a variety of towns and cities, but the propinquity of events and places offered by Swansea, and particularly the Uplands, would surely have resonated with his creative predispositions.

It is around Cwmdonkin Terrace that we can position, among other places of note, the childhood home of Dylan Thomas, the family residence of Kingsley Amis,[14] and the lodgings of Ludwig Wittgenstein from 1944-7. A Welshman, an Englishman and an Austrian – not the first line of a joke, but an instalment of the remarkable true-life tale of literary and philosophical imagination and achievement. All this within a small subdivision of a quasi-bourgeois suburb in an industrial, largely proletariat town – now a city – in Wales.

Poems, propositions and prose were the three writing styles and techniques of these protagonists. The poem never lies. Facts are truths. The novelist always tells fibs. Veracity, rationality and fiction, or at the very least the embellishment of what one believes to be true. All three are traditionalists, in many ways, but were ground-breaking in their fields. All three are accessible artists. Dylan, especially the younger and *Under Milk Wood* incarnations, is more comprehensible than many other wordsmiths. Wittgenstein is a veritable picture of clarity compared to the abstruse Hegel or Heidegger, and Amis is less flowery and ostentatious than many novelists of his time or before. All three would have walked around the Uplands seeking inspiration, and would have found it after inducing perspiration through ascending its sundry hillocks. Were we to apply contemporary technology, we could certainly identify crossed paths. Imagine, for example, a GPS tracker mapping out their peregrinations.

Other elements come into play. Dylan and Wittgenstein, for instance, throw up some quirky numerical factors: 52 metres of separation is the distance between their houses, where these great minds slept and dreamt, their fanciful thoughts swirling in the Swansea night, as a young Dylan may have noted. That figure of 52, ironically, is in between the years of their twentieth century deaths – '51 for Ludwig, '53 for Dylan.

The apocryphal Zola story is another interesting aspect.[15] Kingsley Amis was once invited to visit a coal mine on the outskirts of Swansea. Whilst there, he was shown around the underground workings at the coal face before coming back up to the surface in the cage. During his ascent, one miner asks Amis what he thought of the experience. Amis replied 'Shocking! Very hard conditions.' Another miner immediately interjects, 'a bit like *Germinal*.' Amis responds, in an astonished tone, 'You know *Germinal*?' The miner retorts that 'all the boys have read Zola'. Whether factual or fabricated, this tale exemplifies the zeitgeist of the miners' libraries and the autodidact workers. These are the men who would have heard their sons and daughters, or grandsons and granddaughters, proclaim that they are 'the first generation of my family to go to university'. The old, now deceased, miners must have had a remarkable sense of inner pride and pleasure, combined with a whirling, gnawing anger at what might have been for them. This would have been an anger, contained but conspicuous, which probably would have been exceptionally difficult for an Oxford-educated littérateur like Amis to fully comprehend.

Were he around, Wittgenstein may have seen Amis's Zola episode as a Vitruvian man anecdote. The enlightened proletariat unpretentiously displaying their knowledge in an example of shock value equalitarianism. There was certainly a matrix of identities and personalities for writers like Amis and Wittgenstein to observe within the working classes of Swansea and its surrounding smokestack villages; those honest grafters being the life models for their narrative canvas. Examples of shock value equalitarianism, it could be contended, affected all three in various ways, and the inhabitants of Swansea have the innate ability to level themselves up, when required, but also the skill and prowess to pull down anyone exhibiting bumptious or haughty tendencies.

Swansea is represented to varying degrees in the writings of the three: Dylan's childhood view, Amis's early to middle-aged angst and loathing, and Wittgenstein's words of praise for the Swansea of his sojourns. Dylan attempted to maintain that narrative of romantic innocence throughout his life and writings. Amis desired to be the established academic and esteemed novelist from an early stage, whilst Wittgenstein, no more so than in Swansea, was more becalmed; happy in his own world of thought and generally relaxed in his intellectual environment. All saw similar things around them, in the Uplands and elsewhere, but each reacted very differently.

We must always recall that Wittgenstein experienced wartime Swansea. One can only imagine what the sentiments and emotional thoughts of Wittgenstein, who fought in the First World War, must have been. This is especially so, as he would have seen so many armoured vehicles and uniformed personnel during his time in Swansea. Swansea during wartime represented bipolarity and contrasts of an extreme nature. The beautiful, imperishable Swansea Bay met its antithesis in the horrendous three-night Swansea blitz.[16] *Et in Arcadia ego.*[17] The Prelapsarian idyll came face-to-face with the destructive tendencies of ideologically-warped humankind.

In June 1944, Swansea was an embarkation point for the Normandy landings. Swansea Bay was dotted with various sized craft to transport military forces to war. Wittgenstein would have observed this, and from Mumbles Hill, where six anti-aircraft guns were placed, he would have had a drone like view of the preparing armada. As an ex-serviceman, certain painful, and invariably complex, memories of conflict would have flooded his cortex. To access this viewpoint, on one of Swansea's highest promontories, Wittgenstein would have passed the home where Morfydd Llwyn Owen, the accomplished composer and mezzo-soprano, died at the tender age of twenty-six.[18] It was the abode of the parents of her husband, Ernest Jones, the Gowerton-born neurologist and psychologist who was a close associate of Sigmund Freud. Vienna's star melancholily shining on Mumbles Hill. Wittgenstein enthusiastically discussed Freud with Rush Rhees at the time of his visits to Swansea. Hence, passing Ernest Jones's house, and triggering his thoughts on psychoanalysis, would have provided a point of stimulation for Wittgenstein during his wanderings across Mumbles; another tether to strap him into his Swansea ecosystem.

Another Mumbles-Uplands connection is noteworthy. Rocco Francis Marchegiano, commonly known as Rocky Marciano, billeted in Swansea in 1944. For a period, he slept on the timber decking of Mumbles Pier, which was used as a makeshift camp for US forces. An altruistic Catholic, Marciano regularly caught the Mumbles train to Brynmill Station in order to visit Stella Maris School and Convent in Eaton Crescent, Uplands, where he assisted the nuns with the schoolchildren. Wittgenstein would have been familiar with the elegant, boot-shaped Eaton Crescent[19] and may well have brushed past the future undefeated heavyweight champion of the world.[20] A conversation on the definition of games between those two would have been mesmeric.

Despite his love of being in Mumbles, Langland and the beaches of Gower, Wittgenstein's fulcrum was the Uplands and his Cwmdonkin Terrace lodgings, Swansea University set in Singleton Park, and Brynmill, home to Rush Rhees. These locations are linked, in ley line fashion, by three resplendent parks – Cwmdonkin, Brynmill and Singleton. There is flow and continuity in their green spaces, but each has its unique, distinctive features. Water flows in Singleton through the ever-trickling stream; Brynmill has its wildfowl-rich lake; and there is a Dylan-themed pond-cum-water feature in Cwmdonkin (though Cwmdonkin also used to have a reservoir where the children's play area now stands). Added together, these three parks, where Wittgenstein strolled and where he and Rhees spent countless hours in fruitful discourse, can rightly be seen as verdant havens surrounded by tightly assembled streets of substantial and, in those days, fashionable houses. Town meets gown meets recreation ground. This is Arcadia buried beneath the canopies in the middle of urban Swansea.

On the western side of the three parks, Swansea University rests within Singleton's green majesty. Seagulls hover from Swansea University along the Mumbles Road, and up to Langland. Scavengers with a liking for dropped morsels – not unlike the students to whom Wittgenstein and Rhees would have been both instructors and guides. Singleton is a spacious park, where the entrance to the university takes you past a grand building in Singleton Abbey. Its sibling, Sketty Hall, sits at the north-west tip of the park. Whilst opulent and grandiloquent in Swansea terms, these structures are nowhere near as glittering as the Wittgenstein family palaces in Vienna. Wittgenstein, with his architect's hat on, would have been amused by the Swiss Cottage in Singleton Park, built in 1826, the architecture of which would have contrasted starkly with the surrounding buildings of stone, whose gothic tint and imposing towers protected the new buildings popping up at Swansea University.[21] The Swiss Cottage, with its 'Libertie et patrie' (Freedom and Fatherland) adornment, is the type of delightful out-of-kilter folly that would have a raised a regular smile on Wittgenstein's face as he passed it *en route* to a philosophical engagement with Rhees. He would have invariably contemplated the other inscription on the chalet, 'Lebe so das du wieder leben magst' (Live in such a way that you may live again). The irony of an Austrian reading a German inscription on a 'Swiss' style building in Wales in the middle of wartime takes some imagining, but, in many ways, it reflects the many-hued complexion of Wittgenstein's life course and experiences.

Swansea's parks are mostly trimmed and manicured, but they have a prelapsarian feel. This would have enabled Wittgenstein to envisage things in the raw, as generally there are very few fabricated adornments to despoil the natural environment. If you wish to ponder on elementary languages, mathematical formulae, or the psychology of philosophy, then this is the setting for you. A primitivistic pathway between lodgings and a seat of learning.

Cwmdonkin Terrace, his latter Swansea address, allowed Wittgenstein to experience a different route to his key locations and points of contact. Looking from Cwmdonkin Terrace, with an altitude of a hundred metres above sea level, Wittgenstein would have had a commanding perspective of the bay, peering at Mumbles lighthouse and letting his eyes roll east across the horizon to Sker Point, near Porthcawl. This was an expanse of water as seen from higher up on one of Swansea's multiple hills. Wittgenstein's downward course to the sea, to the water that inspired him at Swansea, resembled his 'up above' years at Skjolden in Norway. As the crow flies, he was nearer to the water at Skjolden than he was while lodging at Cwmdonkin Terrace, but his journey to the seafront in Swansea would have taken a shorter duration – a suburban stroll through tightly packed tall but thin rows of buildings rather than a cragged, rustic ramble. Once again in Wittgenstein's story, there are family resemblances, but they are markedly different in tone and sensation.

Though the delights of the natural environment, and his ability to view them at some leisure, would have pleased Wittgenstein, it was essentially his need to be with Rush Rhees, and to work on his philosophical manuscripts, which he desired from his stays in Swansea. Every day in Swansea was an intellectual, kaleidoscopic quest. Swansea is an invitational space which welcomes those with an open mind and an imaginative streak. The battle between Apollonian and Dionysian feelings and endeavours would have been acted out in those short, scenic walks from his lodgings to the door of Rush Rhees's university office. The palliative, therapeutic nature of the parks would have tempered any building rage, or pessimistic thoughts, within.

There wasn't any artifice in the Wittgenstein-Rhees relationship. They fastidiously sought out facts through lucidity and pushed aside the vagaries of fashion and transient attitudes and commentary. Wittgenstein and Rhees would engage in daily walks, with Wittgenstein supplementing these with individual strolls.[22] Was Wittgenstein an aimless wanderer – a flaneur – or someone for whom the act of *dérive* (an unplanned walk with constant reflection) was a stimulant? He would have customarily appreciated the reality of his walk, in contrast to the mediated, somewhat false, environment of the cocooned academic arena. Talking at a timetabled seminar offers a different sense of place and satisfaction than talking with a trusted associate as one is sauntering along the seashore of Mumbles or Langland. The eyes that gaze out on diverging scenes will allow the mind to produce different thoughts and conclusions. Changing the location, inevitably, modifies the result. Wittgenstein was cordially subverting the status quo.

During these walks, would it be possible to allude that Wittgenstein and Rhees were pre-empting the positions of the *Situationniste*[23] in their ascetic approaches and their rejection of ever-increasing consumerism? At this point in the twentieth century, left-wing and anti-capitalist alignment or flirtations were *de rigueur*. Could Wittgenstein and Rhees have drifted into these modes of thinking or positioning? The lifestyle of the rebel or outlier would certainly have been overtly and covertly applicable, in varying degrees, to both men. Unconventional, with radical interior mechanisms, they certainly would have considered the notion that we have become obsessed with images rather than lived experience, and the creation of our own situations – be they for positive linguistic engagement, social interaction, or in a purely responsive, and seemingly mundane, sense. Wittgenstein and Rhees rejected the *homo economicus* model. Commodity fetishism was not for them. They were looking for answers in their minds, and in the world as it appeared in front of them, and not in any abstract forms. Hence, they were not just seeking linguistic clarity, but they were also exploring the cultural and social interfaces. The Wittgenstein–Rhees walks involved dialectic leading to praxis. They were immersive experiences where the ideas shared were intertwined with the congenial surroundings.

Rush Rhees would spend his evenings writing up his account of that day's encounter with Wittgenstein. Concurrently, Wittgenstein would be at his lodgings, eating, reflecting and at times playing games. The student worked into the night as the master unwound in ways in which only he could.

Philosophical ramblers and seekers of solitude are sprinkled throughout history. Rousseau (*Reveries of the Solitary Walker*), Nietzsche (*Thus Spoke Zarathustra*), and Kant, in his head if not in terms of doing the wide-ranging hard yards, were prolific advocates. Furthermore, we can add creative writers such as the transcendentalist Henry David Thoreau and the literary impressionist Joseph Conrad.[24] Politically, and in terms of life actions and embracing activism, Guy Debord and the Situationists were key drivers, though this was a decade or more after Wittgenstein's demise. Nevertheless, Wittgenstein is an important part of this evolutionary strand, and he has his own matchless place within it.

For Wittgenstein Swansea was a 'borderland':[25] near the sea with its outward and inward transnational connections. Welsh in character, tone and speech, but cosmopolitan, albeit in minority aspects during the 1940s. A place where ennui can be put to good use. A ruminating space that would have then made it, and still makes it to this day, a location to devise and propound ground-breaking ideas. Swansea, for Wittgenstein, could also be viewed as a 'break' – social, cultural, epistemological (or part thereof). In Swansea, Wittgenstein discovered foundations and underpinnings – social, cultural and philosophical developments, which assisted in formulating *Philosophical Investigations*, and a state of mind and quality of life that was different to anything he had previously experienced. For this to occur, and for him to maximise its advantages, Wittgenstein absorbed and immersed himself in his surroundings, using, perhaps unbeknown to him, psychogeographical techniques.

Psychogeography, undertaken in a state of solitude, can induce a form of solipsism. Physical engagements and human interactions, on an everyday basis, are therefore important to pull the individual back from an extreme egocentric interpretation of their surroundings. Did Wittgenstein's sojourns and meanderings foster new narratives across the philosophical field, or is that too far-reaching a supposition? New aperçus, possibly? It certainly allowed him thinking time before his discourse with Rhees and those countless hours in their scriptorium. Psychogeography is not the *deus ex machina* to explain, or even pigeonhole, Wittgenstein's thought process, but the environment would have undoubtedly provided an ambient framework for his cognitive process.

Swansea gave Wittgenstein space and time to subvert, and this led to innovation and production. Matters that may only have been adumbrated at Cambridge could now be refined at Swansea. He may have been a squirrelly soul at Cambridge, but at Swansea he would have felt at ease as he passed the *bona fide* squirrels in Singleton Park. This period in his life would have endorsed his retention of what we know for certain, whilst catering for the pursuance of exploratory angles for addressing the de-complexion of language using logic as his tool. Wittgenstein did not want to commit patricide of his early work – the *Tractatus* – but he wished to prepare a palimpsest that would be a formula for the continuation of language appraisal, and enactment, after his time. Namely, the *Philosophical Investigations*.

All of this took place in the inimitable setting of Swansea, with the indispensable assistance of Rush Rhees. These were integral pieces of Wittgenstein's 1940s' intellectual and human-centred jigsaw. Swansea University's motto is *Gweddw crefft heb ei dawn* (Skill is bereft without culture); Cambridge University's motto is *Hinc lucem et pocula sacra* (From here, we derive light and sacred draughts); the combination of the two perfectly sums up Wittgenstein's view of others, not least Rhees, as well as his own multifaceted persona.

Notes

1 W. H. Auden wrote the poem *Night Mail* to accompany the 24-minute documentary of that name which was released in 1936. It shows the journey taken by postal workers on the overnight postal train from London to Scotland.
2 The photograph of Ludwig Wittgenstein at Brynmill Station is often referred to as 'the Swansea photograph'. It is one of the most famous photographs of him and reflects the mature, at ease Wittgenstein.

3   Swansea has the second highest tidal range in the world at fifteen metres. It is only surpassed by the Bay of Fundy in Canada, which reaches sixteen metres.
4   Thales of Miletus, one of the Seven Sages of Ancient Greece, is credited with the Delphic maxim 'know thyself'.
5   Taken from 'The Philosophy of Language – John Searle and Bryan Magee', in the BBC series 'Men of Ideas', 1978.
6   The etymology of Swansea is contested but some favour the attribution towards Sweyn Forkbeard, a Viking King, who became the first Danish King of England. He allegedly made camp on an islet at the mouth of the river Tawe in what is now the city centre of Swansea. That islet is the 'Ey' in 'Sweyn's Ey'. The islet is currently the land including and encircling the Parc Tawe shopping area down to the Strand (formerly the banks of the river). Interestingly, there have not been any significant archaeological excavations to identify Viking settlements in Swansea.
7   See the essay by this author, 'Am I Glad to Be Here!; Ludwig Wittgenstein and Philosophy at Swansea', *Swansea University Centenary Essays, 2020: Am I Glad To Be Here!*, Swansea University Digital Collections.
8   For an excellent introduction to Mumbles, see Martin Williams's film *Welcome to Mumbles* on YouTube.
9   See Alfred Schmidt's chapter in this volume.
10 'Jacks' are the inhabitants of Swansea; an honour usually granted through birth, but occasionally attained through absorption and allegiance. The term 'Jack' is thought to derive from Jack Tar, as the sailors of Swansea had a global reputation as masters of their craft. It was often said that if you announced yourself in any port worldwide as being a native of Swansea, you would be guaranteed employment. There was also a very famous retriever dog called Swansea Jack, who, in the 1930s, used to jump into the docks and open water to rescue anyone in distress. He is credited with saving twenty-seven lives. Today, the supporters of Swansea City Football Club are known as the Jack Army.
11 See Mario von der Ruhr's informative 'Rhees, Wittgenstein and the Swansea School', in John Edelman (ed.), *Sense and Reality: Essays out of Swansea*, vol. 10 in the series Publications of the Austrian Ludwig Wittgenstein Society (De Gruyter, 2009).
12 The adroit Swansea poet, and Uplands resident, David 'Dai' Hughes, defines the Uplands as being between Rosehill to the east and Glanmor Park Road to the west, Penlan Terrace to the north and Pantygwydr Road, Eaton Crescent and Westbury Street to the south.
13 Daniel Jones owned, and sometimes resided at, 16 Cwmdonkin Terrace. Jones rented out the ground floor flat, which become the wartime home of the skilled artist and printmaker Alan Figg.
14 Kingsley Amis was a lecturer at Swansea University from 1949–61. Though he would not have been in Swansea during Wittgenstein's visits, and as far we know they never met, he would have certainly known Rush Rhees.

15 Amis would often hold classes in one of the local pubs rather than having them on campus.
15 I first heard this illuminating tale during a 1994 lecture at Swansea University by Professor Peter Stead, on the theme of literature within post-Second World War social and cultural history.
16 The Swansea Blitz was three nights of sustained Luftwaffe bombing from 19–21 February 1941. This is the bombed town to which Wittgenstein ventured a year later.
17 'I (deceased) too lived in Arcadia.'
18 Morfydd Llwyn Owen was buried at Oystermouth Cemetery, Mumbles, in 1918. This is also where Rush Rhees was interred in 1989.
19 Rush Rhees later lived at 64A Eaton Crescent (1957–64).
20 Another story centring on Rocky Marciano, albeit one with a less religious slant, concerns the incident at the Adelphi pub in Wind Street, Swansea. The tale goes that Marciano was in this establishment one evening drinking a glass of milk, as he was trying to maintain his fitness. A couple of army servicemen, allegedly Australian, came into the bar and started to ridicule him and make homophobic remarks about his choice of beverage. Marciano ignored them, until one came up to him and swore in his face. By the time the last syllable left the man's mouth, Marciano had floored him with a right hook. The unconscious serviceman was carried outside into the fresh air where his friends took quite a while to bring him round, by which time Marciano had finished his milk in a leisurely fashion, departed the Adelphi, and ambled up the street.
21 The Swiss Cottage was built in 1826 by Peter Frederick Robinson, who also designed Sketty Hall. The Swiss Cottage is now a Grade II listed building.
22 See D. Z. Phillips's 'Rush Rhees, a biographical sketch', in D. Z. Phillips (ed.), *Rush Rhees: Wittgenstein and the Possibility of Discourse* (Oxford: Blackwell Publishing, 2006), p. 274.
23 Operating from 1957–72, the Situationist International, or Situationists, were an assemblage of social revolutionaries, artists and political philosophers, who viewed liberation as achievable through creating situations that disrupted the everyday capitalist and political machinery and mindsets. They advocated rambling, sometimes for days on end, in order to open the mind to different experiences and to foster avant-garde thought.
24 Thoreau's *Walden* (1854) explores simple living in natural surroundings, whilst Conrad's novella *Heart of Darkness* (1899) examines the contrast between the perceived civilised and savage worlds.
25 The notion of Swansea as a borderland was often voiced by the accomplished Swansea and Gower poet and psychogeographer, Nigel Jenkins (1949–2014). He is buried at St Mary's Church, Pennard (originally Llanarthbodu), Gower, which is also the final resting place of two other esteemed poets, Vernon Watkins and Harri Webb.

11

Wittgenstein, Rhees and Philosophy

James Kelman in conversation[1]

When did you first discover Ludwig Wittgenstein?

It would have been early in 1975 when I bought an edition of the *Tractatus* which was published at the end of 1974. It was before I went to university – I went later the same year. That was my introduction and I suppose most people come to his work through the *Tractatus* – it is hard to imagine them coming through the *Philosophical Investigations*, though you never know. I think it is precision for some writers, as well as the exploration of ideas, that you are drawn to philosophy. What you find is philosophers having a real influence on writers of fiction, for instance Descartes, he would be one of the heaviest. Samuel Beckett explicitly refers to Descartes, but you can also see it in the work of people like Goethe. Edgar Allan Poe is another, some of his short stories seem to have begun from a reading of Descartes's *First Meditation*,[2] the solitary man alone in the room, the fire, the shadows, the introspection. The same goes for Kafka.

As a writer how important is it to be precise in your choice of words and language?

There is nothing more important than that and especially so – if you are working in a tradition that is not '*the* tradition', the high English tradition. There is a greater need for precision for writers who are exploring their own rhythms and language patterns. They'll be concerned with things like syntax, phrasing, and so on, phonetics too, different patterns of language, what you expect to find in ordinary speech and probably associate it with orature rather than literature. These are issues for many Scottish writers and in other cultures, who want to make use of their native languages, not to write in it but making use of how their qualities operate within English, their linguistic patterns. Some Welsh writers must be part of it too, wanting to capture a sense of their own Welshness while writing in the English language. Remember that standard English literary form is the voice of the imperialist, the voice of the coloniser, of authority, of the lawmaker and it is full of value, laden down with value although it is so ingrained it appears otherwise, as though value-free.

I don't really know now what it was about Wittgenstein's work that attracted me other than that precision, trying to get to the essence of the thing, and the need to be absolutely clear about what it is you mean, a kind of distillation, especially the early pages of the *Tractatus*, appreciating the need for these numbered paragraphs and so on, and how come that was necessary. Memorable stuff comes from that alone. At one point I encouraged students in Creative Writing to have a go, just to help them get rid of the verbiage, to get to the nub of it. There is nobody more precise in that way than Wittgenstein, but it doesn't mean he gets it all correct which is a different matter and maybe later when Rush Rhees becomes relevant, helping clarify the material.

How important was Rush Rhees to Wittgenstein's legacy as a philosopher?

There has been good work done on Rhees at Swansea University by D. Z. Phillips and others. But I don't think beyond that there has been enough emphasis on Rhees as there should have been, and there's a lot to explore. Waiting in the wings is the influence that came through Edinburgh University, and that was powerful as he said himself, one of the three crucial influences on him was John Anderson. Anderson later moved to Australia and became about the most important philosopher over there in the last hundred years,[3] a position he occupies in both Australia and Scotland.

These are exciting questions. We can ask what was it about Wittgenstein that had such an impact on Rhees but we can also ask about the impact Rhees had on Wittgenstein, not only philosophically but politically and culturally. The Rhees archive is waiting to be explored, and not only by academics and philosophy students. I read there was around 16,000 pages, plus there'll be letters and other materials. It's exciting.

What was it particularly about Rhees's social and political sensibilities that influenced Wittgenstein?

Yes, well, the man himself, his background, his political position, all of that would have had an influence. I don't have any doubt about that, and that Wittgenstein would have admired him. The reason why Rush Rhees ended up leaving the USA was because he was kicked out of university at the age of nineteen. You might say that it is a healthy tradition for great philosophers to be at loggerheads with the establishment. Rhees was expelled from Rochester University because he refused to accept what his professor of philosophy was saying to him. You must remember that this was the 1930s, and it was one of those eras that happens in the States every so often, a major crackdown on radical politics. Anyone who had a radical political outlook would be in a very difficult position. It was a bad time, and people like Nicola Sacco and Bartolomeo Vanzetti – two working class men, immigrants, anarchists – were convicted and executed for something they didn't do.[4] Rush Rhees came out and declared publicly that he was an atheist and an anarchist. That was a brave thing to do. He wasn't working class, and he wasn't an immigrant, he was something like a third generation American.

Complications everywhere – his father was not only a highly regarded theologian, he was the president of Rochester University, the very one that expelled his son. He didn't disown the boy – far from it, he approved his fighting spirit and encouraged him to take his studies further, get his head screwed on properly by studying philosophy properly. Rush Rhees chose to leave the USA. He came to Edinburgh University. You might say when he came to Edinburgh he landed lucky, because the young John Anderson was teaching there and head of the department was Norman Kemp Smith.[5]

You cannot get away from class and politics in Scotland and this is something shared with Wales. That political sensibility never left

Rhees, and his integrity just seems unimpeachable, really, and of course he acted, he took it into his hands, at the age of nineteen – maybe a similar sort of mindset as Wittgenstein himself, who made the move to England at the same age. Rhees's great-great-grandfather was from the south of Wales, and was a Methodist preacher of the later eighteenth century, and a well-known radical. Apparently, he went to France to see how the French Revolution was working! He went with some Welsh friends. After that experience, he decided to head straight to America. This is why the family ended up in the USA.

So Rhees came from a strong religious background but equally strong was an ethical sense, a general integrity in theological, philosophical, and political terms.

Do you think there is a tangible relationship between philosophy and literature?

In a sense it is one hundred per cent. Wittgenstein himself was influenced by art theory and aesthetics. Part of what drew me to Wittgenstein was that he bumped his head against certain issues which many artists and writers were facing during the nineteenth century. What they were trying to do was present a picture of a fact, a sort of pictorial fact, they were trying to create work that made a fact or expressed a fact.

So, what is a fact? Something that can't be disputed. So, you can deny the significance of something but not its existence, and that makes it very political. You see nowadays to what extent the far right strive to deny matters of historical fact. From Cézanne's time in the visual arts[6] – and Zola too in literature, and Kafka – they were trying to find a way of presenting an image, or a piece of art, that was like an autonomous structure that could only exist on its own and that could not be tampered with, or interfered with, or ever properly described. The only thing you could ever do is create a kind of structurally identical thing, trying to convey (or picture) the structure of the original, or expressing that. So, philosophy and art running together in that way, if any of that makes sense, which is how I saw Wittgenstein coming at related issues, it takes you into other areas, space and time, the world of science, physics and so on.

Do you think that Swansea is an inspirational place for creative thinkers?

I am obviously biased because I have been going to Swansea since 1968, when I met my future wife. I've come to know the area pretty well. I am not surprised that Wittgenstein enjoyed it so much. It might have been strange for Rhees because of his background, and although you might say this was the land of his fathers, he was an immigrant, he was an American, so that duality, the place being both his and not his. Maybe at a basic social and cultural level too, because most of south Wales is ordinary people at that level, working class people, and that was not his own background. The tradition-bearers in any indigenous culture are working class people, the language and the culture haven't been educated out of them completely. Not so for the middle and upper classes. For Rush Rhees it was so far gone in his past – to what extent had his family home kept the culture alive?

The class background here between the two is interesting in its own way. Wittgenstein was not just bourgeoisie, he was upper class, minor aristocracy, so when he arrived at Cambridge he was the opposite of out of his depth. That would have applied to Rush Rhees too though in a different way, when he went to Cambridge. His family background seems to have been upper middle class in the American way of it, and intellectually and so on he was ahead of the field. At Edinburgh University he was awarded the highest bursaries available, and I think he won one of them twice, which was unheard of at that time, so he was what they would call nowadays, a high-flier – great things were expected – and he was accepted for further studies at Cambridge. Cambridge wasn't a place to meet ordinary people, not unless they were servants. South Wales was different. Ordinary people were working-class people. They were not there to service rich students and academics, they lived their life and got on with it.

When Wittgenstein came to Swansea, he was encountering ordinary working-class people and they acted ordinary, they weren't tipping their hat to superiors. Along the Mumbles was ordinary, and the Gower villages, right along the old Wind Street, Swansea docks and wharfs. That stretch from the university campus up the Mumbles Road, or along Oxford Street to Swansea Market, areas Wittgenstein and Rhees would have haunted, thinking about the second-hand bookshops too

– and I knew a couple myself, that one in Dillwyn Street where you could spend weeks, Dylan's down the alley off Wind Street, bookshops up Oystermouth Road. Wittgenstein stayed round the corner for a while,[7] a ten-minute walk to Langland, Limeslade Bay – an exciting place. You could walk to Caswell Bay, and that path all the way to Rhossili. These places were within walking distance for Wittgenstein. The Mumbles train was running back then. He said that he never felt so much at home as when he got off the train at Swansea. Then he could relax.

My own lecturer on a basic course in philosophy was from the valleys, although he saw Swansea as his town. Hywel Thomas was his name, and his father was a Methodist minister. He undertook post-graduate work at Leeds, which was strong in Wittgensteinian scholarship, but he never really spoke about that side of it with me, probably because I didn't know enough. A later course I took began from Wittgenstein and Chomsky,[8] but he didn't take that one.

I liked both Wittgenstein and Chomsky for different reasons. Their formative years, like that of Rhees, were not typical and maybe took them into a different type of life than what might have been expected, so they were never quite at home in academia, and you see that throughout their lives, although so different. At certain points in their lives they met with people who were deeply committed and that maybe helped them along, going their own way, no matter how difficult that might have been for them. You could say, in that sense, things were difficult for Rush Rhees although on the surface it might not appear that way, I don't think he ever felt 'at home' and I mean intellectually, there again it's a guess, I don't know enough. Nothing could be taken for granted. I think Wittgenstein encouraged him to stay at Swansea.

So many fields covered there, in terms of totality, and there is this notion of dissent, and the philosophy of dissent. In your conversations with Chomsky, you talk about the philosophy of resisting and reflecting the outsider, and this is where we may see some of Wittgenstein's strengths as an outsider and a man fighting against the system. Is that fair to say?

I think that what you find is that individuals like that usually end up in battles with the authorities. It is not an intentional thing, and neither, to some extent, is it a fault of the authorities, more to do with the structure of society. Rhees is the more important politically between the two, but commitment is a different matter. When I was teaching a Creative Writing course I tried to get something of what real commitment might amount to, getting them to understand about Wittgenstein by reading Van Gogh's letters and notebooks, talking about the level of commitment that Van Gogh was at, a similar type of commitment that Wittgenstein had, a very personal thing, different, and here you need to see his family background too. But that kind of youthful integrity I see in him is shared with Rhees, as also Chomsky who has managed to live all his life within the establishment but somehow on his own terms.

Individuals might be prepared to conform, join in with others but it becomes difficult, having to sublimate all your own thoughts and you would end up in a struggle against all forms of authority, not because of any sort of romanticised or adolescent view but because ultimately it leads you to that, simply because as an individual you are driven by the totality of your own self, or what it means to be a human being and that takes you out of party politics. People don't always choose to be anarchists, others describe them as such, because they don't conform, no matter how hard they try, and they do try. But it means having to sort of cover up yourself, and some folk can't avoid bringing themself sooner or later, because for them there is no other way. Who they are is always there in their philosophy, although it may reveal itself differently. But whatever, the party system can't cope with individuals.

You might get an insight here why Plato sees the greatest expression of humanity in the work of the greatest artists, the way I think of it, because the individual work of the greatest artists is the totality of one unique human being at one unique point in their life. Tomorrow will be different, a minute later is different. But at that particular moment in time, that totality is an expression of every last thing, everything that you are is there, every single piece of intellectualisation, every emotion, every last thing, and nothing can be greater than that. I remember that Hywel Thomas, my first philosophy tutor (who stayed a Christian) was eventually led to the study of Duns Scotus,[9] who brings that sense of the unique individual, the notion of thisness, the uniqueness of this individual.

Do you see Rush Rhees as an underrated figure in this canon of thought?

I have been reading philosophy in one way or another for most of my life. I just never thought about it in these terms, ideas were always the interest. I think what is important with Rush Rhees just now would be to try to get a fuller idea of where he was coming from. I think it would be important to look at where Rush Rhees reached beyond Wittgenstein, and to be aware that G. E. Moore was important for Rhees, as well as Wittgenstein, and can go in a slightly different way. What I would see as crucial here is Moore's own regard and study of Thomas Reid.[10] This would take you into areas of philosophy connecting with the Common Sense tradition, which takes you into the Scottish experience Rhees had. He would have had difficulty with Wittgenstein's work at certain points because of this. I don't see how it could be otherwise. You could see, for example, Wittgenstein's professed inability to get to David Hume. That would have been difficult in his relationship with Moore because Moore would have been so aware of Hume as a primary figure through his work on Thomas Reid. That would have been very useful for Wittgenstein, I think, it might have helped him.

There's a basic thing here. Rush Rhees had the intellectual experience from his time at Edinburgh University and his acquaintance with Norman Kemp Smith as well as John Anderson. The Kant connection to Hume is important here. May be something of that was missed by Wittgenstein. I doubt if he ever looked at Kemp Smith's work on Kant, and the reason for that is straightforward, he read Kant in German. Kemp Smith was a major translator of Kant. Wittgenstein could have come across Kemp Smith because he respected the work of Baron Von Hugel, and Von Hugel and Kemp Smith were close friends. It was in a letter to Von Hugel that Kemp Smith speaks of the nineteen-year-old Rhees arriving at his philosophy department in Edinburgh, looking like 'the young Shelley'. In a sense, whether Rush Rhees is a significant philosopher is not so much irrelevant as redundant. What is important is to get a clear idea of where he is intellectually, philosophically. He expressly names John Anderson as an influence, and this influence is there to be checked out in later works like the *Philosophical Investigations* – at least the way I see it and that work is waiting there to be done, although maybe it has been already, or is in progress.

Anderson's insistence on having a position, each one of us, leads back to Hume and areas to do with perception, explored further by Adam Smith, later by people like Husserl.

D. Z. Phillip's s *Wittgenstein and the Possibility of Discourse*[11] is an interesting book in many ways, but what comes through to me again is Rush Rhees's difficulties with some aspects of what Wittgenstein was arguing. Chomsky made a revolutionary move back in the 1950s re: the acquisition of language and theory of mind generally but it was too late for Wittgenstein. To what extent Rush Rhees was in touch with that and developments since then, I don't have any idea, but through Anderson he must have had. I look forward to seeing the kind of work he was doing when I explore his archive at Swansea University, which I intend doing some time soon. Overall, I think Rhees is important, not because he may be a sort of unsung giant but because his notebooks, letters and so forth help get a better understanding of a much wider context, that leads through and beyond Wittgenstein and will give greater insights into some of Wittgenstein's later work, into that sort of context that cannot exclude the social, the political, the cultural. These areas are exciting.

How does Swansea influence creative people like Wittgenstein and yourself?

I see that photograph of Wittgenstein standing on the Mumbles Road. He's standing at the train stop, near to where there was a footpath over the road – St Helens Road? My wife worked in the Guildhall when she was a girl – but I know where he is going, Mumbles, and he's going to walk up Newton Road to his digs or else take the back route through the woods over Mumbles Hill to Limeslade Bay and meet Rhees for a cup of tea in the café, then heading along the coastal path, maybe taking the route up the steep hill round the back of the café, where you have to squeeze in tight to pass, and hope a rottweiler dog isn't coming the other way.

Anyone who does this tremendous walk to Caswell Bay gets to feel close to the area. It is a wonderful area. But the politics cannot be ignored, you cannot get away from that. Rush Rhees's other influence was John Anderson, and the Celtic connection is vital, seeing the issues around culture and so forth, the language issue in Swansea, the expression of what it means to be Welsh, or what it means to have a dual culture. It is not because you are in any way negative about English, or the Anglo-Saxon tradition. Because you wish to be aware of your own cultural tradition does not mean that you reject the ones of other people. There isn't a competition going on. You have a right to your own culture, your own traditions. Rush Rhees was in an awkward, difficult situation. Did he feel American, Anglo-American, Welsh, American Welsh? I think he would have felt American, but he would have wanted to feel Welsh as well, in the way that I connect with my own people, and my ancestors, who were essentially cleared off their land and mostly went to America, not because of choice but because they were kicked out by the British ruling class. So, there is that sense too when you get to know Wales, a sadness. It is great for me to go up the valleys or farther north, anywhere to hear the voices, hear the language. When you go in a bar and hear someone speaking Welsh, I really like that, even just using English but with strong Welsh voice. Even around Swansea, where my wife grew up. I enjoy going to Carmarthen market because you always get a sense of people coming in from the country. I like driving from Carmarthen to Aberystwyth, for example. I like that sense of Welshness, and I feel a solidarity, to go back to Rush Rhees, the drive from empathy to solidarity that takes you into a politics that demands the rights of human beings to not be exploited. That kind of thing is what you want to get to. These are the things that Wittgenstein was not born into but saw alongside Rush Rhees, and he came to love it and to be within it.

John Anderson taught at Cardiff University before being headhunted by the University of Edinburgh, and while he was in Cardiff he was attached to the WEA (Workers' Educational Association). That was also encouraged at the University of Edinburgh. Norman Kemp Smith, head of the philosophy department, was a leading figure in the WEA. Anderson came from a strong left-wing lower middle-class family where there were always books in the house. His elder brother became a professor of philosophy in New Zealand.[12] Their father was a headmaster, and member of the ILP (Independent Labour Party), and would have known Keir Hardie, later MP for Merthyr Tydfil. He was likely a member of the earlier Scottish Labour Party, and if so would have known its first paid employee, James Connolly.

This is all of tremendous interest as far as Rush Rhees is concerned. The crucial thing about John Anderson is that the politics came with him in philosophy. There is the subject, there is the teaching of the subject, there is yourself. We bring what we are. This is the influence Rush Rhees experienced, that amalgam of stuff, integrity, commitment, the pursuit of ideas, political, philosophical, ethical, theological, the whole range, in addition to the courage he displayed as a young fellow, that had him expelled from Rochester University. If you go back to Greek philosophy, and Rush Rhees was steeped in the study, then how can you absent yourself from personal commitment? Why was Socrates executed? Is philosophy political? That gets asked in academic circles even to this day. It dishonours the study and is a source of wonder to me, given that not one shred of evidence exists to suggest otherwise.

On the theme of politics, the way I was taught Wittgenstein is summed up in the phrase 'gadael y byd fel y mae' (leave the world as it is). It was a phrase emphasised by Walford Gealy, who was a student at Swansea in the 1950s. So, it is interesting to hear you talk about Rhees and Wittgenstein in an explicitly political way. Is there a tension between this philosophy as something therapeutic, in its 'cool place', to quote D. Z. Phillips, or something that is outside of the world and the deep political commitments to which you refer?[13]

In a sense, it can be therapeutic, and I don't feel that is anything to worry about. I see it as supremely political simply because the idea of applying yourself to your full scope as a human being, intellectually, must drive you towards some sense that change is possible. At this level I do not see any way of distinguishing between it, because you are involved in what it is to be human. On so many levels it is intrinsically political. How can the idea of intellectually exploring all you can be as a human being not be political? Part of it is that you are demanding that right for all human beings. This is where the work of Chomsky returns to this discussion. I use Chomsky as the greatest example because of what he has done over this past fifty years or more. This is the way he has spent his life. You cannot come to philosophy without yourself.

Chomsky left Boston when he was eighty-eight years of age, to live and work in Arizona. As a student he attended the classes of James Sledd, in the study of rhetoric. Later in life Sledd worked at the University of Texas. He stopped teaching in 1975, because he could not cope with what was being asked of him by the university authorities, which would have led to the separation between himself from his role as a teacher. He did not see any difference between his work as a philosopher, as an academic, and his life as a human being. Although he was no longer part of the teaching staff, he managed to retain a wee office on campus where he saw students right into the late 1990s.

How can you put up with what is going on nowadays in this right-wing state which is Great Britain? How do we bear that? I don't feel British, and hate to be called British which identifies me in an imperialist context, but I live within Great Britain and Ireland, and I cannot be apart from it. To think about the British State right now, and what it is doing with these attacks on civil rights, citizen rights, and human rights, how can we not be involved in that? We are always people, always human. How do we distance ourselves? Well, that's another matter.

Notes

1. This was originally a two-part conversation/interview which James Kelman adapted for inclusion here. The first part provided material for the Radio Wales documentary, 'Ludwig Wittgenstein: From Austria to Abertawe' (broadcast August 2022). The second part was an interview at the *Ludwig Wittgenstein: An Austrian at Swansea* conference on 16 June 2022. I am indebted to Nigel Crowle for his assistance with the first of these conversations, and to Huw Williams for his question regarding J. R. Jones during the second conversation.
2. René Descartes's *Meditations on First Philosophy, in which the existence of God and the immortality of the soul are demonstrated* was published in Latin in 1641, then in French in 1647. It is often referred to as the First Meditation.
3. John Anderson (1893–1962) advocated 'freethought' across all topics. He was Professor of Philosophy at Sydney University from 1927–58.
4. Woody Guthrie released a series of songs recorded in 1946–7 under the title *Ballads of Sacco and Vanzetti*.
5. Norman Kemp Smith was a Kantian scholar, who was Professor of Logic and Metaphysics at Edinburgh University from 1919–45.
6. Paul Cézanne (1839–1906) was a French Post-Impressionist artist, who influenced Cubism.
7. Wittgenstein stayed with Mrs Mann at 10 Langland Road in 1944.
8. See *Between Thought and Expression Lies a Lifetime: Why Ideas Matter*, with James Kelman and Noam Chomsky (New York: PM Press, 2021).
9. John Duns Scotus (1265–1308) was an influential Scottish theologian and philosopher. He coined the term 'haecceity' to denote thisness – our individual essence against the general.

10 Thomas Reid (1710–96) was a realist philosopher and founder of the Scottish School of Common Sense.
11 D. Z. Phillips, *Wittgenstein and the Possibility of Discourse* (Cambridge: Cambridge University Press, 1998).
12 Willie Anderson was Professor of Philosophy at Auckland University from 1921–55.
13 This question was asked by Huw Williams, whose chapter appears earlier in this collection.

12

Family Recollections of Wittgenstein in Swansea

Jamie Bill

My mother and father were both from Swansea. My mother's parents were Albert and Mary Clement and they lived with my mum, Barbara and her older sister, Joan at 1 Cwmdonkin Terrace, Uplands, Swansea from 1941, having been bombed out of their former home during the Swansea blitz. Albert was a caulker at Swansea Docks, and Mary had a variety of part-time jobs. He was a keen sportsman and supporter, and the couple enjoyed showing dogs and flowers. Revd Morgan from next door along the terrace had connections with Swansea University, and it was via this route that Ludwig Wittgenstein came to lodge with my grandparents during the 1940s. The Clement family stories have been passed down the generations, so now, eight decades on, my nieces know about 'Vicky' and his exploits.

It is clear from my Mum's recollections that Vicky wasn't just a lodger – he was treated in many respects as a family member experiencing and playing his part in everyday family life. We loved hearing that this man with a brain the size of a small planet, and an eponymous school of philosophy, was completely infatuated with the board game Snakes & Ladders, which he played, game after game, with the girls. Such was his fervour that, eventually, Mum became so tired of it that she cunningly suggested to Vicky that Joan really loved playing with him – with the desired result that Joan drew the fire from then on. A Cambridge Don outwitted by a young girl!

Vicky always had his eccentricities, and whilst staying with the Clements he developed some fixed habits. He never missed his evening mug of cocoa, but one night thought he had discovered a slug in it! (He hadn't – it was just a lump). The response of this man with a vast lexicon at his disposal was to jump up shouting 'Bloody bugger! Bloody bugger!' – much to the amusement of the girls who had never heard such language. A similar episode occurred when instead of swallowing his daily cod liver oil tablet he *bit* into it. Same expletive filled result – same level of entertainment for the girls!

Family life wasn't confined to the house. Vicky was included in outings and clearly wasn't put off by the complications attendant with the family not having a car. On one memorable occasion he joined the family on an afternoon trip to the beach. At one point the relaxation was broken by a lady running down towards the group shouting 'Vicky! Vicky!' Wittgenstein leapt to his feet 'Here I am, here I am' – just as the lady regained control of her dog, whose name happened to be Vicky. Once again, there was great general amusement at the confusion, never mind the idea that he should think it at all probable that someone might be running down the beach calling for him.

Naturally, the funny moments loomed large in the memories of the girls. At that age, the mundane doesn't fizz, but they did remember Wittgenstein's kindness, which was notably evinced through gifts of tennis balls and oranges – both spherical gold in times of rationing!

Specific incidents aside, when recollecting their times together, my Granny, Auntie Joan and Mum always spoke of Vicky with great affection. This man whose background and life experience couldn't have been more different – twenty years Albert's senior, with a strong 'German' accent (during the war, amid a family displaced by German bombing), and openly gay (albeit not ostentatiously) – was welcomed as a family member. This, for me, is a source of great pride, a case of apparently ordinary people doing the extraordinary, providing the acceptance his own family seemed unable to give.

Afterword: Wittgenstein's Swansea Legacy and Contemporary Relevance

Alan Sandry

Is Wittgenstein a brand? In today's McLuhanesque[1] global village, he has arguably become one, as is the case with so many other figures (dead or alive). When considering both tone and era, it was certainly easier for people – be they amateur or acolyte – to negotiate and empathise with Wittgenstein in those relatively straightforward, and ordered, black and white times; colour, and media expansion, has unquestionably distorted interpretations across the board and has added unnecessary layers of confusion. Photographs of Wittgenstein in sepia tell us more about Ludwig Wittgenstein – the man, his times, his emotions, his inner workings – than any jazzy coloured snaps. Wittgenstein on TikTok, were he to have been able to create his own personal account, would have been the final slap in the face for those of us who inhabit more traditionalist, pen, pencil, paper and notebook settings. Clickbait and the blogosphere are all a very long way from perusing the archives of Wittgenstein at the Wren Library, Trinity College, Cambridge.

While Wittgenstein undoubtedly remains a consequential global figure, in credit to his philosophical presence and achievements, what, if any, manifestations of him are there still lingering across the city of Swansea? Over the course of the last few years some of the questions that have been floated to the author, and others, consist of enquiries as to what one can observe of Wittgenstein in modern day Swansea, and what, if anything, can one learn about Wittgenstein at those venues. The answers, whilst never entirely positive or negative, often pose additional questions; some answerable, others unanswerable.

Wittgenstein in Swansea

For those Wittgenstein afficionados visiting the city, it is pleasing to note that, in purely physical terms, most of his (and Rush Rhees's) places and attachments still exist. The foremost unseeable location is the Brynmill Station, site of the iconic 1947 photograph. Whilst Wittgensteinians can stand on the spot and use their vivid imaginations to recreate the scene, sadly, due to its demolition several decades ago, there is no longer a graffitied wall, nor a wooden bench, with obligatory splinters to sit on, nor a blackened wooden frame to lean upon.[2] To add insult to historical injury, you will be unable to experience the delight of the Mumbles train rattling past you alongside the promenade. What you will encounter is the impossible to miss Mumbles Road, a busy arterial thoroughfare with its ceaseless procession of cars, lorries, and delivery vans, the latter of which serve the, progressively embourgeoised, shop-from-home student communities of Brynmill and Uplands. These vehicles are joined by the systematic buses for commuters from Mumbles and all suburbs west to Swansea city centre, and, predominantly during the summer months when they pack the open-top buses, the holidaymakers who stare expectantly out to sea as they cruise from the city centre down the, often breezy, four-mile stretch to Oystermouth.

In terms of the three parks – Singleton, Brynmill and Cwmdonkin[3] – with which Wittgenstein would have been most familiar, they have seen mostly cosmetic, infrastructural change: namely, additional seating and licks of paint across all three parks; the installation of the Swansea City of Sanctuary Orchard, and a children's zipwire at Cwmdonkin; the removal of the cricket pitch from Singleton to cater for musical events (generally not of the Viennese variety); and a kiosk selling ice cream for dogs and a Discovery Centre at Brynmill. Overall, therefore, they have undergone relatively conservative, incremental change rather than revolutionary combustion, though the mental image of an impish Wittgenstein on a zipwire in Dylan's cherished Cwmdonkin Park is one that takes some erasing.

The houses where Wittgenstein lodged, and the house that he would have visited the most from 1942–7, Rush Rhees's stable residence in Bryn Road, Brynmill, all remain intact. Taken individually, 10 Langland Road is the preeminent property, where the contemporary owners have fully embraced the historical narrative of the house and are exceedingly proud of its association with Wittgenstein. As part of the legacy and commemoration of this, a blue plaque will be placed at the front of the house to honour Wittgenstein's conceptually productive time there from April to September 1944. This will be a private installation by the owners of the house and a coterie of advocates for Wittgenstein. This is intended to celebrate the significance of this location within the story of Wittgenstein in Swansea.

Blue plaques may be established in future for numbers 1 and 2 Cwmdonkin Terrace. Forming part of the important tale of literary and cultural Uplands, it would appear obvious to have some acknowledgement of these locations, which are adjacent to the childhood home of Dylan Thomas. In actual fact, Cwmdonkin Terrace in its entirety should be given due attention, as it not only boasts the Wittgenstein abodes, but also the house of the Classicist and Communist Benjamin Farrington, and his wife Ruth Schechter, the intellectual and friend of Mahatma Gandhi, at number 4,[4] and the home of the composer and conductor Daniel Jones at number 16; not forgetting the respected printmaker and artist Alan Figg, who also spent his childhood years at that address. Perhaps the very name 'Cwmdonkin', when we add in Dylan's Cwmdonkin Drive and the centrepiece Cwmdonkin Park, should be conferred 'designated status' by Swansea City Council, the Welsh Government, UNESCO, or all three. If so, Bohemia may prosper once more.

At the time of writing, Swansea City Council has graciously granted permission, subject to the usual elongated administrative process, for one of their coveted blue plaques to be accorded to Wittgenstein. The plaque is scheduled to be sited on a salient building on the concrete pathway at Langland Bay. This will sanction civic acknowledgement of the great man and its unveiling will place him at a frequently visited location at the western edge of urban Swansea and at the gateway to Gower. It is an area where natural beauty abounds, and any debutant visitor will immediately understand what would have drawn Wittgenstein to this spot. Let us sincerely hope it is the first of several glistening plaques that link Wittgenstein with the city and, in many ways more importantly, with its convivial inhabitants.

For visitors, residents, and students to view these plaques, and for them to fully appreciate the settings, some Wittgenstein Trails are required. The formation of these would provide opportunities to meander, and contemplate, on the same ground as Wittgenstein. A Brynmill and Uplands route, terminating at Swansea University's Singleton Campus, could be one offering. The other should have a Mumbles and Gower focus with sites around Langland on the itinerary. It would also feature Rush Rhees's grave at Oystermouth Cemetery, which frequently attracts those who are curious about Rhees himself, or those who have read about his connection to Wittgenstein. A two-day 'Wittgenstein Journey' / 'Siwrne Wittgenstein' is feasible for those who want to commingle stunning views with relaxation and philosophical discourse.

Although plaques and trails are unquestionably extremely useful and informative, and certainly shine a light on people and vicinities – indeed there are some murmurings regarding a plaque to observe Wittgenstein, Rhees and the Swansea School, which may be sited on Swansea University's Singleton Campus – it is, in many ways, the more substantial everyday business of Wittgenstein's philosophy that needs to be maintained and encouraged. Accordingly, academic work on Wittgenstein at Swansea requires a regenerative shot in the arm. This could happen in numerous ways, some relatively straightforward, others rather more complex, over several years.

One visible hub that could be developed at Swansea's Singleton Campus is a Wittgenstein-Rush Rhees Centre, or, to give it a working name, a (Rush) Rhees Academy for Wittgenstein Studies. Its acronym RAWS – raw in fundamental terms; raw in the sense that students are beginning to develop their cognitive skills; and 'raws', as in the onomatopoeia 'roars' with approval, or making a loud noise (about something) that is widely audible – provides a majestic play on letters and words. RAWS could also act as an umbrella body for all the Wittgenstein-related material currently held within the Richard Burton Archives – *inter alia* the papers of Rush Rhees, Dewi Zephaniah Phillips, some of the other Swansea School philosophers, and Wittgenstein's reference letter for Rhees, containing his signature.

On the subject of the Swansea School, it is indisputable to many that the time has come to fully reconfigure the Swansea School within a designated Department of Philosophy. Swansea University should make a medium to long term commitment to recruit a mix of young and established Wittgenstein scholars, so that it can re-establish itself as a centre of Wittgenstein (and Rees, and Swansea School of Philosophy) Studies. Swansea boasts a range of excellent philosophers like Mario von der Ruhr, who has contributed an insightful chapter to this volume,

Paddy McQueen, and Patrick Cockburn. Nevertheless, more minds of their eminence are required, and this will only come about through raising the profile of philosophy at Swansea and by way of a declaration of meaningful financial and logistical commitments to expand the scope and activities within Swansea. If this occurs, then Swansea can, once again, achieve global recognition as a Wittgensteinian seat of learning.

In practical terms, therefore, what can be done to promote Wittgenstein at Swansea, through both academic and non-academic expressions? If we start with on-campus proposals, there are a variety of options that could be considered, with themes and specialisations to be assessed. Whilst drawing on current, and projected, expertise, any expansion of Wittgenstein studies, and related activities, should be offered a *tabula rasa* from which to operate. That would invariably provoke the instigation of some innovative programmes, modules, and pursuits. Whilst exegeses of the *Tractatus* and *Philosophical Investigations* would be expected, and would certainly receive assistance, uncommon approaches and angles would be strongly encouraged and nurtured.

Given Wittgenstein's publication of his *Word Book*,[5] some weight should be placed upon the discipline of Lexicography. This could be supplemented with the opening of a Philosophy (and Arts and Humanities) print at Swansea University, or within Swansea, to compile and publish dictionaries and allied manuscripts. This could then, for instance, allow for an emphasis on Paleonymy. How can we explore, in multidisciplinary fashion, the use of words and their transference across different settings and moments in time? The study of periods of creativity and innovation within our human development, and textual explosions that accompanied those forces, could also come into play. In similar vein, Narratology is a possibility for RAWS to include in any menu for study.

Some attention needs to be given to a Wittgensteinian investigation of language as a visceral, slicing tool. A question to ponder may go something like this: do we merely observe the division of language and its interplays, within and between individuals and societies, or has the language of division, *qua* division, become the key driver and signifier? A line of argument that may be assessed is the contention that the binarisation and polarisation of our world is now being expressed through language which is consciously designed to alienate and intimidate in equal measure. Modern societies are ruptured by volatile, often impromptu, arguments about politics, religion, moral matters, and a multitude of, often relatively trivial, issues. Ergo, do we desire to live in an Open or a Closed society? Do we crave freedom of thought, speech, and action? Or are we essentially insouciant, in that we appear content with governments, and swathes of civil societies, who propagate the denial of considerable elements of those critical factors? Thus, do we need to undertake a comprehensive re-examination of Wittgenstein's central questions and assumptions about language, its uses, and, significantly, its misuses?

Unsurprisingly, an obvious module for student enrichment, and scholarly inspection, would be Wittgenstein (and Rhees) in Swansea 1942–7. The subject of this volume could be an area of exploration with chronological subdivisions for each year within that period. Tracking Wittgenstein's philosophical, and personal, expedition in this five-year bloc, as in other comparable interludes, could prove to be a fruitful exercise.

Following on from the above, Wittgenstein and Wales, or Wittgensteinian considerations on Wales, are subjects that should be highlighted. Whilst this volume has primarily focused on Swansea, with sporadic acknowledgements to Wales more broadly, any course of study at a revived Swansea School could pursue a Wittgensteinian study of Wales, at the period of his visits or at other times, with possibilities for interdisciplinary working across Swansea University – i.e. in conjunction with language scholars from Academi Hywel Teifi, or with colleagues from CREW (Centre for Research into the English Literature and Language of Wales). It could be envisaged that RAWS would operate symbiotically with CREW, Academi Hywel Teifi, and other relevant centres, institutions, and units across Swansea University, and potentially beyond.

An obvious area for attention should be Wittgenstein and Culture. Opportunities exist to further explore Wittgenstein's attachment to, and writings on, art, music, and culture in general. Again, a specifically Welsh stream could be coalesced with what is already known of Wittgenstein's interests and opinions on said topics. The cultural aspects of Swansea, highlighted by contributors to this volume, most notably in Jeff Towns's colourful account of 'Kardomah Town', also offer avenues for consideration.

Legacy and Contemporary Relevance

It could be asserted that Wittgenstein and Politics is an underplayed theme. What has emerged from research into Swansea at the time of Wittgenstein's visits has been the predominance of what may be labelled 'intellectual leftism', or, what at a minimum may be described as a scepticism, cynicism or incredulity towards capitalist and imperialist norms and values. Some of this comes out in the life story of Rush Rhees, underpinned as it is with a leitmotif of radicalism. Consequently, a deep dive into Rhees's and Wittgenstein's political ideologies – possibly similar in nature but certainly not carbon copies – would make for a nutritious project.

A theme that may prove revealing, regarding his disposition, could be Wittgenstein 'On the Road'.[6] Could Wittgenstein meet Kerouac in any exploration of the need to be seeking out environments which are conducive to the enhancement of his thought processes? Some people seek, and occasionally find, solace through movement from place to place. That movement, or displacement, then introduces the individual to other social, cultural, and, importantly for someone like Wittgenstein, language ecosystems. From anthropological and sociological perspectives, this adds to the recognition that different settings, be they reached by boat or train, enhance our understanding – epistemological, ontological and existential – of where we are, and who we are with, at any given moment, or during any epoch.

RAWS could also act as a facilitator of extraneous events. For example, a Wittgenstein Day should be established, possibly on his birth date of 26 April. This would be a panoramic annual occurrence, akin to Bloomsday in Dublin[7], where events take place around the Wittgenstein and Rush Rhees-related sites in Swansea. There could also be linking sessions with other Wittgenstein-associated sites in Austria, England, Norway, Ireland, Finland, and so forth. 1940s attire would not be compulsory, but readings from the *Tractatus*, *Philosophical Investigations*, *Word Book*, *On Certainty*, *Culture and Value*, *The Blue and Brown Books*, etc.,[8] could take place at venues far and wide. Apart from furthering knowledge about the protagonist himself, Wittgenstein Day would also provide a welcome Spring boost to the tourism sectors in and around Swansea.

Finally, to return to physical spaces and places, there is a folly with a Wittgenstein twist. The architecturally curious Tower of the Nets, or the Hexagonal Hut as some refer to it, lies in Swansea's

Maritime Quarter, where it keeps a laid-back eye on the Observatory. This mass of concrete poetry, designed by the extraordinary artist Ian Hamilton Finlay, was created out of homage to the overall life and work of Wittgenstein, and not directly because of Wittgenstein's time at Swansea.⁹ The fact that we have the handiwork in Swansea is therefore a case of serendipity rather than prefiguration through association. The Nets theme originated in the 1960s, around the time that Ian Hamilton Finlay came across the *Tractatus*. On the Tower itself, there is a quote from Wittgenstein in the Anaximander Fragment. It is an often-photographed section of the sculpture. Unfortunately, Swansea's saline-infused air, and its slightly discarded position on the seafront, have not been kind to the Tower. Repair work and tender loving care is much needed, and the respected architect Robin Campbell has assembled a team to take matters forward. What this does represent, albeit in its weather-beaten state, is a non-Swansea University-related Wittgenstein site of interest. Hence, it is an important one to add to the list. Furthermore, inspiration from the revitalised Tower could conceivably incite some artists and philosophers to develop the Swansea scene for happenings around ecopoetics – a novel, multidisciplinary approach to writing about poetry, nature and thought, and creating artworks that reflect these moods – with a decidedly Wittgenstein tinge.

When combined, all the above display the extant corpus, added with the possibilities for developing future engagement and activities, which secure Wittgenstein's special place in the memory and reality of Swansea. Though he was never a full-time resident, or held any position at Swansea University, he was, in so many ways, a perfect character for Swansea, due to his blend of quirkiness, individuality, and, despite his privileged upbringing, his compassion for the marginalised, or seemingly weaker, sectors of society. As a result, he can add 'Swansea Jack' to his illustrious CV, and, for the citizens of Abertawe, that is the ultimate accolade.

Notes

1 Marshall McLuhan, who studied under Ivor Richards and Frank Leavis at Cambridge, theorised on how multifarious branches of media would reshape culture and project it into uncharted, potentially dangerous, waters.

2 From the 1970s to our present time, Swansea City Council has admirably sought to improve the seafront by creating open spaces and installing facilities such as the free to use fitness equipment which is visible along the promenade. These tidying up exercises meant that fatigued structures like Brynmill Station inevitably fell by the wayside. On this Wittgenstein-related spot today is a minimalist bus shelter, with an advertising board promoting subscription movies and accompanying burgers.

3 For more information on Singleton, Brynmill and Cwmdonkin parks see: Parks and outdoor activities search – Swansea (*http://swansea.gov.uk/parkssearch*), and Friends of Cwmdonkin Park – A Beautiful Space for Everyone (*http://cwmdonkinpark.com*).

4 After Ruth Schechter's death in 1942, Benjamin Farrington rented a room to Edward Arthur Thompson, his Swansea University colleague. Thompson was a pioneer in the fields of late antiquity and medieval studies. He was also a Marxist, who became active in the Communist Party of Great Britain (CPGB). In later years, Thompson was highly critical of Soviet intervention during the Prague Spring of 1968, and was a vocal opponent of the UK State's policies towards Northern Ireland.

5 Wittgenstein's *Word Book* – original title *Wörterbuch für Volksschulen* (Dictionary for Elementary Schools) – was his dictionary for children. It was composed during his time as a schoolteacher in Austria, and published in 1925.

6 Jack Kerouac's highly influential *On the Road* (1957) was the quintessential novel of the Beat Generation in the USA. It is a tale of travelling in order to find freedom and expression of mind and movement. The story encapsulates the desire within us to seek pastures new, with adventures along the way, in the search for something that makes us smile. Wittgenstein's peripatetic episodes could be gelled with Kerouac's dramatised, semi-realistic prose.

7 Bloomsday is staged every 16 June in Dublin. It is named after Leopold Bloom, the central character in James Joyce's masterpiece *Ulysses*. It is a day of celebration that features cultural events, literary readings, and group pub crawls.

8 Books by Ludwig Wittgenstein, or any publication on Ludwig Wittgenstein, could be used during any Wittgenstein Day activities. An outreach programme for schools and colleges, and a series of community engagement events, may also be appropriate for such a festivity. An essay writing competition for under-eighteens covering some aspect of Wittgenstein's life would be stimulating for those young people who are new to the man. Perhaps it would be obligatory to include some references to his work, and that of other relevant philosophers, and an element of the German language as a nod to his vernacular.

9 Thanks are due to the architect Robin Campbell, the bookseller and author Jeff Towns (who has a chapter in this volume), the curator and lecturer Sally Moss, sculptor and teacher Roger Moss, and Ian Hamilton

Finlay's son, the poet and artist Alec Finlay, for information regarding Ian Hamilton Finlay and The Tower of the Nets. Of additional interest is the fact that Alec Finlay published a poem entitled 'The Wittgenstein House (Skjolden)' in his 2012 work *Be My Reader*. He also co-authored the volume *Ludwig Wittgenstein: There Where You are Not* (2005) with Michael Nedo et al.

Select Bibliography

Works by Ludwig Wittgenstein
Wittgenstein, Ludwig, *Tractatus Logico-Philosphicus* (London: Routledge, 2001).
Wittegsntein, Ludwig, *Philosophical Investigations* (Oxford: Wiley-Blackwell, 2009).
Wittgenstein, Ludwig, *Blue & Brown Books*, 2nd edn (Oxford: Wiley-Blackwell, 1969).
Wittgenstein, Ludwig, *On Certainty* (Oxford: Wiley-Blackwell, 1975).
Wittgenstein, Ludwig, *Word Book* (New York, Badlands Unlimited, 2020).
Wittgenstein, Ludwig, *Culture and Value* (London: Blackwell, 1998).
Wittgenstein, Ludwig, *Remarks on Colour* (Oxford: John Wiley & Sons, 1979).

Selected Works on Ludwig Wittgenstein
Baker, Gordon and Hacker, Peter, *Wittgenstein: Rules, Grammar and Necessity* (London: Wiley-Blackwell, 2009).
Baker, Gordon and Hacker, Peter, *Wittgenstein: Understanding and Meaning, Part II* (London: Wiley-Blackwell, 2009).
McGuinness, Brian (ed.), *Wittgenstein in Cambridge: Letters and Documents 1911–1951* (London: Wiley-Blackwell, 2012).
Monk, Ray, *Wittgenstein. The Duty of Genius* (London: Jonathan Cape, 1990).
Monk, Ray, *How to Read Wittgenstein* (London: Granta, 2005).
Nedo, Michael, Moreton, Guy, and Finlay, Alec, *Ludwig Wittgenstein: There Where You are Not* (London: Black Dog Publishing, 2005).
Perloff, Marjorie (ed.), *Private Notebooks 1914–1916* (New York: Liveright Publishing Corporation, 2022).
Pichler, Alois and Säätelä, Simo (eds), *Wittgenstein: The Philosopher and His Works* (Berlin: De Gruyter, 2006).

Rhees, Rush (ed.), *Recollections of Wittgenstein* (Oxford: Oxford University Press, 1984).

Sandry, Alan, *Am I Glad To be Here!: Ludwig Wittgenstein and Philosophy at Swansea* (Swansea University Centenary Essays, 2020).

Schmidt, Alfred, *I think of you constantly with love: Briefwechsel Ludwig Wittgenstein – Ben Richards 1946–1951* (Vienna: Haymon Verlag, 2023).

Schweitzer, Radmila (ed.), *Ludwig Wittgenstein's Tractatus Odyssey: The Great War and the Writing of the Tractatus Logico-Philosophicus* (Los Angles: DoppelHouse Press, 2023).

Von der Ruhr, Mario, 'Rhees, Wittgenstein, and the Swansea School', in John Edelman (ed.), *Sense and Reality* (Frankfurt: Ontos Verlag, 2009), pp. 219–35.

Von Wright, Georg Henrik, *Wittgenstein* (Oxford: Blackwell, 1982).

Selected Works by the Swansea School

Beardsmore, R. W., *Art and Morality* (London: Macmillan, 1971).

Diamond, Cora, *The Realistic Spirit: Wittgenstein, Philosophy and the Mind* (Cambridge, MA: MIT Press, 1995).

Dilman, Ilham, *Free Will: An Historical and Philosophical Introduction* (London: Routledge, 1999).

Holland, Roy, *Against Empiricism: On Education, Epistemology and Value* (Oxford: Wiley-Blackwell, 1983).

Jones, J. R., *Yr Argyfwng Gwacter Ystyr* (Llandybie: Llyfrau'r Dryw, 1964).

Jones, J. R., *Prydeindod* (Llandybie: Llyfrau'r Dryw, 1966).

Lloyd, Ieuan, 'Teaching Religious Understanding', *Religious Studies*, 17/2 (198), 253–9.

Mounce, H. O., *Wittgenstein's Tractatus: An Introduction* (Chicago: University of Chicago Press, 1989).

Phillips, D. Z., *J. R. Jones* (Writers of Wales) (Cardiff: University of Wales Press, 1995).

Phillips, D. Z. *Faith After Foundationalism* (London: Routledge, 2016).

Rhees, Rush, *Wittgenstein and The Possibility of Discourse*, ed. D. Z. Phillips (Oxford: Blackwell, 2006).

Winch, Peter, *The Idea of a Social Science and its Relation to Philosophy* (London: Routledge, 2007).

Select Bibliography

Selected Works by Contributors

Daniel, Rhianwen, 'The Liberal/Conservative Nationalism Divide: A distinction without a difference?' *Nations and Nationalism*, 28/2 (2022), 523–38.

Kelman, James (with Noam Chomsky), *Between Thought and Expression Lies a Lifetime: Why Ideas Matter* (Oakland, CA: PM Press, 2021).

Kelman, James, *The State Is the Enemy: Essays on Liberation and Racial Justice* (Oakland, CA: PM Press, 2023).

Miles, K. G. and Towns, Jeff, *Bob Dylan and Dylan Thomas: The Two Dylans* (Carmarthen: McNidder & Grace, 2022).

Monk, Ray, *Bertrand Russell; The Spirit of Solitude* (London: Vintage, 1997).

Sandry, Alan, *Plaid Cymru: An Ideological Analysis* (Cardiff, Welsh Academic Press, 2011).

Sandry, Alan, *From Linz to Langland: A Journey with Ludwig Wittgenstein* (Llandeilo: Cambria Publishing, 2024).

Schmidt, Alfred, 'The Wittgenstein Collection of the Austrian National Library', *Nordic Wittgenstein Review*, 3/1 (2014).

Smith, Jonathan, 'Circuitous processes, jigsaw puzzles and indisputable results: Making the best use of the manuscripts of Sraffa's Production of Commodities by Means of Commodities', *Cambridge Journal of Economics*, 36/6 (2012), 1291–301.

Thomas, M. Wynn, *R. S. Thomas: Serial Obsessive* (Cardiff: University of Wales Press, 2013).

Von der Ruhr, Mario, *Simone Weil* (London: Bloomsbury Continuum, 2006).

Williams, Daniel G., *The Centenary Edition: Raymond Williams/ Who Speaks for Wales? Nation, Culture, Identity*, 2nd edn (Cardiff: University of Wales Press, 2021).

Williams, Huw, *On Rawls, Development and Global Justice: The freedom of peoples* (Basingstoke: Palgrave Macmillan, 2013).

Archives

The Richard Burton Archives at Swansea University house the Rush Rhees Collection, which includes his personal papers and works relating to Wittgenstein, including his signed reference letter for Rhees's application to Swansea University. It also includes the correspondence of Rhees with figures such as Elizabeth Anscombe and Maurice O'Connor Drury. The Richard Burton Archives also house the D. Z. Phillips Collection, which contains Phillips's notebooks, correspondence and material related to Rush Rhees.

The Wren Library at Trinity College Cambridge contains the papers of Wittgenstein from 1914–51. These include his wartime notebooks and transcripts from 1927–48, along with material dictated to the likes of G. E. Moore and Moritz Schlick. There are also copies of the 'Blue Book' (1933–4) and the 'Brown Book' (1934–5).

The Austrian National Library in Vienna contains a large amount of Wittgenstein originals, including manuscripts, typescripts, letters, and other correspondence.

The Wittgenstein Archives at the University of Bergen, Norway is a research infrastructure and projects platform. It includes digital and paper copies as well as transcriptions of Wittgenstein's Nachlass, as catalogued by G. H. von Wright in 1969.

Index

A
Aberystwyth 210
Anscombe, Elizabeth 146
   see also Wittgenstein, Ludwig:
   and Elizabeth Anscombe
Amis, Kingsley 77–8, 136, 141,
   191–3
Atkin, Leon 16
Auden, W. H. 187

B
Beardsmore, R. W. 75–8
Bevan, Aneurin 158
Braithwaite, Richard 2
Braque, Georges 14
Brynmill Press 145
Burke, Edmund 140

C
Campbell, Robin 224
Cambridge 28, 38–9, 154, 190, 198,
   205
Cambridge University 1–3, 6, 13,
   19, 143, 198, 215, 217
Cardiff University 210
Carmarthen 210
Cézanne, Paul 204
Chomsky, Noam 145, 206–7, 209,
   211
Clement Family 6, 11, 31, 215–16
Cockburn, Patrick 221

Collingwood, R. G. 133, 145
Communism 154, 177–8
Connolly, James 210

D
Davie, Donald 135
Dekker, George 135
Department of English, Swansea
   University 135, 147
Descartes, René 201
   First Meditation 201
Diamond, Cora 75
Dilman, Ilham 75–7
Dublin 2, 223
Duns Scotus, John 207

E
Eagleton, Terry 154
Eliot T. S. 142, 151, 155, 168
Ellison, Ralph 152
   and Wales 153–4
   Works:
   In a Strange Country 156, 158,
      160, 174, 177
   Invisible Man 152, 154, 157, 163,
      169, 173–4
   The Corn is Green 159
   The Red Cross in Swansea, SW
      152, 155–6, 163–4
   The World and the Jug 167
Erskine-Hill, Howard 135

F

Farrington, Benjamin 4–5, 162, 219
Fichte, J. G. 114
Figg, Alan 219
Finlay, Ian Hamilton 224
Fisher, Charles 15, 17, 19, 29
Fleure, H. J. 125–6, 128
Fouracre, Roy 10
Freud, Sigmund 3–4

G

Gandhi, Mahatma 219
Gealy, Walford 211
Geddes, Patrick 125
Goethe, Johann Wolfgang von 201
Gruffydd, W. J. 159

H

Hardie, Keir 210
Hegel, G. W. F. 191
Heidegger, Martin 191
Herder, J. G. 114, 123
Holland, Roy 75–7
Hume, David 208–9
Hutt, Rowland 3

I

Independent Labour Party (ILP) 210
Ireland 10, 43, 56
Isherwood, Christopher 13

J

Jacobs, Gabriel 138
Janes, Alfred (Fred) 14, 17–21, 23
Jones, Daniel 14, 17–19, 24, 28, 191, 219
Jones, Ernest 30, 193
Jones, J. R. 75, 85–108, 113–14, 134
  Argyfwng Gwacter Ystyr 90
  Christianity 91, 98
  Cristnogaeth a Chenedlaetholdeb 123
  Cymdeithas yr Iaith Gymraeg 89–90, 94, 122
  and Walford Gealy 93–4, 107, 113
  National Identity 104–6
  and D. Z. Phillips 86, 93–4, 96–9, 101, 104, 113
  Plaid Cymru 89
  Prydeindod 99, 122–4
  and Rush Rhees 92, 96, 108
  Troedle 102

K

Kafka, Franz 201, 204
Kant, Immanuel 208
Kardomah Gang 14–15, 17, 24, 30, 222
Kastil, Alfred 1

L

Language and Identity 209–10, 212
Lawrence, D. H. 14, 144
Leavis F. R. 135, 142–6
  'Memories of Wittgenstein' 146
Levy, Mervyn 14, 19
Lewis, Saunders 121–2, 127, 158
Leyshon, Alban 15
Linguistic Patterns 201–2
Llanelli 190
Lloyd, Ieuan 75, 78
Lowry, L. S. 14
Lyotard, Jean-François 165

Index

M

Mann, Mrs 5, 27, 56, 63, 189
Marciano, Rocky 193–4
McQueen, Paddy 221
Moore, G. E. 1–3, 39–43
Morgan, Mrs 5–6, 11
   see also Morgan, Revd Wynford
Morgan, Revd Wynford 5–6, 11
   see also Wittgenstein, Ludwig:
      and Revd Wynford Morgan
Moseley, Oswald 16
Mounce, H. O. 75–9, 81

N

Norway 2, 10, 195
   see also Wittgenstein, Ludwig:
      and Norway

O

Owen, Mabley 15
Owen, Morfydd 193
Oxford 192

P

Phillips, D. Z. 137, 202, 209
   see also Phillips, D. Z.; Rhees,
      Rush
Picasso, Pablo 14, 26
Philosophy of Language 111,
   115–21
   see also Wittgenstein, Ludwig:
      Philosophy of Language
Philosophy of Religion 78–81,
   112–13, 136, 143, 207
   see also Wittgenstein, Ludwig:
      Philosophy of Religion
Plaid Cymru 121, 125–6
   see also Jones, J. R.: Plaid Cymru
Plato 207

Poe, Edgar Allan 201
Porthcawl 195
Prichard, John 15, 18–19, 22
Price, Cecil 137

R

Rambling 196–8
Rees, John 138
Reid, Thomas 208
Richards, Ben (family) 52–3
   see also Wittgenstein, Ludwig:
      and Ben Richards
Richards, Ceri 15
Richards, I. A. 13
Rhees, Benjamin Rush 1–2
Rhees, Rush 1–3, 6, 8, 13, 27, 68,
   69–70, 134, 137–8, 153, 193,
   208
   see also Wittgenstein, Ludwig:
      and Rush Rhees
   Anarchism 203
   and Anderson, John 202, 206,
      209–10
   Atheism 203
   Background 1, 69, 204
   and Bartley, William 146–7
   Bryn Road (home) 27, 188,
      218
   Cambridge University 1–3
   Edinburgh University 1, 202–3,
      206, 210
   Manchester University 1, 69
   and John Ormond 147–8
   Oystermouth Cemetery (grave)
      30, 220
      see also Swansea:
         Oystermouth Cemetery
   and D. Z. Phillips 72, 75–81, 136,
      138, 211, 220

Rhees, Rush (continued)
   Swansea School of Philosophy
      68–72, 75–9, 111, 147, 220
   Swansea University 3, 70,
      134–41, 191, 196, 202, 209,
      220
      see also Swansea: Swansea
        University
   The Philosophical Society 72
   and Simone Weil 79
   Welding 70, 190
   and Peter Winch 68, 76–7
   and Ludwig Wittgenstein 1–2,
      8, 30, 40, 69–71, 80, 161, 193,
      196–8, 206, 222
      see also Wittgenstein, Ludwig:
        and Rush Rhees
   University of Rochester 69, 203,
      211
   Works:
   The Tree of Nebuchadnezzar
      147
   Without Answers 146
   Wittgenstein and the Possibility
      of Discourse 80
Rhys, Morgan John 1
Robinson, Ian 136–48
   Chaucer and the English
      Tradition 140
   The Human World 145–6
   The New Grammarian's'
      Funeral: A critique of Noam
      Chomsky's linguistics 145
   The Survival of English: Essays
      in Criticism of Language 141

S
Sacco, Nicola 203
Savage, D. S. 13

Schechter, Ruth 219
   see also Farrington, Benjamin
Scotland 202–3
Scottish Labour Party 210
Sims, David 136–41, 146–7
Sker Point 195
Skinner, Francis 3, 9
Skjolden 38, 69, 195
   see also Wittgenstein, Ludwig:
      and Norway
Sledd, James 211–12
Smith, Adam 209
Smith, Norman Kemp 208, 210
Smithies, Yorrick 3
Socrates 211
St Augustine 7
   Confessions 7
Stapledon, George 125
Swansea 3–5, 38, 43–4, 151, 179,
   187–94, 197–8, 205–6, 209–10,
   217, 219
   Abertawe 179, 189, 224
   Accent 190
   Bishopston 31
   Blitz 151–3, 193
   Bookshops 24, 206
   Bryn Road 27, 63–4, 188, 218
   Brynmill 56, 60, 188, 191, 194,
      218–19
   Brynmill Park 194, 218
   Brynmill Station 188, 194,
      218
   Caswell Bay 28, 57, 206, 209
   Cinemas 24, 77
   Civic Centre (The Guildhall) 29,
      54–5, 209
   Copperopolis 187
   Cwmbwrla 19
   Cwmdonkin Drive 5, 31, 219

Index

Cwmdonkin Park 44, 191, 194, 218–19
Cwmdonkin Terrace 5, 31, 55, 57, 60–1, 64, 191, 194–5, 215, 219
Dillwyn Street 206
Eaton Crescent 194
Glynn Vivian Art Gallery 22
Gower Peninsula 1, 3, 28, 30, 189–90, 194, 219
  see also Wittgenstein, Ludwig: Gower Peninsula
Gowerton 30
History 188
Langland Bay 5, 28, 57, 189, 194, 196, 206
Langland Road 5, 27, 63, 189, 218
Limeslade Bay 206, 209, 219
Morriston 152
Mount Pleasant 6
Mumbles 5, 20, 30, 189, 193, 196, 205, 209
Mumbles Hill 193, 209
Mumbles Lighthouse 195
Mumbles Pier 194
Mumbles Railway 187, 194, 218
Mumbles Road 80, 194, 209, 218
Newton Road 209
Oxford Street 205
Oystermouth Castle 189
Oystermouth Cemetery 30, 220
  see also Rhees, Rush: Oystermouth Cemetery (grave)
Oystermouth Road 206
Penclawdd 190
Pwll Du 28, 57
Rhossili 206
Rotherslade Bay 28
Royal Institute of South Wales (Swansea Museum) 25
Singleton Abbey 194
Singleton Park 191, 194, 198, 218
Sketty Hall 194
St Helen's Road 209
Stella Maris School and Convent 194
Swansea Bay 188, 193
Swansea Central Library 22
Swansea Docks 205, 215
Swansea Market 205
Swansea School of Art 22–3
Swansea University 194, 198, 220–1, 224
  see also Rhees, Rush: Swansea University
Swiss Cottage 194–5
Terrace Road 6
Theatres 23
Tower of The Nets (Hexagonal Hut) 223–4
Underhill Park 28, 189
Uplands 18, 31–2, 190–1, 193–4, 218–20
Wartime 193
Wind Street 152, 205–6
Working Class 205

T

Taig, Thomas 15–16, 23
  Rhythm and Verse 16
Thomas, Dylan 5, 13–30, 68, 179, 191–2, 218
  and 1930s Poets 25
  Surrealism and Art 26
  Thomas's Family 31–3

Thomas, Dylan (continued)
  Works:
    'The Fight' 14
    Memories of Christmas 32
    Portrait of the Artist as a Young
      Dog 14, 32
    Reminiscences of Childhood 21,
      29, 32
    Return Journey 16, 23–4
    Under Milk Wood 191
Thomas, Hywel 206–7
Thomas R. S. 136
Trick, Bert 16, 30
Turing, Alan 3

U
Upward, Edward 13
University College of Swansea
  15–16, 33, 133–5
  see also Swansea University
University of Wales 133

V
Van Gogh, Vincent 207
Vanzetti, Bartolomeo 203
Vaughan-Thomas, Wynford 15
Vienna 2, 40, 42, 155, 194
Vienna Circle 112

W
Wales 203, 205, 210
Watkins, Vernon 13–14, 18–20, 27
  and Erich Heller 27
Warner, Tom 15, 17
Weill, Simone 135–6
  see also Rhees, Rush: and Simone
    Weill
Welsh Language (Cymraeg) 86–8,
  159–60

Welsh Nationalism 158–9
Winch, Peter 67–8, 75–8, 81, 133–4
  see also Rhees, Rush: and Peter
    Winch; Wittgenstein, Ludwig:
    influence on Peter Winch
Wisdom, John 2, 7
Wishart, Ralph 24
Wittgenstein, Ludwig
  Aesthetics 204
  and Alice Ambrose 41
  and Elizabeth Anscombe 69
  Art Theory 204
  arriving Swansea (1942) 187
  Austria 223
  Brynmill Photograph 60–1,
    188
  Cambridge 28, 38, 48, 61, 74–5
    see also Cambridge University
  Cambridge University 2–3, 6–8,
    40–4, 46, 61, 217
  Cambridge University Press
    43–4
  and Clement Family 6, 11, 31,
    60, 64, 215–16
  departing Swansea (1947) 29
  and Maurice O'Connor Drury
    2, 57, 155, 162
  and Dublin 2, 74
  England 223
  Family Resemblances 168
  Finland 223
  on Freud 3–4
  and Gower Peninsula 1, 29, 44,
    57, 74, 194, 205
  Guy's Hospital 3–4, 10, 44, 148
  and Ireland 154, 223
  and J. M. Keynes 39, 155
  Language Games 139, 165,
    171–3, 176

Index

Lodgings (1944–7) 191
and Norman Malcolm 3, 5, 9, 28
Metaphors 47–8
and G. E. Moore 39–40, 43, 208
and Revd Wynford Morgan 31, 55, 60, 63–4
 see also Morgan, Mrs
and Newcastle 4–5, 30, 44, 61, 153
and Norway 2, 10, 41–2, 51, 154, 195, 223
 see also Skjolden
Philosophy of Language 114, 116–21, 127–8, 137, 139–40, 146, 178, 206
Philosophy of Mathematics 3, 6–7, 45
Philosophy of Psychology 45
and David Pinsent 41
Politics 223
Private Language 142, 160
and Frank Ramsey 39–40, 45
and Basil Reeve 148
Philosophy of Religion 136
and Rush Rhees 1–2, 8, 11, 28–30, 44–5, 48, 63, 69–70, 73–5, 194, 196–8, 206, 222
and Ben Richards 9–10, 28–9, 51–64, 159, 188
and Bertrand Russell 39
and Francis Skinner 3, 9, 41
Skjolden 38, 42–3, 47, 51, 61
 see also Norway
and Piero Sraffa 40, 43
Trinity College 44, 46, 217
 see also Cambridge University
and W. H. Watson 38
influence on Peter Winch 133
and G. H. von Wright 69
Theory of Deterioration 2, 75
Thoughts on Swansea 46–7, 54–7
Time in Swansea 153, 159, 196, 215–16
'Vicky' 215–16
and Welsh Language (Cymraeg) 159–60
Wren Library 217
Works:
 Culture and Value 223
 On Certainty 146, 223
 Philosophical Grammar 7–8
 Philosophical Investigations 2, 6–11, 37–48, 51, 61–2, 74–5, 80–1, 142, 156–7, 160, 176, 178–9, 197–8, 201, 208, 221, 223
 'Remarks on Frazer's Golden Bough' 146, 161
 The Blue Book 138–9, 223
 The Brown Book 41–3, 47, 138, 223
 Tractatus Logico-Philosophicus 39, 81, 154, 178, 198, 201–2, 221, 223–4
 Word Book 223
Workers Educational Association (WEA) 210

Z

Zola, Émile 192, 204
 Germinal 192